Focus on
GRAMMAR 3A

FOURTH EDITION

Focus on GRAMMAR 3A

FOURTH EDITION

Marjorie Fuchs
Margaret Bonner
Miriam Westheimer

ALWAYS LEARNING

PEARSON

To the memory of my parents, Edith and Joseph Fuchs—MF
To my parents, Marie and Joseph Maus, and to my son, Luke Frances—MB
To my husband, Joel Einleger, and my children, Ari and Leora—MW

FOCUS ON GRAMMAR 3A: An Integrated Skills Approach, Fourth Edition

Copyright © 2012, 2006, 2000, 1994 by Pearson Education, Inc.
All rights reserved.

Pearson Education, 10 Bank Street, White Plains, NY 10606

Staff credits: The people who made up the *Focus on Grammar 3A, Fourth Edition,*
team, representing editorial, production, design, and manufacturing, are Elizabeth Carlson,
Tracey Cataldo, Aerin Csigay, Dave Dickey, Christine Edmonds, Nancy Flaggman, Ann France,
Françoise Leffler, Lise Minovitz, Barbara Perez, Robert Ruvo, and Debbie Sistino.

Cover image: Shutterstock.com
Text composition: ElectraGraphics, Inc.
Text font: New Aster

PEARSON LONGMAN ON THE **WEB**

Pearsonlongman.com offers online
resources for teachers and students. Access
our Companion Websites, our online catalog,
and our local offices around the world.

Visit us at **pearsonlongman.com**.

Printed in the United States of America

ISBN 10: 0-13-216058-7
ISBN 13: 978-0-13-216058-2

8   17

ISBN 10: 0-13-216059-5 (with MyLab)
ISBN 13: 978-0-13-216059-9 (with MyLab)

Contents

WELCOME TO *FOCUS ON GRAMMAR*

Now in a new edition, the popular five-level *Focus on Grammar* course continues to provide an integrated-skills approach to help students understand and practice English grammar. Centered on thematic instruction, *Focus on Grammar* combines controlled and communicative practice with critical thinking skills and ongoing assessment. Students gain the confidence they need to speak and write English accurately and fluently.

NEW for the FOURTH EDITION

VOCABULARY

Key vocabulary is highlighted, practiced, and recycled throughout the unit.

PRONUNCIATION

Now, in every unit, pronunciation points and activities help students improve spoken accuracy and fluency.

LISTENING

Expanded listening tasks allow students to develop a range of listening skills.

UPDATED CHARTS and NOTES

Target structures are presented in a clear, easy-to-read format.

NEW READINGS

High-interest readings, updated or completely new, in a variety of genres integrate grammar and vocabulary in natural contexts.

NEW UNIT REVIEWS

Students can check their understanding and monitor their progress after completing each unit.

MyFocusOnGrammarLab

An easy-to-use online learning and assessment program offers online homework and individualized instruction anywhere, anytime.

Teacher's Resource Pack   One compact resource includes:

THE TEACHER'S MANUAL: General Teaching Notes, Unit Teaching Notes, the Student Book Audioscript, and the Student Book Answer Key.

TEACHER'S RESOURCE DISC: Bound into the Resource Pack, this CD-ROM contains reproducible Placement, Part, and Unit Tests, as well as customizable Test-Generating Software. It also includes reproducible Internet Activities and PowerPoint® Grammar Presentations.

THE *FOCUS ON GRAMMAR* APPROACH

The new edition follows the same successful four-step approach of previous editions. The books provide an abundance of both controlled and communicative exercises so that students can bridge the gap between identifying grammatical structures and using them. The many communicative activities in each Student Book provide opportunities for critical thinking while enabling students to personalize what they have learned.

- **STEP 1: GRAMMAR IN CONTEXT** highlights the target structures in realistic contexts, such as conversations, magazine articles, and blog posts.
- **STEP 2: GRAMMAR PRESENTATION** presents the structures in clear and accessible grammar charts and notes with multiple examples of form and usage.
- **STEP 3: FOCUSED PRACTICE** provides numerous and varied controlled exercises for both the form and meaning of the new structures.
- **STEP 4: COMMUNICATION PRACTICE** includes listening and pronunciation and allows students to use the new structures freely and creatively in motivating, open-ended speaking and writing activities.

Recycling

Underpinning the scope and sequence of the *Focus on Grammar* series is the belief that students need to use target structures and vocabulary many times, in different contexts. New grammar and vocabulary are recycled throughout the book. Students have maximum exposure and become confident using the language in speech and in writing.

Assessment

Extensive testing informs instruction and allows teachers and students to measure progress.

- **Unit Reviews** at the end of every Student Book unit assess students' understanding of the grammar and allow students to monitor their own progress.
- Easy to administer and score, **Part and Unit Tests** provide teachers with a valid and reliable means to determine how well students know the material they are about to study and to assess students' mastery after they complete the material. These tests can be found on MyFocusOnGrammarLab, where they include immediate feedback and remediation, and as reproducible tests on the Teacher's Resource Disc.
- **Test-Generating Software** on the Teacher's Resource Disc includes a bank of *additional* test items teachers can use to create customized tests.
- A reproducible **Placement Test** on the Teacher's Resource Disc is designed to help teachers place students into one of the five levels of the *Focus on Grammar* course.

COMPONENTS

In addition to the Student Books, Teacher's Resource Packs, and MyLabs, the complete *Focus on Grammar* course includes:

Workbooks Contain additional contextualized exercises appropriate for self-study.

Audio Program Includes all of the listening and pronunciation exercises and opening passages from the Student Book. Some Student Books are packaged with the complete audio program (mp3 files). Alternatively, the audio program is available on a classroom set of CDs and on the MyLab.

THE *FOCUS ON GRAMMAR* UNIT

Focus on Grammar introduces grammar structures in the context of unified themes. All units follow a **four-step approach**, taking learners from grammar in context to communicative practice.

STEP 1 GRAMMAR IN CONTEXT

This section presents the target structure(s) in a natural context. As students read the **high-interest texts**, they encounter the form, meaning, and use of the grammar. **Before You Read** activities create interest and elicit students' knowledge about the topic. **After You Read** activities build students' reading vocabulary and comprehension.

Vocabulary exercises improve students' command of English. Vocabulary is **recycled** throughout the unit.

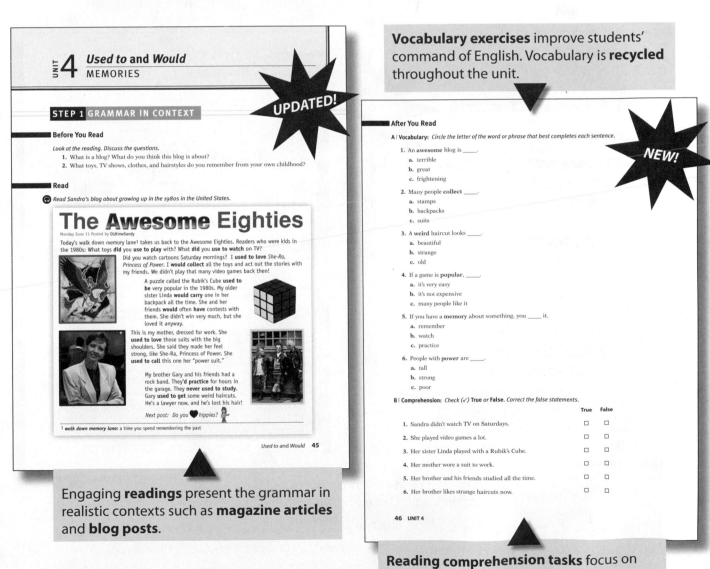

Engaging **readings** present the grammar in realistic contexts such as **magazine articles** and **blog posts**.

Reading comprehension tasks focus on the meaning of the text and draw students' attention to the target structure.

This section gives students a comprehensive and explicit overview of the grammar with detailed **Grammar Charts** and **Grammar Notes** that present the form, meaning, and use of the structure(s).

Grammar Charts present the structure in a clear, easy-to-read format.

Grammar Notes give concise, simple **explanations** and **examples** to ensure students' understanding.

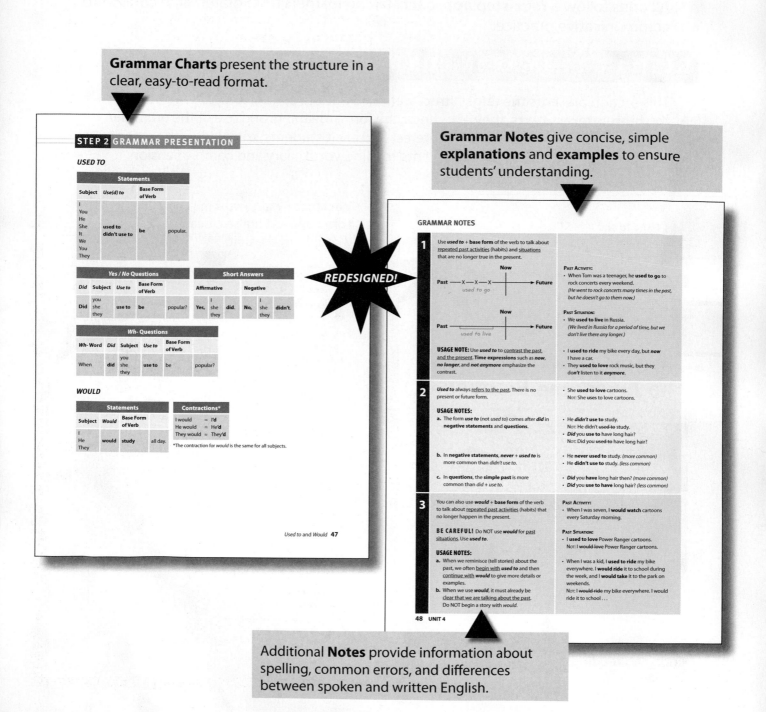

Additional **Notes** provide information about spelling, common errors, and differences between spoken and written English.

STEP 3 FOCUSED PRACTICE

Controlled practice activities in this section lead students to master form, meaning, and use of the target grammar.

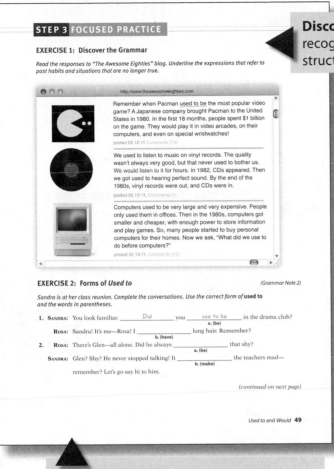

STEP 3 FOCUSED PRACTICE

EXERCISE 1: Discover the Grammar

Read the responses to "The Awesome Eighties" blog. Underline the expressions that refer to past habits and situations that are no longer true.

http://www.theawesomeeighties.com

Remember when Pacman used to be the most popular video game? A Japanese company brought Pacman to the United States in 1980. In the first 18 months, people spent $1 billion on the game. They would play it in video arcades, on their computers, and even on special wristwatches!
posted 02.12.11 Comments (14)

We used to listen to music on vinyl records. The quality wasn't always very good, but that never used to bother us. We would listen to it for hours. In 1982, CDs appeared. Then we got used to hearing perfect sound. By the end of the 1980s, vinyl records were out, and CDs were in.
posted 02.13.11, Comments (7)

Computers used to be very large and very expensive. People only used them in offices. Then in the 1980s, computers got smaller and cheaper, with enough power to store information and play games. So, many people started to buy personal computers for their homes. Now we ask, "What did we use to do before computers?"
posted 02.14.11, Comments (11)

EXERCISE 2: Forms of *Used to* (Grammar Note 2)

Sandra is at her class reunion. Complete the conversations. Use the correct form of **used to** *and the words in parentheses.*

1. **SANDRA:** You look familiar. ___Did___ you ___use to be___ in the drama club?
    a. (be)
   ROSA: Sandra! It's me—Rosa! I _____ long hair. Remember?
    b. (have)
2. **ROSA:** There's Glen—all alone. Did he always _____ that shy?
    a. (be)
   SANDRA: Glen? Shy? He never stopped talking! It _____ the teachers mad—
    b. (make)
   remember! Let's go say hi to him.

(continued on next page)

Used to and Would **49**

Discover the Grammar activities develop students' recognition and understanding of the target structure before they are asked to produce it.

An **Editing** exercise ends every Focused Practice section and teaches students to find and correct typical mistakes.

EXERCISE 5: Editing

Read the journal entry about a high school reunion in Timmins, Ontario, a small town 500 miles north of Toronto. There are nine mistakes in the use of **used to** *and* **would**. *The first mistake is already corrected. Find and correct eight more.*

Shania Twain

The high school reunion tonight was awesome! I
      talked
used to talk to Eileen Edwards for a long time. Well,
she's the famous country pop singer Shania Twain now.
In high school, she was used to be just one of us, and
tonight we all called her Eileen. She graduated in 1983,
the same year as me. Today she uses to live in a
chateau in Switzerland and has her own perfume
brand, but her life didn't use to be like that at all! She
uses to be very poor, and her grandma used to made all her clothes because her
family couldn't afford to buy them. She was always a good musician, though. In fact, she
used to earns money for her family that way. On Saturday nights, she would performed
with a local rock band, and my friends and I would go hear her. She could really sing!
Her new name, Shania, means "on my way" in Ojibwa (her stepfather's Native American
language). After she left Timmins, I would think that Timmins wasn't important to her
anymore—but I was wrong. Now that she's famous, she has a lot of power, and she
uses it to do good things for our community. And tonight she was just the way she
used be in high school—simple and friendly!

A school reunion

52 UNIT 4

A **variety of exercise types** engage students and guide them from recognition and understanding to accurate production of the grammar structures.

The *Focus on Grammar* Unit **x**

STEP 4 COMMUNICATION PRACTICE

This section provides practice with the structure in **listening** and **pronunciation** exercises as well as in communicative, open-ended **speaking** and **writing** activities that move students toward fluency.

Listening activities allow students to hear the grammar in natural contexts and to practice a range of listening skills.

STEP 4 COMMUNICATION PRACTICE

EXERCISE 6: Listening

🎧 **A** | *Two friends are talking about their past. Listen to their conversation.*

🎧 **B** | *Read the statements. Then listen again to the conversation and circle the letter of the correct information.*

1. The friends are at a _____.
   a. rock concert   (b.) school reunion

2. Their present lives are very _____ their past lives.
   a. similar to   b. different from

3. They have _____ memories about their past.
   a. good   b. bad

4. They used to play a lot of _____.
   a. video games   b. music CDs

5. The friends are enjoying talking about _____.
   a. a trip   b. the past

🎧 **C** | *Listen again to the conversation. Check (✓) the things the friends used to do in the* **past** *and the things they do now.*

	Past	Now
1. get up very early without an alarm clock	✓	☐
2. use an alarm clock	☐	☐
3. have a big breakfast	☐	☐
4. have a cup of coffee	☐	☐
5. look at the newspaper	☐	☐
6. have endless energy	☐	☐
7. do aerobics	☐	☐
8. take car trips on weekends	☐	☐
9. meet at class reunions	☐	☐

EXPANDED!

Pronunciation Notes and **exercises** improve students' spoken fluency and accuracy.

EXERCISE 7: Pronunciation

🎧 **A** | *Read and listen to the Pronunciation Note.*

> **Pronunciation Note**
>
> We often pronounce **used to** like "usta." Notice that the pronunciation of **used to** and **use to** is the same.
>
> **EXAMPLES:** I **used to** play chess.   →   "I **usta** play chess."
> What games did you **use to** play?   →   "What games did you **usta** play?"
>
> Be sure to write **used to** or **use to**, NOT "usta."
>
> We often use the contraction of **would** (**'d**) in both **speech** and **writing**.
>
> **EXAMPLE:** We **would** play for hours.   →   "We**'d** play for hours."

NEW!

🎧 **B** | *Listen to the sentences. Notice the pronunciation of* **used to** *and the contraction of* **would.**

1. I **used to** live in a small town.
2. I didn't **use to** have a lot of friends.
3. I**'d** spend hours alone.
4. On weekends, my sister **used to** play cards with me.
5. She**'d** always win.
6. We**'d** have a lot of fun.

🎧 **C** | *Listen again and repeat the sentences.*

EXERCISE 8: Picture Discussion

Work with a partner. Look at the pairs of pictures and talk about how the people have changed. Then write sentences that describe the changes. Compare your sentences with those of your classmates.

Then	Now

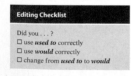 

1. Sharifa *used to be very busy, but now she is more relaxed. She would always be in a hurry.*
   Now she takes things more slowly. She used to wear glasses, but now she doesn't . . .

C: *Everybody* used to have long hair then.

EXERCISE 10: Writing

A | *Write a two-paragraph essay. Contrast your life in the past with your life now. In the first paragraph, describe how your life used to be at some time in the past. In the second paragraph, describe your life today. Remember: We often begin with* **used to** *and then change to* **would.**

EXAMPLE: I used to live in Russia. I attended St. Petersburg University. I would ride my bike there every day. In those days I used to . . . Today I am living in Florida and attending Miami University . . .

B | *Check your work. Use the Editing Checklist.*

> **Editing Checklist**
>
> Did you . . . ?
> ☐ use **used to** correctly
> ☐ use **would** correctly
> ☐ change from **used to** to **would**

NEW!

Writing activities encourage students to produce meaningful writing that integrates the grammar structure.

An **Editing Checklist** teaches students to correct their mistakes and revise their work.

Speaking activities help students synthesize the grammar through discussions, debates, games, and problem-solving tasks, developing their fluency.

UNIT 4 Review

Check your answers on page UR-1.
Do you need to review anything?

NEW!

A | *Circle the correct words to complete the sentences.*

1. What <u>did / would</u> you use to like to do when you were a kid?

2. I <u>used to / would</u> love reading comic books when I was younger.

3. <u>Do / Did</u> you use to go to concerts?

4. My sister would <u>plays / play</u> video games for hours.

5. I never <u>used to / would</u> like them before, but now I love them.

6. Life <u>used to / would</u> be so different back then.

B | *Complete the conversations with **used to** or **would** and the verb in parentheses.*

- **AMY:** Hey, is that Jorge? He _____ very different. I almost didn't recognize him!
  1. (look)

  BEN: Yes. He _____ long hair, but he cut it last month.
  2. (have)

- **MIA:** I _____ my hair grow very long in the summer.
  3. (let)

  LEE: Me too. Sometimes I _____ a haircut for a whole year!
  4. (not get)

- **AMY:** I _____ the guitar. I'm sorry I quit.
  5. (play)

  BEN: I had a guitar too. I _____ for hours.
  6. (practice)

- **TOM:** _____ you _____ to concerts when you were a student?
  7. (go)

  MIA: Yes. I _____ the free concerts in the park. I even once heard Celine Dion!
  8. (love)

C | *Find and correct six mistakes.*

Celine Dion was born in Quebec, Canada. When she used to be five, her family opened a
club, and Celine used to sang there. People from t[...]
perform. At the age of 12, Celine wrote her first so[...]
it to a manager. At first Celine used to singing only[...]
became known in more countries. As a child, Celi[...]
to be a singer. Today she is one of the most succes[...]

PART I

From Grammar to Writing
COMBINING SENTENCES WITH TIME WORDS

You can often improve your writing by combining two short sentences into one longer sentence that connects the two ideas. **The two sentences can be combined by using time words** such as *while*, *when*, *as soon as*, *before*, *after*, or *until*. The new, longer sentence is made up of a main clause and a time clause.

EXAMPLE: I was shopping. I saw the perfect dress for her. →

TIME CLAUSE   MAIN CLAUSE
While I was shopping, I saw the perfect dress for her.

MAIN CLAUSE   TIME CLAUSE
I saw the perfect dress for her **while** I was shopping.

The time clause can come first or second. When it comes first, a **comma** separates the two clauses.

1 | *Read the paragraph. Underline all the sentences that are combined with a time word. Circle the time words.*

> I always exchange holiday presents with my girlfriend, Shao Fen. Last year, (while) I was shopping for her, I saw an umbrella in her favorite color. As soon as I saw it, I thought of her. I bought the umbrella and a scarf in the same color. When Shao Fen opened the present, she looked really upset. She didn't say anything, and she didn't look at me. I felt hurt and confused by her reaction. Later she explained that in Chinese, the word for "umbrella" sounds like the word for "separation." When she saw the umbrella, she misunderstood. She thought I wanted to end the relationship. After I heard that, I was very upset! When we both felt calmer, we talked about our misunderstanding. At the end, we laughed about it, and I think we're better friends because of it. I discovered something new about Shao Fen's culture. Now I want to learn more about cross-cultural communication.

SCOPE AND SEQUENCE

UNIT	READING	WRITING	LISTENING
1 page 2 **Grammar:** Present Progressive and Simple Present **Theme:** Different Cultures	An article: *What's Your Cross-Cultural IQ?*	A paragraph about a new experience	Interviews of foreign students studying in the United States
2 page 16 **Grammar:** Simple Past **Theme:** Poets	A biography: *Matsuo Basho, 1644–1694*	A paragraph about important events in your life	An interview with a poet
3 page 31 **Grammar:** Past Progressive and Simple Past **Theme:** Accidents	A newspaper article: *Disaster at Sea*	A paragraph about an event you witnessed	A witness describing a traffic accident
4 page 45 **Grammar:** *Used to* and *Would* **Theme:** Memories	A blog: *The Awesome Eighties*	A two-paragraph essay comparing your life in the past with your life now	Two friends talking about their past
5 page 58 **Grammar:** *Wh-* Questions **Theme:** In Court	An excerpt from a court transcript: *State of Illinois vs. Harry M. Adams*	Interview questions and the interview	A telephone conversation about an accident
PART I **From Grammar to Writing,** page 69 **Combining Sentences with Time Words:** Write a paragraph about a misunderstanding or mistake.			
6 page 74 **Grammar:** Future **Theme:** Space Travel	A radio program transcript: *Space Tourists: Not Just Science Fiction*	A paragraph about your life five years from now	Conversations about future plans and about something happening now
7 page 91 **Grammar:** Future Time Clauses **Theme:** Setting Goals	An article: *Go For It! What are your dreams for the future?*	A goal-planning worksheet	A telephone call to an employment agency
PART II **From Grammar to Writing,** page 103 **Showing the Order of Events:** Write a blog post about your weekend plans.			

SPEAKING	PRONUNCIATION	VOCABULARY	
Find Someone Who . . . *Picture Discussion:* Understanding gestures and facial expressions *Compare and Contrast:* Appropriate cultural questions	Reduction of *What do you* and *What are you* ("Whaddaya")	abroad culture* distance	event misunderstanding native
Compare and Contrast: Two poets *Information Gap:* Celebrity Profile	*Wh-* questions with *did* ("Why'd")	admirer emotion journey	restless topic*
Game: Are You a Good Witness? *Role Play:* Alibi	Pausing after time clauses	alarmed area* calm (adj)	disaster sink (v) survivor*
Picture Discussion: Then and now *Compare and Contrast:* How you used to be and how you are now	Reduction of *used to* ("usta") and contraction of *would* ('d)	awesome collect memory	popular power weird
Role Play: On the Witness Stand *Game:* To Tell the Truth	Intonation of *Wh-* questions asking for information or asking for repetition	defendant frightened in a hurry	indicate* record (n)
Making Plans: Finding a time when you and your partner are both free *Reaching Agreement:* Deciding which events to attend	Contraction of *will* ('ll) and reduction of *going to* ("gonna")	edge experience (v) float	incredible sold out takeoff (n)
What About You? Comparing your plans with your classmates' plans *Game:* What's Next?	Intonation in sentences with time clauses	achieve* catalog degree	download goal* interview (n)

* = AWL (Academic Word List) items

UNIT	READING	WRITING	LISTENING
8 page 108 **Grammar:** Present Perfect: *Since* and *For* **Theme:** Careers	An article: *King of Skate* A sports card: *Bob Burnquist*	A paragraph about someone's accomplishments	A job interview for a radio sports announcer
9 page 121 **Grammar:** Present Perfect: *Already*, *Yet*, and *Still* **Theme:** Party Planning	An article: *It's Party Time!*	Two paragraphs about things you've already done and haven't done yet	A conversation about plans for a party
10 page 133 **Grammar:** Present Perfect: Indefinite Past **Theme:** Adventure Travel	A travel magazine article: *Been There? Done That?*	A paragraph explaining a quotation about travel	A conversation with a travel agent
11 page 146 **Grammar:** Present Perfect and Simple Past **Theme:** Long-Distance Relationships	An article: *An Ocean Apart*	Two paragraphs about a long-distance relationship	An interview with a couple who had a long-distance relationship
12 page 159 **Grammar:** Present Perfect Progressive and Present Perfect **Theme:** Climate Change	An article: *Global Warming: A Hot Topic*	An email about what you've been doing lately	Conversations about recent finished and unfinished activities

PART III From Grammar to Writing, page 173
The Topic Sentence and Paragraph Unity: Write a personal statement about your accomplishments.

UNIT	READING	WRITING	LISTENING
13 page 176 **Grammar:** Ability: *Can, Could, Be able to* **Theme:** Dance	An article: *Born to Dance*	One or two paragraphs about someone who was successful in spite of a disability or problem	A job interview for office manager at a dance studio
14 page 190 **Grammar:** Permission: *Can, Could, May, Do you mind if* **Theme:** Roommates	An article: *Always Ask First*	Short notes asking permission and giving or refusing permission	Short conversations asking and giving permission

SPEAKING	PRONUNCIATION	VOCABULARY	
Role Play: A Job Interview	Intonation in *yes / no* questions and *wh-* questions	consider dramatically* opportunity	positive* residence support (v)
Information Gap: Chores *What About You?* Things you've already done and things you haven't done yet	Contractions of *have* in the present perfect	available* organized professional*	specific* successful
Find Someone Who . . .	Reduction of auxiliary *have* ("books of") and *has* ("hotelz") after a noun	adventure affordable ancient	annual* survey* transportation*
Compare and Contrast: Events last year and this year *Interview:* Asking your partner about a long-distance relationship	Pronunciation of *-ed* in the simple past and past participle of regular verbs	apart arrangement manage	solution temporary* turn down
Find Someone Who . . . *Picture Discussion:* Global warming *Discussion:* Recent changes in your life	Stress in present perfect and present perfect progressive verb phrases	climate design (v)* develop	energy* expert* pollution
Information Gap: Can they do the tango? *Ask and Answer:* Finding someone who can do each task	Distinguishing unstressed *can* /kən/ and stressed *can't* /kænt/	aspiration confused dedication	integrated* perception* talent
Problem Solving: Asking permission *Role Play:* Could I . . . ?	Linking final consonants with *I* or *he:* *can I, could he, may I*	annoyed assume* establish*	guidelines* neat presentation

* = AWL (Academic Word List) items

SPEAKING	PRONUNCIATION	VOCABULARY	
Making Plans: Requesting help with things on your schedule	Reductions of *you* in requests ("couldja," "wouldja," "willya," and "canya")	appreciate* cheer up deliver	distribute* text (v)
Cross-Cultural Comparison: Advice about customs *Problem Solving:* Discussing everyday situations *Picture Discussion:* Improving a classroom	Reductions of *ought to* ("oughta") and *had better* ("'d better" or "better")	avoid behavior communication*	identity* normal* protect
Quotable Quotes: Time *Problem Solving:* Creating a time capsule	Dropping unstressed vowels ("histry")	civilization create* impressed	intentional interpret* occasion
Game: Quiz Show *Information Gap:* Story Time *Discussion:* What the morals of stories mean; tell a story that illustrates a moral	Two ways to pronounce *the*: /ði/ and /ðə/	enormous* famous immediately	struggle wonderful
What About You? Describing where you live *Compare and Contrast:* Different types of housing *Discussion:* Describing your ideal home *Game:* A Strange Story	Stressing contrasting or new information	charming convenient ideal	located* peaceful satisfied
Compare and Contrast: Pizzas from around the world *Role Play:* Your Restaurant	Reduction of *as* /əz/ and *than* /ðən/	crowded delicious fresh	relaxed* traditional* varied*

* = AWL (Academic Word List) items

UNIT	READING	WRITING	LISTENING
21 page 296 **Grammar:** Adjectives: Superlatives **Theme:** Cities	A travel brochure about Toronto: *A Superlative City*	A fact sheet for your hometown or city	A couple comparing three hotels
22 page 307 **Grammar:** Adverbs: *As . . . as,* Comparatives, Superlatives **Theme:** Sports	A transcript of a TV sports program: *The Halftime Report*	A paragraph comparing two sports figures	Sportscasters describing a horse race
PART VI From Grammar to Writing, page 319 **Using Descriptive Adjectives:** Write a paragraph describing a room.			
23 page 322 **Grammar:** Gerunds: Subject and Object **Theme:** Health Issues	An article: *No Smoking: Around the World from A–Z*	A two-paragraph opinion essay for or against a health or safety issue	A doctor giving advice to a patient
24 page 334 **Grammar:** Infinitives after Certain Verbs **Theme:** Friends and Family	Letters from a newspaper advice column: *Ask Annie*	Emails to two or three friends inviting them to join you for an event	A couple talking to a family counselor
25 page 344 **Grammar:** More Uses of Infinitives **Theme:** Smart Phones	An article: *The World in Your Pocket*	A post for an online bulletin board about using an electronic device	A TV ad for a new phone
26 page 357 **Grammar:** Gerunds and Infinitives **Theme:** Procrastination	An excerpt from an article: *Stop Procrastinating— Now!*	A goals worksheet Three paragraphs about accomplishing each of your goals	An interview with a student about her study habits
PART VII From Grammar to Writing, page 372 **Combining Sentences with *And, But, So, Or*:** Write an email to a friend describing your present life.			

SPEAKING	PRONUNCIATION	VOCABULARY	
What About You? Describing a city you have visited *Discussion:* Some cities in your country	Dropping the final *-t* sound before an initial consonant sound	dynamic* feature* financial*	multicultural public
Compare and Contrast: Famous athletes *Questionnaire:* Work and Play	Linking final consonants to beginning vowels in *as* + adverb + *as*	aggressively consistently* effectively	frequently intensely*
Survey: Opinions about smoking *For or Against:* Smoking in public and private places	Linking final *-ing* with an initial vowel sound	approve of ban (v) illegal*	in favor of permit (v) prohibit*
What About You? Describing childhood relationships *Cross-Cultural Comparison:* How do young people in your culture socialize?	Stress in infinitive phrases	focus (v)* interact* obviously*	similar* solve
Survey: Opinions about cell phones *For or Against:* Pros and cons of new technology *Problem Solving:* Other uses for everyday objects *Discussion:* New uses for a smart phone	Stress in adjective + infinitive phrases	combine device* function (n)*	major* multipurpose old-fashioned
Brainstorming: Ideas for work breaks *Information Gap:* At the Support Group *Quotable Quotes:* Procrastination *Problem Solving:* Ways of stopping clutter	Reduction of *to* /tə/, *for* /fər/, and *on* /ən/	anxious discouraging project (n)*	put off task* universal

* = AWL (Academic Word List) items

UNIT	READING	WRITING	LISTENING
27 page 376 **Grammar:** Reflexive and Reciprocal Pronouns **Theme:** Self-Talk	An article from a psychology magazine: *Self-Talk*	An advice column entitled "Help Yourself with Self-Talk"	Conversations at an office party
28 page 391 **Grammar:** Phrasal Verbs **Theme:** Animal Intelligence	An article about animal behavior expert Cesar Millan: *When He Whispers, They Tune In*	A paragraph about a pet or an animal you've read about or observed	Conversations about a college science class
PART VIII From Grammar to Writing, page 403 Using pronouns for Coherence: Write instructions to someone taking care of your home while you are away.				
29 page 408 **Grammar:** Necessity: *Have (got) to, Must, Don't have to, Must not, Can't* **Theme:** Transportation	An article: *Know Before You Go*	A paragraph about an application procedure	Short conversations about driving
30 page 422 **Grammar:** Expectations: *Be supposed to* **Theme:** Wedding Customs	A page from an etiquette book: *Wedding Wisdom*	A short essay about an important life event	Short conversations about a wedding
31 page 434 **Grammar:** Future Possibility: *May, Might, Could* **Theme:** Weather	A transcript of a TV weather report: *Weather Watch*	An email to a friend about your weekend plans	A weather forecast
32 page 446 **Grammar:** Conclusions: *Must, Have (got) to, May, Might, Could, Can't* **Theme:** Mysteries	The beginning of a Sherlock Holmes mystery: *The Red-Headed League*	Possibilities and conclusions based on a story outline	A radio play: the end of *The Red-Headed League*
PART IX From Grammar to Writing, page 461 Combining Sentences with *Because, Although, Even though*: Write a letter of complaint.				

SPEAKING	PRONUNCIATION	VOCABULARY	
Questionnaire: Are you an optimist or a pessimist? *Game:* Who Remembers More? *Picture Discussion:* Imagining people's self-talk *Problem Solving:* Feeling better in difficult situations	Stress in reflexive and reciprocal pronouns	fault finally* impact (v)*	maintain* reaction* realize
Making Plans: Organizing a class field trip *For or Against:* Owning a pet	Stress on noun and pronoun objects of phrasal verbs	figure out give up keep on	straighten out take over turn on
Picture Discussion: Traffic signs *Game:* Invent a Sign *What About You?* Describing tasks you have to and don't have to do *Discussion:* Rules and Regulations	Reductions of *have to* ("hafta" and "hasta") and *have got to* ("have gotta" and "gotta")	equipment* hassle (n) inspect*	regulation* strict valid*
Discussion: Important plans that you changed *Cross-Cultural Comparison:* Customs for important life events	Reductions of *supposed to* ("supposta") and *going to* ("gonna")	assistant* ceremony certificate	etiquette role* select*
Conversation: Your weekend plans *Problem Solving:* Predicting what two students might do in the future	Stress in short answers with modals	affect (v)* bundle up exceed*	forecast local trend*
Picture Discussion: Making guesses about a family *Problem Solving:* Giving possible explanations for several situations	Stress on modals that express conclusions	advertisement amazed encyclopedia method*	millionaire position salary

* = AWL (Academic Word List) items

ABOUT THE AUTHORS

Marjorie Fuchs has taught ESL at New York City Technical College and LaGuardia Community College of the City University of New York and EFL at the Sprach Studio Lingua Nova in Munich, Germany. She has a master's degree in Applied English Linguistics and a certificate in TESOL from the University of Wisconsin-Madison. She has authored and co-authored many widely used books and multimedia materials, notably *Crossroads, Top Twenty ESL Word Games: Beginning Vocabulary Development, Families: Ten Card Games for Language Learners, Focus on Grammar 4: An Integrated Skills Approach, Focus on Grammar 3 CD-ROM, Focus on Grammar 4 CD-ROM, Longman English Interactive 3* and *4, Grammar Express Basic, Grammar Express Basic CD-ROM, Grammar Express Intermediate, Future 1: English for Results,* and workbooks for *The Oxford Picture Dictionary High Beginning* and *Low Intermediate, Focus on Grammar 3* and *4,* and *Grammar Express Basic.*

Margaret Bonner has taught ESL at Hunter College and the Borough of Manhattan Community College of the City University of New York, at Taiwan National University in Taipei, and at Virginia Commonwealth University in Richmond. She holds a master's degree in library science from Columbia University, and she has done work toward a PhD in English literature at the Graduate Center of the City University of New York. She has authored and co-authored numerous ESL and EFL print and multimedia materials, including textbooks for the national school system of Oman, *Step into Writing: A Basic Writing Text, Focus on Grammar 4: An Integrated Skills Approach, Focus on Grammar 4 Workbook, Grammar Express Basic, Grammar Express Basic CD-ROM, Grammar Express Basic Workbook, Grammar Express Intermediate, Focus on Grammar 3 CD-ROM, Focus on Grammar 4 CD-ROM, Longman English Interactive 4,* and *The Oxford Picture Dictionary Low-Intermediate Workbook.*

Miriam Westheimer taught EFL at all levels of instruction in Haifa, Israel, for a period of six years. She has also taught ESL at Queens College, at LaGuardia Community College, and in the American Language Program of Columbia University. She holds a master's degree in TESOL and a doctorate in Curriculum and Teaching from Teachers College of Columbia University. She is the co-author of a communicative grammar program developed and widely used in Israel.

ACKNOWLEDGMENTS

Before acknowledging the many people who have contributed to the fourth edition of *Focus on Grammar*, we wish to express our gratitude to those who worked on the first, second, and third editions, and whose influence is still present in the new work. Our continuing thanks to:

- **Joanne Dresner**, who initiated the project and helped conceptualize the general approach of *Focus on Grammar*
- Our editors for the first three editions: **Nancy Perry**, **Penny Laporte**, **Louisa Hellegers**, **Joan Saslow**, **Laura Le Dréan**, and **Françoise Leffler**, for helping to bring the books to fruition
- **Sharon Hilles**, our grammar consultant, for her insight and advice on the first edition

In the fourth edition, *Focus on Grammar* has continued to evolve as we update materials and respond to the valuable feedback from teachers and students who have been using the series. We are grateful to the following editors and colleagues:

- The entire Pearson FOG team, in particular **Debbie Sistino** for overseeing the project and for her down-to-earth approach based on years of experience and knowledge of the field; **Lise Minovitz** for her enthusiasm and alacrity in answering our queries; and **Rosa Chapinal** for her courteous and competent administrative support.
- **Françoise Leffler**, our multi-talented editor, for her continued dedication to the series and for helping improve *Focus on Grammar* with each new edition. With her ear for natural language, eye for detail, analytical mind, and sense of style, she is truly an editor *extraordinaire*.
- **Robert Ruvo**, for piloting the book through its many stages of production
- **Irene Schoenberg** and **Jay Maurer** for their suggestions and support, and Irene for generously sharing her experience in teaching with the first three editions of this book
- **Ellen Shaw** for being a fan and for her insightful and thorough review of the previous edition
- **Sharon Goldstein** for her intelligent, thoughtful, and practical suggestions

Finally, we are grateful, as always, to **Rick Smith** and **Luke Frances**, for their helpful input and for standing by and supporting us as we navigated our way through our fourth *FOG*.

Reviewers

We are grateful to the following reviewers for their many helpful comments:

Aida Aganagic, Seneca College, Toronto, Canada; **Aftab Ahmed**, American University of Sharjah, Sharjah, United Arab Emirates; **Todd Allen**, English Language Institute, Gainesville, FL; **Anthony Anderson**, University of Texas, Austin, TX; **Anna K. Andrade**, ASA Institute, New York, NY; **Bayda Asbridge**, Worcester State College, Worcester, MA; **Raquel Ashkenasi**, American Language Institute, La Jolla, CA; **James Bakker**, Mt. San Antonio College, Walnut, CA; **Kate Baldrige-Hale**, Harper College, Palatine, IL; **Leticia S. Banks**, ALCI-SDUSM, San Marcos, CA; **Aegina Barnes**, York College CUNY, Forest Hills, NY; **Sarah Barnhardt**, Community College of Baltimore County, Reisterstown, MD; **Kimberly Becker**, Nashville State Community College, Nashville, TN; **Holly Bell**, California State University, San Marcos, CA; **Anne Bliss**, University of Colorado, Boulder, CO; **Diana Booth**, Elgin Community College, Elgin, IL; **Barbara Boyer**, South Plainfield High School, South Plainfield, NJ; **Janna Brink**, Mt. San Antonio College, Walnut, CA; **AJ Brown**, Portland State University, Portland, OR; **Amanda Burgoyne**, Worcester State College, Worcester, MA; **Brenda Burlingame**, Independence High School, Charlotte, NC; **Sandra Byrd**, Shelby County High School and Kentucky State University, Shelbyville, KY; **Edward Carlstedt**, American University of Sharjah, Sharjah, United Arab Emirates; **Sean Cochran**, American Language Institute, Fullerton, CA; **Yanely Cordero**, Miami Dade College, Miami, FL; **Lin Cui**, William Rainey Harper College, Palatine, IL; **Sheila Detweiler**, College Lake County, Libertyville, IL; **Ann Duncan**, University of Texas, Austin, TX; **Debra Edell**, Merrill Middle School, Denver, CO; **Virginia Edwards**, Chandler-Gilbert Community College, Chandler, AZ; **Kenneth Fackler**, University of Tennessee, Martin, TN; **Jennifer Farnell**, American Language Program, Stamford, CT; **Allen P. Feiste**, Suwon University, Hwaseong, South Korea; **Mina Fowler**, Mt. San Antonio Community College, Rancho Cucamonga, CA; **Rosemary Franklin**, University of Cincinnati, Cincinnati, OH; **Christiane Galvani**, Texas Southern University, Sugar Land, TX; **Chester Gates**, Community College of Baltimore County, Baltimore, MD; **Luka Gavrilovic**, Quest Language Studies, Toronto, Canada; **Sally Gearhart**, Santa Rosa Community College, Santa Rosa, CA; **Shannon Gerrity**, James Lick Middle School, San Francisco, CA; **Jeanette Gerrity Gomez**, Prince George's Community College, Largo, MD; **Carlos Gonzalez**, Miami Dade College, Miami, FL; **Therese Gormley Hirmer**, University of Guelph, Guelph, Canada; **Sudeepa Gulati**, Long Beach City College, Long Beach, CA; **Anthony Halderman**, Cuesta College, San Luis Obispo, CA; **Ann A. Hall**, University of Texas, Austin, TX; **Cora Higgins**, Boston Academy of English, Boston, MA; **Michelle Hilton**, South Lane School District, Cottage Grove, OR; **Nicole Hines**, Troy University, Atlanta, GA; **Rosemary Hiruma**, American Language Institute, Long Beach, CA; **Harriet Hoffman**, University of Texas, Austin, TX; **Leah Holck**, Michigan State University, East Lansing, MI; **Christy Hunt**, English for Internationals, Roswell, GA; **Osmany Hurtado**, Miami Dade College, Miami, FL; **Isabel Innocenti**, Miami Dade College, Miami, FL; **Donna Janian**, Oxford Intensive School of English, Medford, MA; **Scott Jenison**, Antelope Valley College, Lancaster, CA; **Grace Kim**, Mt. San Antonio College, Diamond Bar, CA; **Brian King**, ELS Language Center, Chicago, IL; **Pam Kopitzke**, Modesto Junior College, Modesto, CA; **Elena Lattarulo**, American Language Institute, San Diego, CA; **Karen Lavaty**, Mt. San Antonio College, Glendora, CA; **JJ Lee-Gilbert**, Menlo-Atherton High School, Foster City, CA; **Ruth Luman**, Modesto Junior College, Modesto, CA; **Yvette Lyons**, Tarrant County College, Fort Worth, TX; **Janet Magnoni**, Diablo Valley College, Pleasant Hill, CA; **Meg Maher**, YWCA Princeton, Princeton, NJ; **Carmen Marquez-Rivera**, Curie Metropolitan High School, Chicago, IL; **Meredith Massey**, Prince George's Community College, Hyattsville, MD; **Linda Maynard**, Coastline Community College, Westminster, CA; **Eve Mazereeuw**, University of Guelph, Guelph, Canada; **Susanne McLaughlin**, Roosevelt University, Chicago, IL; **Madeline Medeiros**, Cuesta College, San Luis Obispo, CA; **Gioconda Melendez**, Miami Dade College, Miami, FL; **Marcia Menaker**, Passaic County Community College, Morris Plains, NJ; **Seabrook Mendoza**, Cal State San Marcos University, Wildomar, CA; **Anadalia Mendoza**, Felix Varela Senior High School, Miami, FL; **Charmaine Mergulhao**, Quest Language Studies, Toronto, Canada; **Dana Miho**, Mt. San Antonio College, San Jacinto, CA; **Sonia Nelson**, Centennial Middle School, Portland, OR; **Manuel Niebla**, Miami Dade College, Miami, FL; **Alice Nitta**, Leeward Community College, Pearl City, HI; **Gabriela Oliva**, Quest Language Studies, Toronto, Canada; **Sara Packer**, Portland State University, Portland, OR; **Lesley Painter**, New School, New York, NY; **Carlos Paz-Perez**, Miami Dade College, Miami, FL; **Ileana Perez**, Miami Dade College, Miami, FL; **Barbara Pogue**, Essex County College, Newark, NJ; **Phillips Potash**, University of Texas, Austin, TX; **Jada Pothina**, University of Texas, Austin, TX; **Ewa Pratt**, Des Moines Area Community College, Des Moines, IA; **Pedro Prentt**, Hudson County Community College, Jersey City, NJ; **Maida Purdy**, Miami Dade College, Miami, FL; **Dolores Quiles**, SUNY Ulster, Stone Ridge, NY; **Mark Rau**, American River College, Sacramento, CA; **Lynne Raxlen**, Seneca College, Toronto, Canada; **Lauren Rein**, English for Internationals, Sandy Springs, GA; **Diana Rivers**, NOCCCD, Cypress, CA; **Silvia Rodriguez**, Santa Ana College, Mission Viejo, CA; **Rolando Romero**, Miami Dade College, Miami, FL; **Pedro Rosabal**, Miami Dade College, Miami, FL; **Natalie Rublik**, University of Quebec, Chicoutimi, Quebec, Canada; **Matilde Sanchez**, Oxnard College, Oxnard, CA; **Therese Sarkis-Kruse**, Wilson Commencement, Rochester, NY; **Mike Sfiropoulos**, Palm Beach Community College, Boynton Beach, FL; **Amy Shearon**, Rice University, Houston, TX; **Sara Shore**, Modesto Junior College, Modesto, CA; **Patricia Silva**, Richard Daley College, Chicago, IL; **Stephanie Solomon**, Seattle Central Community College, Vashon, WA; **Roberta Steinberg**, Mount Ida College, Newton, MA; **Teresa Szymula**, Curie Metropolitan High School, Chicago, IL; **Hui-Lien Tang**, Jasper High School, Plano, TX; **Christine Tierney**, Houston Community College, Sugar Land, TX; **Ileana Torres**, Miami Dade College, Miami, FL; **Michelle Van Slyke**, Western Washington University, Bellingham, WA; **Melissa Villamil**, Houston Community College, Sugar Land, TX; **Elizabeth Wagenheim**, Prince George's Community College, Lago, MD; **Mark Wagner**, Worcester State College, Worcester, MA; **Angela Waigand**, American University of Sharjah, Sharjah, United Arab Emirates; **Merari Weber**, Metropolitan Skills Center, Los Angeles, CA; **Sonia Wei**, Seneca College, Toronto, Canada; and **Vicki Woodward**, Indiana University, Bloomington, IN.

PRESENT AND PAST

UNIT	GRAMMAR FOCUS	THEME
1	Present Progressive and Simple Present	Different Cultures
2	Simple Past	Poets
3	Past Progressive and Simple Past	Accidents
4	*Used to* and *Would*	Memories
5	*Wh-* Questions	In Court

Present Progressive and Simple Present
DIFFERENT CULTURES

Before You Read

Look at the cartoons. Discuss the questions.

1. What are the people doing?
2. How do they feel?

Read

🎧 *Read the article about cross-cultural communication.*

WHAT'S YOUR CROSS-CULTURAL IQ?[1]

Are you **living** in your native country or in another country? **Do** you ever **travel** abroad? **Do** you **understand** the misunderstandings below?

SITUATION 1

Jason **is standing** at Dan's door. He **thinks** he's on time for the party, but he **doesn't see** any guests, and Dan **is wearing** shorts and a T-shirt! Dan **looks** surprised. In his culture, people never **arrive** at the exact start of a social event. They often **come** at least 30 minutes later.

SITUATION 2

Ina and Marty **are talking**. They **are** both **feeling** very uncomfortable. In Marty's culture, people usually **stand** quite close. This **seems** friendly to them. In Ina's culture, people **prefer** to have more distance between them. This **doesn't mean** they **are** unfriendly.

[1] ***What's your cross-cultural IQ?:*** How much do you know about other people's cultures?
[2] ***What's the matter?:*** What's wrong?

After You Read

A | Vocabulary: *Circle the letter of the word or phrase closest in meaning to the word in* **blue.**

1. Are you living in your **native** country?
   a. first
   b. new
   c. favorite

2. Do you ever travel **abroad**?
   a. by boat
   b. to foreign countries
   c. on expensive trips

3. What was the **misunderstanding** about?
   a. fight
   b. argument
   c. confusion

4. They come from different **cultures**.
   a. schools
   b. climates
   c. ways of life

5. They prefer to have more **distance** between them.
   a. streets
   b. space
   c. time

6. There are a lot of parties and other **events** at the Students' Club.
   a. members
   b. languages
   c. activities

B | Comprehension: *Complete each sentence with the correct name.*

1. _____ doesn't have shoes on.

2. _____ isn't expecting people to arrive at 8:00.

3. _____ thinks he's on time.

4. _____ is wearing perfume.

5. _____ wants to stand farther away.

6. _____ probably thinks the other person is a little unfriendly.

PRESENT PROGRESSIVE

Affirmative Statements

Subject	Be	Base Form of Verb + -ing	
I	am		
You	are		
He She It	is	traveling	now.
We You They	are		

Negative Statements

Subject	Be	Not	Base Form of Verb + -ing	
I	am			
He	is	not	traveling	now.
We	are			

Yes / No Questions

Be	Subject	Base Form of Verb + -ing	
Is	he	traveling	now?

Short Answers

Yes,	he	is.
No,		isn't.

Wh- Questions

Wh- Word	Be	Subject	Base Form of Verb + -ing	
Where	are	you	traveling	now?

SIMPLE PRESENT

Affirmative Statements

Subject		Verb
I You		travel.
He She It	often	travels.
We You They		travel.

Negative Statements

Subject	Do	Not	Base Form of Verb	
I	do			
He	does	not	travel	often.
We	do			

Yes / No Questions

Do	Subject	Base Form of Verb	
Does	he	travel	often?

Short Answers

Yes,	he	does.
No,		doesn't.

Wh- Questions

Wh- Word	Do	Subject		Base Form of Verb
Where	do	you	usually	travel?

GRAMMAR NOTES

1 Use the **present progressive** to describe:

a. something that is happening <u>right now</u> (for example, *now, at the moment*)

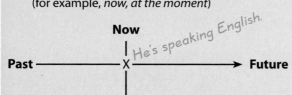

b. something that is happening in a <u>longer present time</u> (for example, *this month, this year, these days, nowadays*), even if it's not happening right now

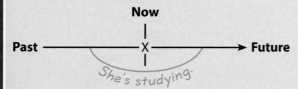

- Diego **is speaking** English *now*.
- He**'s wearing** shorts *at the moment*.

- We**'re studying** U.S. history *this month*. (But we aren't studying it right now.)
- Laura**'s studying** in France *this year*.
- **Are** you **studying** hard *these days*?

2 Use the **simple present** to describe what <u>regularly</u> happens (for example, *usually, often, every day, always*).

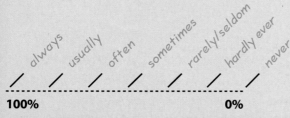

- Diego **speaks** Spanish at home.
- He **wears** jeans *every day*.

3 Use the **simple present** with **adverbs of frequency** to express <u>how often</u> something happens.

always usually often sometimes rarely/seldom hardly ever never

/ / / / / / /

100%   **0%**

Adverbs of frequency usually go <u>before</u> the main verb. However, some adverbs, such as *sometimes* and *usually*, can go at the <u>beginning</u> of the sentence too.

BE CAREFUL! Adverbs of frequency always go <u>after</u> the verb *be*.

- In Spain, women *always* **kiss** on both cheeks.
- In France, women *often* **kiss** on both cheeks.
- We *rarely* **stand** very close to each other.
- In China, children *never* **call** adults by their first names.

- I *sometimes* **wear** shorts at home.
OR
- *Sometimes* I **wear** shorts at home.

- They **are** *never* late.
Not: They ~~never are~~ late.

(continued on next page)

4 Use the **simple present** with most **non-action verbs**. Do NOT use the present progressive—even when the verb describes a situation that exists at the moment of speaking.

Non-action verbs usually describe <u>states</u> or <u>situations</u> but not actions. We use them to:

- Jane **wants** to go home *now*.
  Not: Jane ~~is wanting~~ to go home now.

a. express **emotions** (*like, love, hate, want, feel, fear, trust*)

- We **like** Claude a lot.
- We **love** his sense of humor.

b. describe **mental states** (*know, remember, believe, think [= believe], understand*)

- I **know** a lot of U.S. customs now.
- Ari **remembers** your number.

c. show **possession** (*have, own, possess, belong*)

- Cesar **has** two brothers.
- Some students **own** cars.

d. describe **senses** and **perceptions** (*hear, see, smell, taste, feel, notice, seem, look [= seem], be, appear, sound*)

- I **hear** the telephone.
- Dina **seems** tired.

5 Some verbs that describe senses and perceptions, such as ***taste***, ***smell***, ***feel***, and ***look***, can have both a **non-action** and an **action** meaning.

NON-ACTION	ACTION
The soup **tastes** good. *(It's good.)*	He**'s tasting** the soup. *(He's trying it.)*
His car **looks** great. *(It's beautiful.)*	I**'m looking** at his car. *(I'm examining it.)*

Other verbs that have both **non-action** and **action** meaning are ***have*** and ***think***.

I **have** a new watch. *(I own a new watch.)*	I**'m having** fun. *(I'm experiencing fun.)*
I **think** he's right. *(My opinion: He's right.)*	I**'m thinking** of going. *(I'm considering going.)*

USAGE NOTE: We often use ***feel*** in the progressive form to express emotion. The meaning is the same as when we use the simple present form.

- I **feel** tired. OR I**'m feeling** tired.

REFERENCE NOTES

For **spelling rules** on forming the **present progressive**, see Appendix 21 on page A-10.
For **spelling rules** on forming the third person singular of the **simple present**, see Appendix 20 on page A-9.
For **pronunciation rules** for the **simple present**, see Appendix 29 on page A-14.
For **contractions** of *I am, you are*, etc., see Appendix 26 on page A-12.
For a list of **non-action verbs**, see Appendix 2 on page A-2.
For use of the **present progressive** and the **simple present** to talk about the **future**, see Unit 6.

EXERCISE 1: Discover the Grammar

*Read the blog postings by Brian, a Canadian summer exchange student studying in Argentina. Circle all the verbs that describe what is happening **now**. Underline the verbs that describe what **regularly** happens.*

JUNE 28: I'm sitting in a seat 30,000 feet above the Earth en route to Argentina! I usually have dinner at this time, but right now I have an awful headache from all the excitement. My seatmate is eating my food. I guess it's good. She looks happy.

JUNE 30: It's 7:30 P.M. My host parents are still working. Carlos, my father, works at home. My little brother, Ricardo, is cute. He looks (and acts) a lot like Bobby. Right now, he's looking over my shoulder and trying to read my journal.

JULY 4: The weather is cold here in the summer. I usually spend the first weekend of July at the beach. Today I'm walking around in a heavy sweater.

AUGUST 6: I usually feel great in the evening, but tonight I feel really tired.

AUGUST 25: I'm feeling very comfortable here now—but it's almost time to go home! My host parents usually cook a light dinner, but tonight is a special event. They're having a party for me to say goodbye. I miss them already!

EXERCISE 2: Present Progressive or Simple Present   *(Grammar Notes 1–5)*

Some students are talking outside of a classroom. Complete their conversations. Choose between the present progressive and the simple present forms of the verbs in parentheses.

A.   **TARO:** There's Miguel. He _____'s talking_____ to Luisa.
   1. (talks / 's talking)

   MARISA: Yes. They _____ a class together
   2. (take / 're taking)
   this semester.

   TARO: They _____ very close to
   3. (stand / 're standing)
   each other. _____ they
   4. (Do you think / Are you thinking)
   _____?
   5. (date / 're dating)

   MARISA: No. I _____ it _____ anything
   6. (don't think / 'm not thinking)   **7. (means / 's meaning)**
   special. I _____ from Costa Rica, and people usually
   8. (come / 'm coming)
   _____ that close to each other there.
   9. (stand / are standing)

B. **LI-WU:** Hi, Paulo. What _____?
     1. (do you do / are you doing)

PAULO: Oh, I _____ for class to begin.
     2. (wait / 'm waiting)

LI-WU: What's the matter? You _____ a
     3. (seem / 're seeming)

little down.

PAULO: I'm just tired. I _____ evenings this
     4. (work / 'm working)

semester. Hey, is that your teacher over there?

LI-WU: Yes. She _____ to a classmate.
     5. (talks / 's talking)

PAULO: What's wrong? He _____ at her. He
     6. (doesn't look / 's not looking)

_____ uncomfortable.
     7. (seems / 's seeming)

LI-WU: Oh. That _____ anything. In some
     8. (doesn't mean / isn't meaning)

countries it's not respectful to look directly at your teacher.

EXERCISE 3: Questions and Statements
(Grammar Notes 1–5)

Other students are talking outside of a classroom. Complete the conversations. Use the present progressive or the simple present form of the verbs in parentheses.

A. **RASHA:** There's Hans. Why _____*is*_____ he

_____*walking*_____ so fast? Class _____ at
     1. (walk)   **2. (start)**

9:00. He still _____ 10 minutes!
                    3. (have)

CLAUDE: He always _____ fast. I think Swiss people
                         4. (walk)

often _____ to be in a hurry.
          5. (appear)

B. **IZUMI:** Isn't that Sergio and Luis? Why _____

they _____ hands? They already
          1. (shake)

_____ each other!
     2. (know)

LI-JING: In Brazil, men _____ hands every time they
                              3. (shake)

_____. It's normal in their culture.
     4. (meet)

IZUMI: _____ women _____ hands too?
                                         5. (shake)

EXERCISE 4: Affirmative and Negative Statements

(Grammar Notes 1–2, 5)

Look at Brian's schedule in Argentina. He usually has a regular schedule, but today some things are different. Complete the sentences. Use the present progressive or the simple present. Choose between affirmative and negative.

7:00–8:00	~~run in the park~~	get ready for a field trip
8:30–12:30	~~attend class~~	go on a field trip to the museum
1:00–2:00	eat lunch	
2:00–3:00	~~study with my classmates~~	work on the family Web page
3:00–5:00	work in the cafeteria	
5:00–6:30	~~do homework~~	play tennis
6:30–8:30	~~play tennis~~	watch a video with Eva
8:30–9:30	have dinner	
9:30–10:00	~~write letters~~	take a walk with the family
10:00–10:30	~~take a shower~~	do homework

1. Brian always _runs in the park_ early in the morning,

   but today he _'s getting ready for a field trip_ .

2. Brian usually _____ between 8:30 and 12:30,

   but today he _____ .

3. He always _____ between 1:00 and 2:00.

4. It's 1:30. He _____ .

5. He normally _____ after lunch,

   but today he _____ .

6. Every day from 3:00 to 5:00, he _____ .

7. It's 5:00, but he _____ now.

   He _____ instead.

8. It's 6:45, but he _____ .

   He _____ .

9. It's 8:30. Brian _____ .

10. He always _____ at 8:30.

11. After dinner, Brian usually _____ ,

    but tonight he _____ .

12. It's 10:15, but he _____ .

    He _____ .

EXERCISE 5: Present Progressive or Simple Present

(Grammar Notes 1–5)

Complete the paragraph. Use the correct form of the verbs from the box.

cause	feel	go	live	~~make~~	travel

New food, new customs, new routines—they all _____*make*_____ international travel

1.

interesting. But they also _____ culture shock for many travelers going abroad.

2.

_____ you now _____ or _____ in a culture different

3.   **4.**

from your own? If so, why _____ you _____ so good (or so bad)?

5.

Some experts say that we often _____ through four stages of culture shock:

6.

Honeymoon Stage:	In the first weeks, everything seems great.
Rejection Stage:	You have negative feelings about the new culture.
Adjustment Stage:	Things are getting better these days.
Adaptation Stage:	You are finally comfortable in the new culture.

EXERCISE 6: Affirmative and Negative Statements

(Grammar Notes 1–5)

A | *Complete the statements in the quiz. Use the correct form of the verbs from the box.*

annoy	improve	~~love~~	think	understand
feel	live	make	treat	want

☐ 1. I _____*love*_____ it here!

☐ 2. People always _____ me very nicely.

☐ 3. The customs here often _____ me.

☐ 4. I _____ here now, but I _____ I'll stay.
(negative)

☐ 5. Sometimes, I just _____ to go home!

☐ 6. My language skills _____ a lot each month.

☐ 7. I _____ a lot of new friends these days.

☐ 8. I still _____ everything, but I _____ at home here.
(negative)

B | *Are you living in a culture different from your own? If yes, take the quiz. Check (✓) the statements that are true for you* **now**. *Then check your quiz results on page 14.*

EXERCISE 7: Editing

Read the student's journal. There are eleven mistakes in the use of the present progressive or simple present. The first mistake is already corrected. Find and correct ten more.

> I'm sitting
> It's 12:30 and ~~I sit~~ in the library right now. My classmates are eating lunch together, but I don't feel hungry yet. At home, we eat never this early. Today our journal topic is culture shock. It's a good topic for me right now because I'm being pretty homesick. I miss speaking my native language with my friends. And I miss my old routine. At home we always are eating a big meal at 2:00 in the afternoon. Then we rest. But here in Toronto I'm having a 3:00 conversation class. Every day I almost fall asleep in class, and my teacher ask me, "Are you bored?" Of course I'm not bored. I just need my afternoon nap! This class always is fun. This semester we work on a project with video cameras. My team is filming groups of people from different cultures at social events. We are analyze "personal space." That means how close to each other these people stand. According to my new watch, it's 12:55, so I leave now for my 1:00 class. Teachers here really aren't liking tardiness!

STEP 4 COMMUNICATION PRACTICE

EXERCISE 8: Listening

A | You are going to listen to short interviews of foreign students studying at a six-week language program in the United States. Before you listen, try to complete the sentences. Then listen and check your answers.

1. You're living in a new country and experiencing a new _____culture_____.

2. In Turkey, I _____ in a very small town, but now I'm living in New York. New York is huge!

3. How do you _____ life in the big city, Eva? Are you experiencing _____ shock?

4. You don't usually _____ a watch? How do you _____ the time?

5. This summer, I _____ grammar and pronunciation.

B | *Listen again to the interviews and check (✓) the things the students **Usually** do and the things they are doing **Now or These Days**.*

Students . . .	Usually	Now or These Days
1. a. speak English	☐	✓
b. speak Spanish	☐	☐
2. a. live in a small town	☐	☐
b. live in a big city	☐	☐
3. a. walk slowly	☐	☐
b. move quickly	☐	☐
4. a. wear a watch	☐	☐
b. ask other people for the time	☐	☐
5. a. study grammar and pronunciation	☐	☐
b. study English literature	☐	☐

EXERCISE 9: Pronunciation

A | *Read and listen to the Pronunciation Note.*

Pronunciation Note

In **informal, fast American English**, people often pronounce ***What do you . . . ?*** and ***What are you . . . ?*** the same way: "Whaddaya."

EXAMPLES: **What do you** read? → "**Whaddaya** read?"
What are you reading? → "**Whaddaya** reading?"

B | *Listen and repeat the questions.*

1. **What are you** studying this semester?
2. **What do you** do after school?
3. **What are you** thinking about?
4. **What do you** usually eat for lunch?
5. **What are you** reading these days?

C | *Work with a partner. Practice asking and answering the questions. Use your own information.*

EXERCISE 10: Find Someone Who . . .

A | *Walk around your classroom. Ask your classmates questions. Find someone who . . .*

Name

- isn't living in a dormitory

  _____

- likes visiting foreign countries

  _____

- speaks more than two languages

  _____

- is studying something in addition to English

  _____

- doesn't watch sports on TV

  _____

- is planning to travel abroad this year

  _____

- _____

  (add your own)

  _____

  EXAMPLE: **A:** Are you living in a dormitory?
  B: No, I'm not. I'm living with a family.

B | *Report back to the class.*

  EXAMPLE: Tania and José aren't living in a dormitory.

EXERCISE 11: Picture Discussion

Work in pairs. Look at the photographs. Describe them. What's happening? How do the people feel? Discuss possible explanations for each situation. Compare your answers with those of your classmates.

  EXAMPLE: **A:** He's pointing. He looks angry.
  B: Maybe he's just explaining something.

EXERCISE 12: Compare and Contrast

A | *Work in small groups. Look at the questions. In your culture, which questions are appropriate to ask someone you just met? Which are not appropriate? Compare your choices with those of your classmates.*

- Are you married?
- How much rent do you pay?
- How old are you?
- What are you studying?
- What do you do?
- Where do you live?

B | *What are other examples of inappropriate questions in your culture?*

EXERCISE 13: Writing

A | *Write a paragraph about a new experience you are having. Maybe you are living in a new country, taking a new class, or working at a new job. Describe the situation. How is it different from what you usually do? How do you feel in the situation?*

> **EXAMPLE:** I usually live at home with my parents, but this month I'm living with my aunt and uncle. Everything seems different. My aunt . . .

B | *Check your work. Use the Editing Checklist.*

Editing Checklist

Did you use . . . ?
- ☐ the present progressive to describe something that is happening right now
- ☐ the simple present to describe what regularly happens
- ☐ the simple present with non-action verbs such as **be**, **like**, **want**, and **know**
- ☐ adverbs of frequency in the correct position

QUIZ RESULTS FOR EXERCISE 6

If you checked . . .   *you are in the . . .*

1 and **2**	**Honeymoon Stage**
3 and **4** and **5**	**Rejection Stage**
6 and **7**	**Adjustment Stage**
8	**Adaptation Stage**

UNIT 1 Review

Check your answers on page UR-1.
Do you need to review anything?

A | *Circle the correct words to complete the sentences.*

1. What courses <u>are you taking / do you take</u> this semester?

2. I <u>don't / 'm not</u> understand this phrase. What's *culture shock*?

3. At home, we <u>often speak / speak often</u> Spanish.

4. Look! That's my teacher. He<u>'s talking / talks</u> to Andrea, one of my classmates.

5. <u>Are / Do</u> you feel better today?

B | *Complete the conversation with the present progressive or simple present form of the verbs in parentheses.*

A: What _____ you _____ right now?
        1. (do)

B: Not much. I _____ just _____ a video game. Why?
        2. (play)

A: _____ you _____ to get some lunch?
        3. (want)

B: Sure. I usually _____ this early, but I _____
        4. (not eat)   **5. (feel)**

   pretty hungry right now.

A: Mmm, mushroom soup. It _____ good.
        6. (look)

B: It _____ good, though. I had it yesterday.
        7. (not taste)

A: Hey, there's Costa and Libby. Why _____ they _____ like
        8. (shout)

   that? _____ they angry?
        9. (be)

B: I don't think so. They always _____ like that. Let's go sit with them.
        10. (talk)

   They're fun.

C | *Find and correct five mistakes.*

I live in Qatar, but right now I stay in Wisconsin. I'm studying English here. I have a good

time this summer, but in some ways it's a pretty strange experience. Summer in Wisconsin feel

like winter in Qatar! Every weekend, I go to the beach with some classmates, but I go never

into the water—it's too cold! I'm enjoy my time here though, and my culture shock is going

away fast.

Simple Past
POETS

Before You Read

Look at the picture and the text above it. Discuss the questions.

1. What did Matsuo Basho do?
2. How long did he live?

Read

Read the short biography of Basho.

Matsuo Basho, 1644–1694

Matsuo Basho **wrote** more than 1,000 *haiku* (three-line poems). He **chose** topics from nature, daily life, and human emotions. He **became** one of Japan's most famous poets, and his work **established** haiku as an important art form.

Basho **was** born Matsuo Munefusa near Kyoto in 1644. ("Basho" is the name he later **used** as a poet.) He **did not want** to become a samurai[1] like his father. Instead, he **moved** to Edo (present-day Tokyo) and **studied** poetry. Then he **became** a teacher, and by 1681 he **had** many students and admirers.

Basho, however, **was** restless. Starting in 1684, he **traveled** on foot and on horseback all over Japan. Sometimes his friends **joined** him, and they **wrote** poetry together. Travel **was** difficult in the 17th century, and Basho often **got** sick. He **died** in 1694 during a journey to Osaka. At that time, he **had** 2,000 students.

---

[1] *samurai:* in past times, a member of the soldier class in Japan

As for that flower
By the road —
My horse ate it!
— Matsuo Basho

After You Read

A | Vocabulary: *Complete the sentences with the words from the box.*

| admirers | emotions | journey | restless | topic |

1. Basho wrote about everyday things. A frog is the _____ of one of his most famous poems.

2. Basho's students and _____ loved him and called him a great poet.

3. On his first _____, Basho traveled a long way and visited his native village.

4. Basho became _____ and did not want to stay in one place for very long.

5. Basho felt all kinds of strong _____ in his travels, such as fear, loneliness, and happiness.

B | Comprehension: *Check (✓) the boxes to complete the sentences. Check **all** the true information about Basho.*

1. Basho wrote about _____.
   - ☐ flowers
   - ☐ animals
   - ☐ samurai

2. Before Basho, *haiku* _____.
   - ☐ was an important kind of poetry
   - ☐ did not exist
   - ☐ was not an important kind of poetry

3. In Edo, Basho _____.
   - ☐ studied poetry
   - ☐ became a teacher
   - ☐ became a samurai

4. On his journeys, he _____.
   - ☐ traveled in boats
   - ☐ walked
   - ☐ rode horses

5. At the end of his life, Basho _____.
   - ☐ had only a few students
   - ☐ traveled to Osaka
   - ☐ was famous

SIMPLE PAST: *BE*

Affirmative Statements

Subject	*Be*	
I	**was**	
You	**were**	
He She It	**was**	famous.
We You They	**were**	

Negative Statements

Subject	*Be + Not*	
I	**wasn't**	
You	**weren't**	
He She It	**wasn't**	famous.
We You They	**weren't**	

Yes / No Questions

Be	Subject	
Was	I	
Were	you	
Was	he she it	famous?
Were	we you they	

Short Answers

Affirmative			Negative		
	you	**were.**		you	**weren't.**
	I	**was.**		I	**wasn't.**
Yes,	he she it	**was.**	**No,**	he she it	**wasn't.**
	you we they	**were.**		you we they	**weren't.**

Wh- Questions

Wh- Word	*Be*	Subject	
	was	I	
	were	you	
Where When Why	**was**	he she it	famous?
	were	we you they	

SIMPLE PAST: REGULAR AND IRREGULAR VERBS

Affirmative Statements

Subject	Verb	
I You He She It We You They	**moved** **traveled**	to Japan.
	came **left**	in 1684.

Negative Statements

Subject	*Did not*	Base Form of Verb	
I You He She It We You They	**didn't**	**move** **travel**	to Japan.
		come **leave**	in 1684.

Yes / No Questions

Did	Subject	Base Form of Verb	
Did	I you he she it we you they	**move** **travel**	to Japan?
		come **leave**	in 1684?

Short Answers

	Affirmative			Negative	
Yes,	you I he she it you we they	**did**.	**No**,	you I he she it you we they	**didn't**.

Wh- Questions

Wh- Word	*Did*	Subject	Base Form of Verb	
When Why	**did**	I you he she it we you they	**move** **travel**	to Japan?
			come? **leave**?	

GRAMMAR NOTES

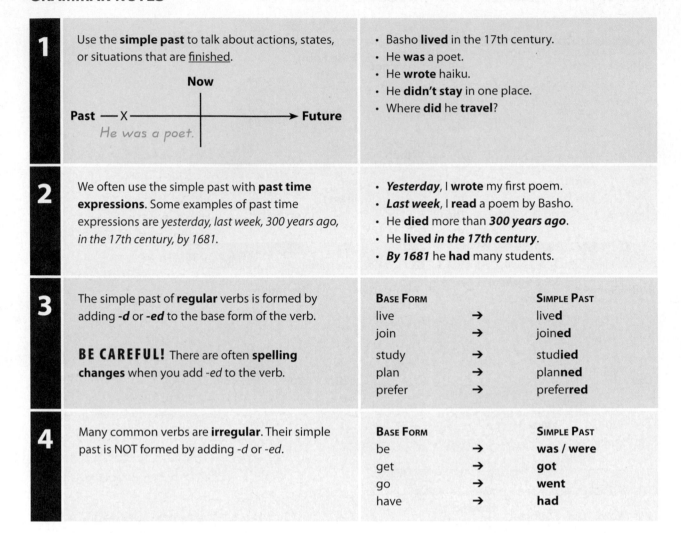

| 1 | Use the **simple past** to talk about actions, states, or situations that are <u>finished</u>.

Now

Past —X————\|————→ Future
    He was a poet. | • Basho **lived** in the 17th century.
• He **was** a poet.
• He **wrote** haiku.
• He **didn't stay** in one place.
• Where **did** he **travel**? |

| 2 | We often use the simple past with **past time expressions**. Some examples of past time expressions are *yesterday, last week, 300 years ago, in the 17th century, by 1681*. | • *Yesterday*, I **wrote** my first poem.
• *Last week*, I **read** a poem by Basho.
• He **died** more than *300 years ago*.
• He **lived** *in the 17th century*.
• *By 1681* he **had** many students. |

| 3 | The simple past of **regular** verbs is formed by adding **-d** or **-ed** to the base form of the verb.

BE CAREFUL! There are often **spelling changes** when you add *-ed* to the verb. | **BASE FORM**   **SIMPLE PAST**
live → live**d**
join → join**ed**
study → stud**ied**
plan → plan**ned**
prefer → prefer**red** |

| 4 | Many common verbs are **irregular**. Their simple past is NOT formed by adding -d or -ed. | **BASE FORM**   **SIMPLE PAST**
be → **was / were**
get → **got**
go → **went**
have → **had** |

REFERENCE NOTES

For **spelling rules** for the **simple past of regular verbs**, see Appendix 22 on page A-10.

For **pronunciation rules** for the **simple past of regular verbs**, see Appendix 30 on page A-15.

For a list of **irregular verbs**, see Appendix 1 on page A-1.

EXERCISE 1: Discover the Grammar

Read more about Basho. Underline all the verbs in the simple past. Then complete the timeline on the left.

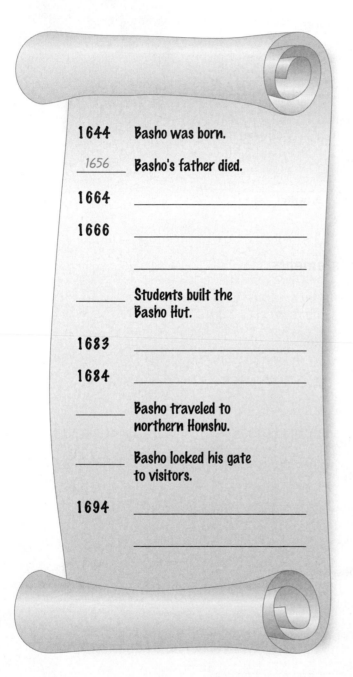

1644   Basho was born.

1656   Basho's father died.

1664   _____

1666   _____

_____

_____   Students built the Basho Hut.

1683   _____

1684   _____

_____   Basho traveled to northern Honshu.

_____   Basho locked his gate to visitors.

1694   _____

_____

As the son of a samurai, Basho <u>grew up</u> in the household of Todo Yoshitada, a young lord. After his father's death in 1656, Basho stayed in the Yoshitada household. He and Todo wrote poetry together, and in 1664, they published some poems. Two years later, Todo died suddenly. Basho left the area.

Basho was a restless young man, and he moved around for several years. In the 1670s, he went to Edo and stayed there. He found friendship and success once again. Basho judged poetry contests, published his own poetry, and taught students. His students built him a home outside the city in 1681. They planted a banana tree (*basho* in Japanese) in front and called his home "Basho Hut." That is how the poet got his name: Basho.

In spite of this success, Basho became unhappy. He often wrote about loneliness. His mother died in 1683, and he began his travels a year later. His trip to the northern part of Honshu in 1689 was difficult, but his travel diary about this journey, *Narrow Road to the Deep North*, became one of Japan's greatest works of literature.

As a famous poet, Basho had many visitors—too many, in fact. In 1693 he locked his gate for a month, stayed alone, and wrote. The following year he took his final journey, to Osaka. He died there among his friends and admirers.

EXERCISE 2: Affirmative Statements

(Grammar Notes 1–4)

Complete the biography of American poet Emily Dickinson. Use the simple past form of the verbs in parentheses. Go to Appendix 1 on page A-1 for help with the irregular verbs.

Emily Dickinson, one of the most famous American poets,

_____ *lived* _____ from 1830 to 1886. Her favorite topics
1. (live)

_____ nature, time, and human emotions.
2. (be)

Dickinson _____ an unusual life. During the 1860s, she
3. (lead)

_____ a recluse[1]—she almost never _____
4. (become)   5. (leave)

her house in Amherst, Massachusetts, and she only _____
6. (wear)

white. Dickinson _____ very few people to visit her, but she
7. (allow)

_____ a lot of friends, and she _____ them
8. (have)   9. (write)

many letters.

EXERCISE 3: Affirmative and Negative Statements

(Grammar Notes 1–4)

Complete the list of facts about Emily Dickinson. Use the simple past form of the verbs in parentheses. Go to Appendix 1 on page A-1 for help with the irregular verbs.

1. Dickinson _____ *wasn't* _____ only interested in poetry.
   (not be)

2. She also _____ science.
   (like)

3. She _____ topics from science in many of her poems.
   (use)

4. She never _____ far from home, but she _____ many people.
   (go)   (know)

5. Dickinson _____ only poetry.
   (not write)

6. She _____ her friends and admirers hundreds of letters.
   (send)

7. Her letters _____ full of jokes, recipes, cartoons, and poems.
   (be)

8. But she _____ the envelopes—other people _____ that for her.
   (not address)   (do)

9. Dickinson _____ a typewriter.
   (not own)

10. She _____ the first drafts[2] of her poems on the back of old grocery lists.
    (write)

11. During her lifetime, 7 of her 1,700 poems _____ in print.
    (appear)

12. She _____ about this, and no one _____ her permission.
    (not know)   (ask)

---

[1] *recluse:* someone who stays away from other people

[2] *first draft:* first copy of a piece of writing, with no corrections

EXERCISE 4: Regular and Irregular Verbs (Grammar Notes 1–4)

Complete the lines from a poem by Emily Dickinson. Use the simple past form of the verbs from the box. Go to Appendix 1 on page A-1 for help with the irregular verbs.

bite	~~come~~	drink	eat	hop	not know

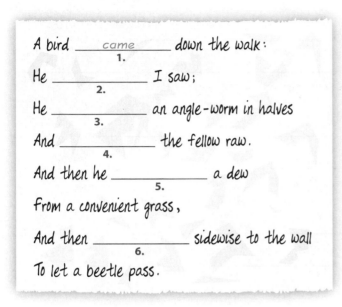

A bird ____came____ down the walk:
1.
He _____ I saw;
2.
He _____ an angle-worm in halves
3.
And _____ the fellow raw.
4.
And then he _____ a dew
5.
From a convenient grass,
And then _____ sidewise to the wall
6.
To let a beetle pass.

EXERCISE 5: Questions and Answers (Grammar Notes 1–4)

Read the statements about Basho. Then write questions about Emily Dickinson. Write a **yes/no** *question if a verb is underlined or a* **wh-** *question if other words are underlined. Then answer your questions using the information from Exercises 2 and 3.*

1. Basho <u>was</u> a poet.

Q: _Was Dickinson a poet?_

A: _Yes, she was._

2. He was born <u>in 1644</u>.

Q: _When was Dickinson born?_

A: _She was born in 1830._

3. He lived <u>in Japan</u>.

Q: _____

A: _____

4. He <u>became</u> famous during his lifetime.

Q: _____

A: _____

(continued on next page)

5. Basho's admirers often <u>visited</u> him.

Q: _____

A: _____

6. He <u>traveled</u> a lot.

Q: _____

A: _____

7. Basho wrote <u>more than 1,000 poems</u>.

Q: _____

A: _____

8. He wrote <u>about nature</u>.

Q: _____

A: _____

9. He died <u>in 1694</u>.

Q: _____

A: _____

EXERCISE 6: Affirmative and Negative Statements

(Grammar Notes 2–4)

A | *Read the article about a modern writer.*

ANA CASTILLO is a modern poet, novelist, short story writer, and teacher. She was born in Chicago in 1953, and she lived there for 32 years. *Otro Canto*, her first book of poetry, appeared in 1977.

In her work, Castillo uses humor and a lively mixture of Spanish and English (Spanglish). She got her special writer's "voice" by living in a neighborhood with many different ethnic groups. She also thanks her father for her writing style. "He had an outgoing and easy personality, and this . . . sense of humor. I got a lot from him . . ."

Castillo attended high school, college, and graduate school in Chicago. In the 1970s, she taught English and Mexican history. She received a Ph.D. in American Studies from Bremen University in Germany in 1992.

B | *Read the statements. Write **That's right** or **That's wrong**. Correct the incorrect statements.*

1. Ana Castillo was born in Mexico City.

   That's wrong. She wasn't born in Mexico City. She was born in Chicago.

2. She lived in Chicago until 1977.

   _____

3. Her father was very shy.

   _____

4. She grew up among people of different cultures.

   _____

5. Castillo got most of her education in Chicago.

   _____

6. She taught Spanish in the 1970s.

   _____

7. She went to France for her Ph.D.

   _____

EXERCISE 7: Editing

Read the student's journal. There are ten mistakes in the use of the simple past. The first mistake is already corrected. Find and correct nine more.

> Today in class we read a poem by the American poet Robert Frost.
>   *enjoyed*
> I really ~~enjoy~~ it. It was about a person who choosed between two roads
> in a forest. Many people believed the person were Frost. He thinked
> about his choice for a long time. The two roads didn't looked very
> different. Finally, he didn't took the road most people take. He took
> the one less traveled on. At that time, he didn't thought it was an
> important decision, but his choice change his life.
>
>   Sometimes I feel a little like Frost. Two years ago I decide to
> move to a new country. It was a long journey and a big change. Did I
> made the right decision?

EXERCISE 8: Listening

A | *Read the statements. Then listen to the interview with a poet. Listen again and circle the correct information.*

1. Murat came to the United States <u>before</u> / <u>after</u> his parents.

2. He had a wonderful life with his grandparents in <u>Baltimore</u> / <u>Turkey</u>.

3. In Baltimore, he had no friends, so he <u>wrote poems</u> / <u>read books</u>.

4. He wrote his first poem in <u>English</u> / <u>Turkish</u>.

5. In college, Murat studied <u>farming</u> / <u>poetry</u>.

B | *Read the information in the timeline. Then listen again to the interview and write the year for each event.*

| was born | parents left Turkey | moved to the U.S. | began to write poetry | graduated from college | won a poetry award | became a teacher |

1970

EXERCISE 9: Pronunciation

A | *Read and listen to the Pronunciation Note.*

Pronunciation Note
In **wh- questions**, we often pronounce **did** "d" after the *wh-* word.
EXAMPLES: Why **did** she write the poem? → "Why**'d** she write the poem?"   Who **did** they show it to? → "Who**'d** they show it to?"   How **did** he like it? → "How**'d** he like it?"
Notice that **How'd he** sounds like "Howdy."

B | *Listen to the short conversations. Then listen again and complete the conversations with the words that you hear. Use full forms.*

1. **A:** _____ live?

    B: In Japan.

2. **A:** _____ talk to?

    B: A famous poet.

3. **A:** _____ move?

    B: To be near school.

4. A: _____ feel about their new home?

   B: Not great at first.

5. A: _____ study poetry?

   B: He loves it.

6. A: _____ go to school?

   B: In Mexico.

C | *Listen again to the conversations and repeat the questions. Use short forms. Then practice the conversations with a partner.*

EXERCISE 10: Compare and Contrast

Work in small groups. Reread the information about Matsuo Basho (see pages 16 and 21) and Emily Dickinson (see page 22). In what ways were the two poets similar? How were they different? With your group, write as many ideas as you can. Compare your ideas with those of your classmates.

> **EXAMPLE:** **A:** Both Basho and Dickinson were poets.
> **B:** Basho lived in the 17th century. Dickinson lived in the 19th century.
> **C:** Dickinson stayed at home, but Basho was restless and traveled a lot.

EXERCISE 11: Writing

A | *Write a paragraph about some important events in your life. Do not put your name on your paper. Your teacher will collect all the papers, mix them up, and redistribute them to the class.*

B | *Check your work. Use the Editing Checklist.*

> ### Editing Checklist
>
> Did you . . . ?
> ☐ use the simple past
> ☐ spell regular past verbs correctly
> ☐ use the correct form of irregular past verbs

C | *Read the paragraph your teacher gives you. Then ask your classmates questions to try to find its writer.*

> **EXAMPLE:** Did you come here in 1990? OR When did you come here?

EXERCISE 12: Information Gap: Celebrity Profile

Work in pairs (A and B). **Student A,** *follow the instructions on this page.* **Student B,** *turn to page 30 and follow the instructions there.*

1. Read the profile of an actor who is also a poet, painter, and musician. Ask your partner questions to complete the missing information.

   EXAMPLE: **A:** When was Viggo born?
                B: He was born on October 25, 1958.

2. Answer your partner's questions.

   EXAMPLE: **B:** Where was Viggo born?
                A: He was born in New York.

3. If you don't know how to spell something, ask your partner.

   EXAMPLE: **A:** How do you spell Argentina?
                B: Capital A, R, G, E, N, T, I, N, A.

SCREEN-TIME PROFILE

Date of Birth: *October 25, 1958*

Place of Birth: New York

Mini Bio:

★ lived in Argentina, Venezuela,

   and _____ as a child

★ attended school in Argentina

★ spoke Spanish, _____, and English

★ returned to the United States in 19_____

★ became a movie actor in 1985

★ first movie was *Witness*

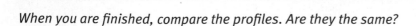

Viggo Mortensen: actor, poet, painter, musician

★ played the part of _____ in *Lord of the Rings* (This movie made him famous.)

★ finished his first _____ in 1993 (The title was *Ten Last Night*.)

★ created the paintings for the movie *A Perfect Murder* (He played the part of the artist.)

★ wrote music for *Lord of the Rings*

When you are finished, compare the profiles. Are they the same?

A | *Circle the letter of the correct answer to complete each sentence.*

1. Last night I _____ a poem for my English class.

   a. write   **b.** wrote   **c.** written

2. It _____ about my childhood.

   a. be   **b.** were   **c.** was

3. At first, I didn't _____ what to write about.

   a. know   **b.** knowing   **c.** knew

4. My roommate _____ a good suggestion.

   a. makes   **b.** did make   **c.** made

5. Did you _____ a poem for your class?

   a. write   **b.** writing   **c.** wrote

6. I really _____ the experience.

   a. enjoy   **b.** enjoys   **c.** enjoyed

B | *Complete the conversation with the simple past form of the verbs in parentheses and a short answer.*

A: _____ you _____ out last night? I _____ you, but
                           1. (go)   **2. (call)**

     you _____.
         3. (not answer)

B: _____, I _____. I _____ to the movies.
                      4.   **5. (go)**

A: What _____ you _____?
                          6. (see)

B: I _____ *Dead Poets Society*. I _____ it very much, though.
       7. (see)   **8. (not like)**

C | *Find and correct six mistakes.*

The poet Elizabeth Alexander was born in New York City, but she didn't grew up there. Her father taked a job with the government, and her family moved to Washington, D.C. As a child, she have a loving family. Her parents were active in the civil rights movement, and Elizabeth gots interested in African-American history. In her first book, she wrote about important African leaders. She met Barack Obama at the University of Chicago. They both teached there in the 1990s. On January 20, 2009, she reads a poem at President Obama's inauguration.

1. Read the profile of an actor who is also a poet, painter, and musician. Ask your partner questions to complete the missing information.

   EXAMPLE: **A:** When was Viggo born?
   B: He was born on October 25, 1958.

2. Answer your partner's questions.

   EXAMPLE: **B:** Where was Viggo born?
   A: He was born in New York.

3. If you don't know how to spell something, ask your partner.

   EXAMPLE: **B:** How do you spell Argentina?
   A: Capital A, R, G, E, N, T, I, N, A.

SCREEN-TIME PROFILE

Date of Birth: October 25, 1958

Place of Birth: _New York_

Mini Bio:

Viggo Mortensen: actor, poet, painter, musician

★ lived in Argentina, Venezuela, and Denmark as a child

★ attended school in _____

★ spoke Spanish, Danish, and English

★ returned to the United States in 1969

★ became a movie actor in 19____

★ first movie was _____

★ played the part of Aragorn in *Lord of the Rings* (This movie made him famous.)

★ finished his first book of poems in 1993 (The title was *Ten Last Night.*)

★ created _____ for the movie *A Perfect Murder* (He played the part of the artist.)

★ wrote _____ for *Lord of the Rings*

When you are finished, compare the profiles. Are they the same?

Before You Read

Look at the picture. Discuss the questions.

1. What do you know about the *Titanic?*
2. What happened to the ship?

Read

🎧 *Read the newspaper article about the sinking of the* Titanic.

VOL CCXII, NO 875   MONDAY, APRIL 15, 1912   PRICE ONE CENT

■ DISASTER AT SEA ■

NEW YORK, April 15—It **was** a clear night. The sea **was** calm. The *RMS Titanic*, the largest luxury ship[1] in the world, **was sailing** from Southhampton, England, to New York City. This **was** its first voyage,[2] and it **was carrying** more than 2,200 passengers and crew.[3] At around 11:30 P.M. crew member Frederick Fleet **was looking** at the sea when, suddenly, he **saw** a huge white form in front of the ship. When he **saw** it, Fleet immediately **rang** the ship's bell three times and **shouted**, "Iceberg ahead!" But it **was** too late. The great ship **crashed** into the mountain of ice.

When the *Titanic* **hit** the iceberg, people **were sleeping**, **reading**, and **playing** cards. Some passengers **heard** a loud noise, but they **were** not alarmed. They **believed** the ship **was** unsinkable.[4] But soon it **became** clear that the *Titanic* **was** in danger. There **was** a hole in the

side of the ship. Water **was entering** fast, and it **was starting** to sink. There **were** lifeboats, but only 1,178 spaces for 2,224 people. In an attempt to keep everyone calm, the ship's band **played** a lively tune while people **were getting** into the boats.

(continued on next page)

---

[1] *luxury ship:* a boat that has many great things (beautiful rooms, swimming pools, restaurants, etc.)
[2] *voyage:* a long trip, usually on a ship
[3] *crew:* the people who work on a ship or airplane
[4] *unsinkable:* cannot go underwater

DISASTER AT SEA

The *Titanic* **was not** the only ship on the sea that night. There **were** several other ships in the area. The *Californian* **was** nearby, but it **did not hear** the *Titanic's* calls for help. And then there **was** the *Carpathia*. While the *Titanic* **was sailing** toward New York, the *Carpathia* **was traveling** from New York to the Mediterranean. When it **heard** the *Titanic's* distress signals,[5] the *Carpathia* **turned** around and **headed** back toward the sinking ship. By the time the *Carpathia* **arrived**, the *Titanic* **was** already at the bottom of the sea, but there **were** 18 lifeboats full of cold and frightened survivors. Thanks to the *Carpathia*, more than 700 people **lived** to tell the story of that terrible night.

[5] ***distress signals:*** calls for help

After You Read

A | Vocabulary: *Match the words with their definitions.*

_____ 1. disaster   **a.** one part of a larger place

_____ 2. calm   **b.** someone who continues to live after an accident

_____ 3. area   **c.** afraid

_____ 4. survivor   **d.** to go under water

_____ 5. alarmed   **e.** a terrible accident

_____ 6. sink   **f.** quiet

B | Comprehension: *Number the events in order (1–8).*

_____ Water entered the *Titanic*.

_____ Frederick Fleet rang the ship's bell.

_____ The *Titanic* hit an iceberg.

_____ The *Carpathia* arrived and saved the survivors.

_____ The *Titanic* was sailing to New York.

_____ The *Titanic* sank.

_____ Frederick Fleet saw an iceberg.

_____ The *Carpathia* heard the *Titanic's* distress signals.

PAST PROGRESSIVE

		Statements		
Subject	*Was / Were*	*(Not)*	Base Form of Verb + *-ing*	
I	**was**			
You	**were**			
He She	**was**	(not)	**reading** **eating** **sleeping**	yesterday at 11:30 P.M. when he **called**. while he **was talking**.
We You They	**were**			

		Yes / No Questions		
Was / Were	Subject	Base Form of Verb + *-ing*		
Was	I			
Were	you			
Was	he she	**reading** **eating** **sleeping**	yesterday at 11:30 P.M.? when he **called**? while he **was talking**?
Were	we you they			

	Short Answers			
Affirmative			**Negative**	
	you	**were.**		you	**weren't.**
	I	**was.**		I	**wasn't.**
Yes,	he she	**was.**	**No,**	he she	**wasn't.**
	you we they	**were.**		you we they	**weren't.**

		Wh- Questions		
Wh- Word	*Was / Were*	Subject	Base Form of Verb + *-ing*	
	was	I		
	were	you		
Why	**was**	he she	**reading** **eating** **sleeping**	yesterday at 11:30 P.M? when he **called**? while he **was talking**?
	were	we you they		

GRAMMAR NOTES

1 Use the **past progressive** to focus on the <u>duration</u> of a past action, not its completion.

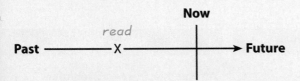

USAGE NOTE: We often use the past progressive with a specific time in the past.

- Paul **was reading** a book last night.
  (We don't know if he finished it.)

- He **was reading** a book *at 11:30 P.M.*

2 Use the **simple past** to focus on the <u>completion</u> of a past action.

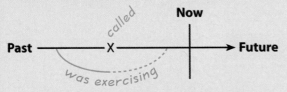

BE CAREFUL! **Non-action verbs** are NOT usually used in the progressive.

- Paul **read** a book last night.
  (He finished it.)

- She **heard** about the disaster.
  NOT: She ~~was hearing~~ about the disaster.

3 Use the **past progressive** with the **simple past** to talk about an action that was <u>interrupted</u> by another action. Use the simple past for the interrupting action.

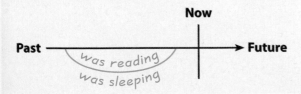

- Use *when* to introduce the **simple past** action.
- Use *while* to introduce the **past progressive** action.

- I **was exercising** when he **called**.
  (I was exercising. The phone rang and interrupted my exercising.)

- He was running **when** he **fell**.
- **While** he **was running**, he fell.

4 Use the **past progressive** with *while* to talk about two actions in progress <u>at the same time</u> in the past. Use the past progressive in both clauses.

Past ———— was reading / was sleeping ———— Now ————→ Future

- **While** I **was reading**, Amy **was sleeping**.
  OR
- Amy **was sleeping** *while* I **was reading**.

5 | **BE CAREFUL!** A sentence with both clauses in the simple past has a very <u>different meaning</u> from a sentence with one clause in the simple past and one clause in the past progressive.

a. Both clauses in the **simple past**:

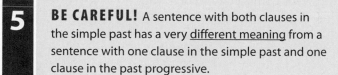

- She **drove** home when she **heard** the news.
  (First she heard the news; then she drove home.)

b. One clause in the **simple past**, the other in the **past progressive**:

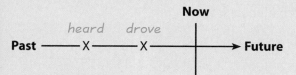

- She **was driving** home when she **heard** the news.
  (First she was driving home; then she heard the news.)

6 | Notice that the **time clause** (the part of the sentence with **when** or **while**) can come at the beginning or the end of the sentence.

Use a **comma** after the time clause when it comes at the beginning. Do NOT use a comma when it comes at the end.

- ***When you called**, I was eating.*
  OR
- *I was eating **when you called**.*

  NOT: I was eating⨯when you called.

REFERENCE NOTES

For **spelling rules** on forming the **past progressive**, see Appendix 21 on page A-10.
For a list of **non-action verbs**, see Appendix 2 on page A-2.

STEP 3 FOCUSED PRACTICE

EXERCISE 1: Discover the Grammar

Read the question. Then circle the letter of the correct sentence.

1. In which sentence did the passengers arrive before the ship left?
   a. When the passengers arrived, the ship was leaving.
   (b.) When the passengers arrived, the ship left.

2. Which sentence tells us that the ship reached New York?
   a. It was sailing to New York.
   b. It sailed to New York.

(continued on next page)

3. In which sentence do we know that the ship went completely under water?

    a. It was sinking.

    b. It sank.

4. Which sentence talks about two actions that were in progress at the same time?

    a. While the ship was sinking, passengers were getting into lifeboats.

    b. When the ship sank, passengers got into lifeboats.

5. In which sentence was the phone call interrupted?

    a. When he heard the news, he called me.

    b. When he heard the news, he was calling me.

6. In which sentence did the woman leave after the phone call?

    a. When he called her, she left the house.

    b. When he called her, she was leaving the house.

EXERCISE 2: Past Progressive Statements

(Grammar Note 1)

Douglas is sailing to Europe on the SS Atlantic. *Look at his schedule for yesterday. Complete the sentences. Use the past progressive form of the verbs in parentheses. Choose between affirmative and negative.*

> ⚓ *S.S. Atlantic*
>
> 10:00 breakfast - Sea Breezes - Donna
> 11:00 exercise - gym - Michel
> 12:00 swimming contest - Olympic pool
> 1:00 lunch - Oceania - Raul
> 2:30 lecture on Italian art - library
> 4:00 coffee - Café Rose - Natasha
> 5:00 haircut - Jean-Georges Salon - Alain
> 7:00 dinner - Thalassa - Kim and Jason
> 9:00 card game - Casino Royal - Massimo

1. At 10:15 Douglas _____*wasn't sleeping*_____ in his cabin.
                       a. (sleep)

  He _____ breakfast at Sea Breezes with Donna.
          b. (have)

2. At 11:05 he _____ in the ship's gym with Michel.
               a. (exercise)

  He _____ in the pool.
          b. (swim)

3. At 1:10 he _____ coffee at Café Rose.
              a. (drink)

  He _____ lunch at Oceania with Raul.
          b. (eat)

4. At 2:40 he _____ for a book in the ship's library.
　　　　　　　　　　　a. (look)

　　He _____ to a lecture on Italian art.
　　　　　　　　　　b. (listen)

5. At 4:05 he _____ a haircut at the Jean-Georges Salon.
　　　　　　　　　　　a. (get)

6. At 7:10 he _____ in his room.
　　　　　　　　　　　a. (rest)

　　He _____ dinner at Thalassa with Kim and Jason.
　　　　　　　　b. (enjoy)

7. At 9:15 he _____ cards at the Casino Royal with Massimo
　　　　　　　　　　　a. (play)

and other friends.

EXERCISE 3: Past Progressive or Simple Past
(Grammar Notes 1–5)

Complete the information about the Titanic *disaster. Use the past progressive or simple past form of the verbs in parentheses. Go to Appendix 1 on page A-1 for help with irregular verbs.*

Eyewitness Accounts[1]

⚓ According to eyewitness Lawrence Beesley, when the ship _____*hit*_____ the iceberg,
　　　　　　　　　　　　　　　　　　　　　　　　　　1. (hit)

the engines _____. Minutes later, when Professor Beesley _____ on
　　　　　2. (stop)　　　　　　　　　　　　　　　　　　　　　　　**3. (go)**

deck, he _____ only a few other passengers there. Everyone was calm. A few people
　　　　4. (find)

_____ cards in the smoking room. When he _____ out the window,
　　5. (play)　　　　　　　　　　　　　　　　　　　　**6. (look)**

he _____ an iceberg at the side of the ship.
　　7. (see)

⚓ Another survivor, Washington Dodge, said that it _____ 11:30 P.M. when the crash
　　　　　　　　　　　　　　　　　　　　　　　　　　8. (be)

_____. He _____ to go on deck. While the ship _____,
　　9. (happen)　　　　　　**10. (decide)**　　　　　　　　　　　　　　　**11. (sink)**

the band _____ a lively tune. At 1:55 A.M. the ship _____ completely
　　　　12. (play)　　　　　　　　　　　　　　　　　　　　　　**13. (sink)**

into the sea.

⚓ While passenger Elizabeth Shutes _____ a chicken sandwich in her cabin, she
　　　　　　　　　　　　　　　　　　14. (eat)

"_____ a shudder travel through the ship." Shortly after, she _____ in
　　15. (feel)　　　　　　　　　　　　　　　　　　　　　　　　　**16. (sit)**

a lifeboat in the middle of the ocean with 34 other people. Hours later, someone shouted "a light,

a ship!" When Shutes _____, she _____ a ship with bright lights
　　　　　　　　17. (look)　　　　　　　**18. (see)**

coming toward them. It was the *Carpathia*—the only ship in the area that came to help.

⚓ When Harold Bride, one of the ship's two radio operators, _____ some lights in the
　　　　　　　　　　　　　　　　　　　　　　　　　　19. (notice)

distance, he _____ it was a steamship. It _____ to rescue them. When
　　　　20. (know)　　　　　　　　　　　　**21. (come)**

the *Carpathia* _____, it _____ all of the survivors—including Mr. Bride.
　　　　　　22. (arrive)　　　　**23. (pick up)**

---

[1] ***eyewitness account:*** a report by someone who saw an accident or crime

EXERCISE 4: *Yes/No* and *Wh-* Questions

(Grammar Notes 1–5)

A newspaper is interviewing a Titanic *survivor. Read the survivor's answers. Write the interviewer's questions. Use the words in parentheses and the past progressive or simple past.*

1. **INTERVIEWER:** _What were you doing Sunday night?_____
   (what / you / do / Sunday night)

   PASSENGER: I was playing cards with some other passengers.

2. **INTERVIEWER:** _____
   (your wife / play / with you)

   PASSENGER: No, she wasn't. My wife wasn't with me at the time.

3. **INTERVIEWER:** _____
   (what / she / do / while you / play cards)

   SURVIVOR: She was reading in our room.

4. **INTERVIEWER:** _____
   (you / feel / the crash)

   SURVIVOR: Not really. But I heard a very loud noise.

5. **INTERVIEWER:** _____
   (what / you / do / when you / hear the noise)

   SURVIVOR: At first, we all continued to play. We weren't alarmed. Everyone stayed calm.

6. **INTERVIEWER:** _____
   (what / you / do / when the lights / go out)

   SURVIVOR: I tried to find my wife.

7. **INTERVIEWER:** _____
   (what / she / do / while you / look for her)

   SURVIVOR: She was looking for *me*. Thank goodness we found each other!

8. **INTERVIEWER:** _____
   (what / you / do / when you / find her)

   SURVIVOR: We tried to get into a lifeboat.

EXERCISE 5: Statements with *When* and *While*

(Grammar Notes 1–6)

Combine the pairs of sentences. Use the past progressive or the simple past form of the verb. Keep the order of the two sentences. Remember to use commas when necessary.

1. The storm started. Mr. Taylor attended a party.

   When _the storm started, Mr. Taylor was attending a party._____.

2. The electricity went out. The wind began to blow.

   _____ when _____.

3. He drove home. He listened to his car radio.

   While _____.

4. He pulled over to the side of the road. He couldn't see anything.

_____ when _____.

5. He listened to the news. He heard about a car crash near his home.

While _____.

6. It stopped raining. Mr. Taylor drove home in a hurry.

When _____.

EXERCISE 6: Editing

Read the journal entry. There are ten mistakes in the use of the past progressive and the simple past. The first mistake is already corrected. Find and correct nine more. Remember to look at punctuation!

April 15

    This afternoon I ~~was going~~ went to a movie at school. It was <u>Titanic</u>. They were showing it because it was the anniversary of the 1912 disaster. What a beautiful and sad film! Jack (Leonardo DiCaprio) was meeting Rose (Kate Winslet) while they both sailed on the huge ship. It was the <u>Titanic's</u> first voyage.

    Rose was from a very rich family; Jack was from a poor family. They fell in love, but Rose's mother wasn't happy about it. When the ship was hitting the iceberg, the two lovers were together, but then they got separated. Rose was finding Jack while the ship was sinking. Seconds before the ship went under, they held hands and were jumping into the water. Rose survived, but Jack didn't. It was so sad. When I left the theater, I still was having tears in my eyes.

    That wasn't my only adventure of the day. When the movie was over I left the school auditorium. While I walked home, I saw an accident between two pedestrians and a car. I was the only one in the area, so while I saw the accident, I immediately called the police. When the police got there, they asked me a lot of questions — there were no other witnesses. I'm glad to say that the accident had a happier ending than the movie!

EXERCISE 7: Listening

A | *You're going to hear a witness describe a traffic accident. Before you listen, look at the pictures. The pictures show three versions of what happened. Work with a partner and describe what happened in each of the three stories.*

1.

2.

3.

B | *Listen to the witness describe the traffic accident. According to the witness, which set of pictures is the most accurate? Circle the number.*

C | *Read the statements. Then listen again to the witness's description and check (✓)* **True** *or* **False**. *Correct the false statements.*

	True	False
1. The woman ~~was in~~ ^{saw} the accident.	☐	☑
2. She was driving down the street.	☐	☐
3. The car was driving very fast.	☐	☐
4. The two men were watching the traffic.	☐	☐
5. The car hit the two men.	☐	☐

EXERCISE 8: Pronunciation

A | *Read and listen to the Pronunciation Note.*

> **Pronunciation Note**
>
> When a **time clause begins a sentence**, we usually **pause** briefly **at the end** of the time clause. In **writing**, we put a **comma** where the pause is.
>
> **EXAMPLE:** When I saw the movie, I cried.   →   "When I saw the movie [PAUSE] I cried."

B | *Listen to the sentences. Put a comma where you hear the pause.*

1. When the phone rang she answered it.

2. While she was talking I was watching TV.

3. When she saw the storm clouds she drove home.

4. While she was driving home she was listening to the news.

5. When she got home she put the TV on.

C | *Listen again and repeat the sentences.*

EXERCISE 9: Game: Are You a Good Witness?

A | *Look at the picture for 30 seconds. Then close your book and write down what was happening. See how many details you can remember. What were the people doing? What were they wearing? Was anything unusual going on?*

> **EXAMPLE:**   A man and a woman were standing by the fireplace. The woman was wearing . . .

B | *When you are finished, compare your list with those of your classmates. Who remembered the most?*

EXERCISE 10: Role Play: Alibi[1]

There was a robbery at the bank yesterday at 2:15 P.M. The thieves stole $100,000. The police are investigating this crime.

A | *Work in groups of three to six. One or two students are police officers; one or two students are witnesses; one or two students are suspects.[2] The police officers are questioning the witnesses and the suspects. Use your imagination to ask and answer questions.*

> **EXAMPLE:**   **OFFICER:** What were you doing when the robbery took place?
>
> **WITNESS 1:** I was standing in line at the bank.
>
> **WITNESS 2:** I was crossing the street in front of the bank. I saw everything.
>
> **OFFICER:** What was happening in the bank? . . .

---

[1] **alibi:** the proof that someone was not at the location of a crime at the time of the crime

[2] **suspect:** someone who may be guilty of a crime

EXAMPLE:	OFFICER:	Where were you yesterday at 2:15 P.M.?
	SUSPECT 1:	At 2:15? I was sitting in class.
	SUSPECT 2:	I was at home. I was watching TV.
	OFFICER:	Were there other people with you?

B | *In your group, discuss these questions:*

- What happened at the bank?

- What were the witnesses doing?

- Do the suspects have good alibis?

- What were they doing when the robbery occurred?

C | *Do you believe their alibis? Why or why not?*

EXAMPLE: Suspect 1 said that she was sitting in class yesterday at 2:15. I don't believe her because there was no school yesterday.

EXERCISE 11: Writing

A | *Write a paragraph describing an event that you witnessed: an accident, a crime, a bad storm, a reunion, a wedding, or another event. Use the past progressive and the simple past to describe what was happening and what happened during the event.*

EXAMPLE: While I was going to lunch today, I saw a wedding party. People were waiting for the bride and groom outside a temple. When they saw the couple, they . . .

B | *Check your work. Use the Editing Checklist.*

Editing Checklist

Did you use . . . ?
- ☐ the simple past
- ☐ the past progressive
- ☐ *when* or *while*
- ☐ commas after time clauses at the beginning of a sentence

A | Complete the conversation with the past progressive or simple past form of the verbs in parentheses.

A: _____ you _____ about the big storm last night?
1. (hear)

B: Yes, I _____ the pictures when I _____ on the news.
2. (see)   3. (turn)

_____ you _____ home during the storm?
4. (drive)

A: No. At 6:00, I _____ in my office. So while it _____ really
5. (work)   6. (rain)

hard, I _____ a report. And just when I _____ work, the rain
7. (finish)   8. (leave)

_____!
9. (stop)

B: I'm glad. Those pictures on the news _____ pretty bad.
10. (look)

B | Combine the sentences. Use the past progressive or simple past form of the verbs.

1. While _____.
(Danielle watched TV. At the same time, I studied.)

2. _____ when _____.
(I closed my book. The show *Dr. Davis* came on.)

3. _____ when _____.
(Dr. Davis talked to his patient. The electricity went off.)

4. When _____.
(The electricity went off. We lit some candles.)

5. _____ while _____.
(We talked about a lot of things. We waited for the lights to come on.)

C | Find and correct five mistakes.

When I turned on the TV for the first episode of *Dr. Davis,* I unpacked boxes in my freshman

dorm room. I stopped and watched for an hour. After that, I wasn't missing a single show while

I was attending school. While I was solving math problems, Dr. Davis was solving medical

mysteries. And *just* while my dumb boyfriend broke up with me, the beautiful Dr. Grace left

Davis for the third time. I even watched the show from the hospital when I was breaking my

leg. The show just ended. I was sad when I see the last episode, but I think it's time for some

real life!

Used to and *Would*
MEMORIES

STEP 1 GRAMMAR IN CONTEXT

Before You Read

Look at the reading. Discuss the questions.

1. What is a blog? What do you think this blog is about?
2. What toys, TV shows, clothes, and hairstyles do you remember from your own childhood?

Read

Read Sandra's blog about growing up in the 1980s in the United States.

The Awesome Eighties

Monday June 11 Posted by OldtimeSandy

Today's walk down memory lane[1] takes us back to the Awesome Eighties. Readers who were kids in the 1980s: What toys **did** you **use to play** with? What **did** you **use to watch** on TV?

Did you watch cartoons Saturday mornings? I **used to love** *She-Ra, Princess of Power*. I **would collect** all the toys and act out the stories with my friends. We didn't play that many video games back then!

A puzzle called the Rubik's Cube **used to be** very popular in the 1980s. My older sister Linda **would carry** one in her backpack all the time. She and her friends **would** often **have** contests with them. She didn't win very much, but she loved it anyway.

This is my mother, dressed for work. She **used to love** those suits with the big shoulders. She said they made her feel strong, like She-Ra, Princess of Power. She **used to call** this one her "power suit."

My brother Gary and his friends had a rock band. They**'d practice** for hours in the garage. They **never used to study**. Gary **used to get** some weird haircuts. He's a lawyer now, and he's lost his hair!

Next post: Do you ♥ hippies?

---

[1] ***walk down memory lane:*** a time you spend remembering the past

After You Read

A | Vocabulary: *Circle the letter of the word or phrase that best completes each sentence.*

1. An **awesome** blog is _____.
   a. terrible
   b. great
   c. frightening

2. Many people **collect** _____.
   a. stamps
   b. backpacks
   c. suits

3. A **weird** haircut looks _____.
   a. beautiful
   b. strange
   c. old

4. If a game is **popular**, _____.
   a. it's very easy
   b. it's not expensive
   c. many people like it

5. If you have a **memory** about something, you _____ it.
   a. remember
   b. watch
   c. practice

6. People with **power** are _____.
   a. tall
   b. strong
   c. poor

B | Comprehension: *Check (✓)* **True** *or* **False**. *Correct the false statements.*

	True	False
1. Sandra didn't watch TV on Saturdays.	☐	☐
2. She played video games a lot.	☐	☐
3. Her sister Linda played with a Rubik's Cube.	☐	☐
4. Her mother wore a suit to work.	☐	☐
5. Her brother and his friends studied all the time.	☐	☐
6. Her brother likes strange haircuts now.	☐	☐

USED TO

Statements			
Subject	*Use(d) to*	Base Form of Verb	
I You He She It We You They	used to didn't use to	be	popular.

Yes / No Questions				
Did	Subject	*Use to*	Base Form of Verb	
Did	you she they	use to	be	popular?

Short Answers					
Affirmative			Negative		
Yes,	I she they	did.	No,	I she they	didn't.

Wh- Questions					
Wh- Word	*Did*	Subject	*Use to*	Base Form of Verb	
When	did	you she they	use to	be	popular?

WOULD

Statements			
Subject	*Would*	Base Form of Verb	
I He They	would	study	all day.

Contractions*		
I would	=	I'd
He would	=	He'd
They would	=	They'd

*The contraction for *would* is the same for all subjects.

GRAMMAR NOTES

1 Use **used to** + **base form** of the verb to talk about <u>repeated past activities</u> (habits) and <u>situations</u> that are no longer true in the present.

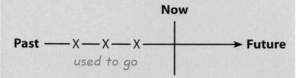

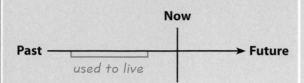

USAGE NOTE: Use **used to** to <u>contrast the past and the present</u>. **Time expressions** such as **now**, **no longer**, and **not anymore** emphasize the contrast.

PAST ACTIVITY:
- When Tom was a teenager, he **used to go** to rock concerts every weekend.
  (He went to rock concerts many times in the past, but he doesn't go to them now.)

PAST SITUATION:
- We **used to live** in Russia.
  (We lived in Russia for a period of time, but we don't live there any longer.)

- I **used to ride** my bike every day, but **now** I have a car.
- They **used to love** rock music, but they do**n't** listen to it **anymore**.

---

2 **Used to** always <u>refers to the past</u>. There is no present or future form.

USAGE NOTES:

a. The form **use to** (not *used to*) comes after **did** in **negative statements** and **questions**.

b. In **negative statements**, **never** + **used to** is more common than *didn't use to*.

c. In **questions**, the **simple past** is more common than *did* + *use to*.

- She **used to love** cartoons.
  NOT: She ~~uses~~ to love cartoons.

- He **didn't use to** study.
  NOT: He didn't ~~used to~~ study.
- **Did** you **use to** have long hair?
  NOT: Did you ~~used to~~ have long hair?

- He **never used to** study. *(more common)*
- He **didn't use to** study. *(less common)*

- **Did** you **have** long hair then? *(more common)*
- **Did** you **use to have** long hair? *(less common)*

---

3 You can also use **would** + **base form** of the verb to talk about <u>repeated past activities</u> (habits) that no longer happen in the present.

BE CAREFUL! Do NOT use **would** for <u>past situations</u>. Use **used to**.

USAGE NOTES:

a. When we reminisce (tell stories) about the past, we often <u>begin with **used to**</u> and then <u>continue with **would**</u> to give more details or examples.

b. When we use **would**, it must already be <u>clear that we are talking about the past</u>. Do NOT begin a story with *would*.

PAST ACTIVITY:
- When I was seven, I **would watch** cartoons every Saturday morning.

PAST SITUATION:
- I **used to love** Power Ranger cartoons.
  NOT: I ~~would love~~ Power Ranger cartoons.

- When I was a kid, I **used to ride** my bike everywhere. I **would ride** it to school during the week, and I **would take** it to the park on weekends.
  NOT: I ~~would ride~~ my bike everywhere. I would ride it to school . . .

EXERCISE 1: Discover the Grammar

Read the responses to "The Awesome Eighties" blog. Underline the expressions that refer to past habits and situations that are no longer true.

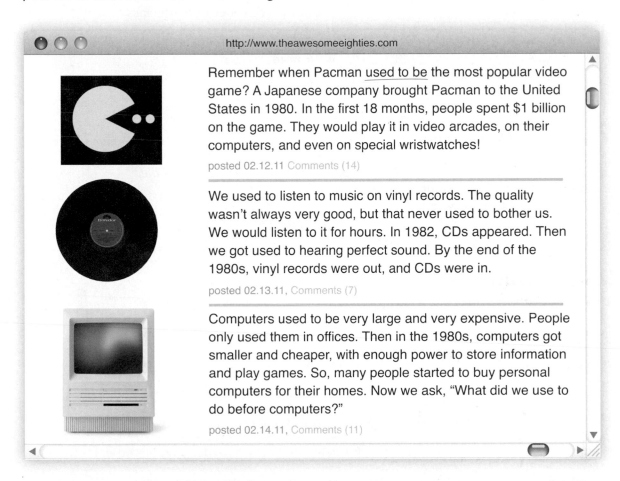

http://www.theawesomeeighties.com

Remember when Pacman used to be the most popular video game? A Japanese company brought Pacman to the United States in 1980. In the first 18 months, people spent $1 billion on the game. They would play it in video arcades, on their computers, and even on special wristwatches!

posted 02.12.11 Comments (14)

We used to listen to music on vinyl records. The quality wasn't always very good, but that never used to bother us. We would listen to it for hours. In 1982, CDs appeared. Then we got used to hearing perfect sound. By the end of the 1980s, vinyl records were out, and CDs were in.

posted 02.13.11, Comments (7)

Computers used to be very large and very expensive. People only used them in offices. Then in the 1980s, computers got smaller and cheaper, with enough power to store information and play games. So, many people started to buy personal computers for their homes. Now we ask, "What did we use to do before computers?"

posted 02.14.11, Comments (11)

EXERCISE 2: Forms of *Used to*   *(Grammar Note 2)*

Sandra is at her class reunion. Complete the conversations. Use the correct form of **used to** *and the words in parentheses.*

1. **SANDRA:** You look familiar. _____*Did*_____ you _____*use to be*_____ in the drama club?
   a. (be)

   ROSA: Sandra! It's me—Rosa! I _____ long hair. Remember?
   b. (have)

2. **ROSA:** There's Glen—all alone. Did he always _____ that shy?
   a. (be)

   SANDRA: Glen? Shy? He never stopped talking! It _____ the teachers mad—
   b. (make)

   remember? Let's go say hi to him.

(continued on next page)

3. **ROSA:** _____ you _____ with Gary's band, the Backyard Boys?
    a. (play)

    GLEN: Sometimes. We _____ in Gary's garage after school.
    b. (practice)

4. **GLEN:** There's Jim and Laura. I think they got married a couple of years ago.

    SANDRA: Really? In high school, they _____ any time together.
    a. (never / spend)

5. **LAURA:** I see Sandra! We _____ next to each other in math class.
    a. (sit)

    JIM: She looks so different now. She _____ glasses.
    b. (not wear)

    LAURA: We all look different now. We _____ a lot younger back then.
    c. (be)

EXERCISE 3: *Used to* or *Would* *(Grammar Notes 1–3)*

*Read CityGal's blog. Circle <u>all</u> the correct answers. Sometimes only **used to** is possible.
Sometimes both **used to** and **would** are possible.*

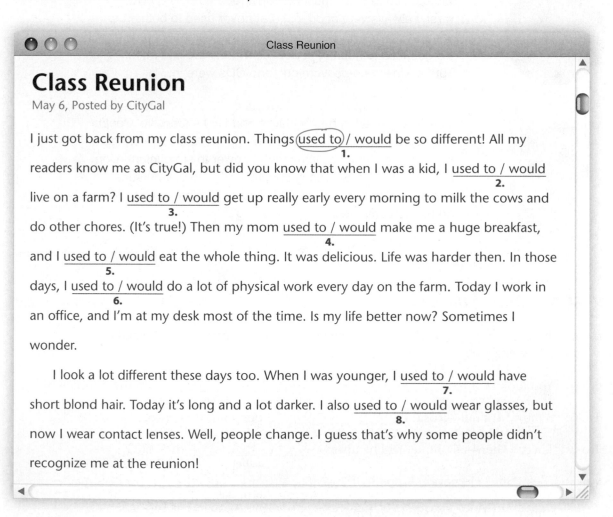

Class Reunion
May 6, Posted by CityGal

I just got back from my class reunion. Things (used to) / would be so different! All my
1.
readers know me as CityGal, but did you know that when I was a kid, I used to / would
2.
live on a farm? I used to / would get up really early every morning to milk the cows and
3.
do other chores. (It's true!) Then my mom used to / would make me a huge breakfast,
4.
and I used to / would eat the whole thing. It was delicious. Life was harder then. In those
5.
days, I used to / would do a lot of physical work every day on the farm. Today I work in
6.
an office, and I'm at my desk most of the time. Is my life better now? Sometimes I

wonder.

   I look a lot different these days too. When I was younger, I used to / would have
7.
short blond hair. Today it's long and a lot darker. I also used to / would wear glasses, but
8.
now I wear contact lenses. Well, people change. I guess that's why some people didn't

recognize me at the reunion!

EXERCISE 4: Contrast: *Used to* or *Would*

(Grammar Notes 1–3)

Sandra is showing her daughter Megan an old photo album. Complete their conversation.
*Use **used to** or **would** and the correct verb from the box. Sometimes both are possible.*

| be | drive | ~~have~~ | love | play | visit | wear |

MEGAN: Wow! Look at that! Uncle Gary ___used to have___ a lot of hair! He really looks kind of
     1.

weird in this picture.

SANDRA: Well, right after this photo, he shaved his head.

MEGAN: In this picture, were you going to the gym?

SANDRA: No. We _____ exercise clothes everywhere.
     2.

MEGAN: You looked cute!

SANDRA: This was your Aunt Linda's new car. After she got it, she _____ her friends to
     3.

school every day.

MEGAN: That's not Uncle Fred with her.

SANDRA: No, that's Glen. He _____ her boyfriend before she met Fred and fell in love.
     4.

MEGAN: Oh! You had a Barbie doll!

SANDRA: Of course. I _____ with it every day.
     5.

MEGAN: And that's me with Grandma and Grandpa!

SANDRA: Right. You _____ them at the beach every summer. You _____
     6.   **7.**

the water.

A 1980s sports car: the Chevrolet Corvette

EXERCISE 5: Editing

Read the journal entry about a high school reunion in Timmins, Ontario, a small town 500 miles north of Toronto. There are nine mistakes in the use of **used to** and **would**. The first mistake is already corrected. Find and correct eight more.

Shania Twain

>   The high school reunion tonight was awesome! I
> ~~used to talk~~ *talked* to Eileen Edwards for a long time. Well,
> she's the famous country pop singer Shania Twain now.
> In high school, she was used to be just one of us, and
> tonight we all called her Eileen. She graduated in 1983,
> the same year as me. Today she uses to live in a
> chateau in Switzerland and has her own perfume
> brand, but her life didn't use to be like that at all! She
> uses to be very poor, and her grandma used to made all her clothes because her
> family couldn't afford to buy them. She was always a good musician, though. In fact, she
> used to earns money for her family that way. On Saturday nights, she would performed
> with a local rock band, and my friends and I would go hear her. She could really sing!
> Her new name, Shania, means "on my way" in Ojibwa (her stepfather's Native American
> language). After she left Timmins, I would think that Timmins wasn't important to her
> anymore — but I was wrong. Now that she's famous, she has a lot of power, and she
> uses it to do good things for our community. And tonight she was just the way she
> used be in high school — simple and friendly!

A school reunion

EXERCISE 6: Listening

A | *Two friends are talking about their past. Listen to their conversation.*

B | *Read the statements. Then listen again to the conversation and circle the letter of the correct information.*

1. The friends are at a _____.

   a. rock concert　　**(b.)** school reunion

2. Their present lives are very _____ their past lives.

   a. similar to　　　**b.** different from

3. They have _____ memories about their past.

   a. good　　　　　**b.** bad

4. They used to play a lot of _____.

   a. video games　　**b.** music CDs

5. The friends are enjoying talking about _____.

   a. a trip　　　　　**b.** the past

C | *Listen again to the conversation. Check (✓) the things the friends used to do in the **past** and the things they do **now**.*

	Past	Now
1. get up very early without an alarm clock	✓	☐
2. use an alarm clock	☐	☐
3. have a big breakfast	☐	☐
4. have a cup of coffee	☐	☐
5. look at the newspaper	☐	☐
6. have endless energy	☐	☐
7. do aerobics	☐	☐
8. take car trips on weekends	☐	☐
9. meet at class reunions	☐	☐

EXERCISE 7: Pronunciation

A | *Read and listen to the Pronunciation Note.*

> ### Pronunciation Note
>
> We often pronounce **used to** like "usta." Notice that the pronunciation of **used to** and **use to** is the same.
>
> **EXAMPLES:** I **used to** play chess. → "I **usta** play chess."
> What games did you **use to** play? → "What games did you **usta** play?"
>
> Be sure to write **used to** or **use to**, NOT "usta."
>
> We often use the contraction of **would** (**'d**) in both **speech** and **writing**.
>
> **EXAMPLE:** We **would** play for hours. → "We**'d** play for hours."

B | *Listen to the sentences. Notice the pronunciation of **used to** and the contraction of **would**.*

1. I **used to** live in a small town.
2. I didn't **use to** have a lot of friends.
3. I**'d** spend hours alone.
4. On weekends, my sister **used to** play cards with me.
5. She**'d** always win.
6. We**'d** have a lot of fun.

C | *Listen again and repeat the sentences.*

EXERCISE 8: Picture Discussion

Work with a partner. Look at the pairs of pictures and talk about how the people have changed. Then write sentences that describe the changes. Compare your sentences with those of your classmates.

Then	Now

1. Sharifa _used to be very busy, but now she is more relaxed. She would always be in a hurry._

   Now she takes things more slowly. She used to wear glasses, but now she doesn't . . .

Then	**Now**

2. Jean-Marc _____

_____

_____

Then	**Now**

3. Lyric _____

_____

_____

Then	**Now**

4. Mike _____

_____

_____

EXERCISE 9: Compare and Contrast

Work in small groups. Talk about how you used to be and how you are now. Answer the following questions. If you have a picture of yourself from that time, you can bring it in to class and show it to your group.

- How did you use to look?

- What types of things would you do?

- How did you use to dress?

  EXAMPLE: **A:** I used to have very long hair. Now I wear my hair short.
  B: Anton, did you use to have long hair?
  C: *Everybody* used to have long hair then.

EXERCISE 10: Writing

A | *Write a two-paragraph essay. Contrast your life in the past with your life now. In the first paragraph, describe how your life used to be at some time in the past. In the second paragraph, describe your life today. Remember: We often begin with* **used to** *and then change to* **would**.

EXAMPLE: I used to live in Russia. I attended St. Petersburg University. I would ride my bike there every day. In those days I used to . . . Today I am living in Florida and attending Miami University . . .

B | *Check your work. Use the Editing Checklist.*

Editing Checklist
Did you . . . ?   ☐ use ***used to*** correctly   ☐ use ***would*** correctly   ☐ change from ***used to*** to ***would***

A | *Circle the correct words to complete the sentences.*

1. What <u>did / would</u> you use to like to do when you were a kid?

2. I <u>used to / would</u> love reading comic books when I was younger.

3. <u>Do / Did</u> you use to go to concerts?

4. My sister would <u>plays / play</u> video games for hours.

5. I never <u>used to / would</u> like them before, but now I love them.

6. Life <u>used to / would</u> be so different back then.

B | *Complete the conversations with* **used to** *or* **would** *and the verb in parentheses.*

- **AMY:** Hey, is that Jorge? He _____ very different. I almost didn't recognize him!
  1. (look)

  BEN: Yes. He _____ long hair, but he cut it last month.
  2. (have)

- **MIA:** I _____ my hair grow very long in the summer.
  3. (let)

  LEE: Me too. Sometimes I _____ a haircut for a whole year!
  4. (not get)

- **AMY:** I _____ the guitar. I'm sorry I quit.
  5. (play)

  BEN: I had a guitar too. I _____ for hours.
  6. (practice)

- **TOM:** _____ you _____ to concerts when you were a student?
  7. (go)

  MIA: Yes. I _____ the free concerts in the park. I even once heard Celine Dion!
  8. (love)

C | *Find and correct six mistakes.*

Celine Dion was born in Quebec, Canada. When she used to be five, her family opened a club, and Celine used to sang there. People from the community would to come to hear her perform. At the age of 12, Celine wrote her first songs. Her family used to record one and sent it to a manager. At first Celine used to singing only in French. After she learned English, she became known in more countries. As a child, Celine Dion would be poor, but she had a dream— to be a singer. Today she is one of the most successful singers in the history of pop music.

Wh- Questions
IN COURT

Before You Read

A lawyer is questioning a crime witness. Look at the drawing by a courtroom artist. Discuss the questions.

1. Who is the lawyer? The judge? The witness?
2. What do you think the lawyer is asking?

Read

Read the excerpt from a court transcript.

STATE OF ILLINOIS VS.[1] HARRY M. ADAMS	MARCH 31, 2011

LAWYER: **What happened on the night of May 12?** Please tell the court.[2]

WITNESS: I went to Al's Grill.

LAWYER: **Who did you see there?**

WITNESS: I saw one of the defendants.

LAWYER: **Which one did you see?**

WITNESS: It was that man.

LAWYER: Let the record show that the witness is indicating the defendant, Harry Adams. OK, you saw Mr. Adams. Did he see you?

WITNESS: No, no, he didn't see me.

LAWYER: But somebody saw you. **Who saw you?**

WITNESS: A woman. He was talking to a woman. She saw me.

LAWYER: OK. **What happened next?**

WITNESS: The woman gave him a box.

LAWYER: A box! **What did it look like?**

WITNESS: It was about this long . . .

LAWYER: So, about a foot and a half. **What did Mr. Adams do then?**

WITNESS: He took the box. He looked frightened.

LAWYER: **Why did he look frightened? What was in the box?**

WITNESS: I don't know. He didn't open it. He just took it and left in a hurry.

LAWYER: **Where did he go?**

WITNESS: Toward the parking lot.

LAWYER: **When did the woman leave?**

WITNESS: She was still there when we heard his car speed away.

---

[1] *vs.* (written abbreviation of *versus*): against
[2] *court:* the people (judge, lawyers, jury) who decide if someone is guilty of a crime

After You Read

A | Vocabulary: *Circle the letter of the word or phrase closest in meaning to the word in* **blue.**

1. I saw one of the **defendants**.
   a. people who saw a crime
   b. people who possibly broke a law
   c. people who work in the court

2. It's for the **record**.
   a. music CD
   b. box
   c. written report

3. He looked **frightened**.
   a. dangerous
   b. afraid
   c. unhappy

4. He left **in a hurry**.
   a. quickly
   b. in a storm
   c. by bus

5. The witness is **indicating** Harry Adams.
   a. smiling at
   b. speaking about
   c. pointing to

B | Comprehension: *Check (✓)* **True** *or* **False.** *Correct the false statements.*

	True	False
1. The lawyer is questioning Harry Adams.	☐	☐
2. The witness saw Harry Adams.	☐	☐
3. Harry Adams saw the witness.	☐	☐
4. The witness saw a woman.	☐	☐
5. The woman saw the witness.	☐	☐
6. The witness gave Adams a box.	☐	☐
7. Adams took the box.	☐	☐
8. The woman left before the car sped away.	☐	☐

WH- QUESTIONS: *WHO, WHAT*

Questions About the Subject			Answers		
Wh- Word Subject	Verb	Object	Subject	Verb	Object
Who	saw	Harry?	Marta	saw	him.
		the box?			it.

Questions About the Object				Answers		
Wh- Word Object	Auxiliary Verb	Subject	Main Verb	Subject	Verb	Object
Who(m)	did	Marta	see?	She	saw	Harry.
What						the box.

WH- QUESTIONS: *WHICH, WHOSE, HOW MANY*

Questions About the Subject			Answers		
Wh- Word + Noun	Verb	Object	Subject	Verb	Object
Which witness			**Mr. Ho**		
Whose lawyer	saw	you?	**Harry's lawyer**	saw	me.
How many people			**Five people**		

Questions About the Object				Answers		
Wh- Word + Noun	Auxiliary Verb	Subject	Main Verb	Subject	Verb	Object
Which witness						the first witness.
Whose lawyer	did	you	see?	I	saw	Harry's lawyer.
How many people						five people.

WH- QUESTIONS: *WHEN, WHERE, WHY*

Questions				Answers		
Wh- Word	Auxiliary Verb	Subject	Main Verb	Subject	Verb	Time/Place/Reason
When						yesterday.
Where	did	Marta	go?	She	went	to the police.
Why						because she was frightened.

GRAMMAR NOTES

1 Use **wh- questions** (also called *information questions*) to ask for specific information.

Wh- questions begin with **wh- words** such as *who, what, when, where, why, which, whose, how, how many, how much,* and *how long.*

A: *Who* did you see at Al's Grill?
B: Harry Adams.

A: *When* did you go there?
B: On May 12.

A: *How many* people saw you?
B: Two.

2 To ask **basic information** about people and things, use *who* and *what.*

a. For questions about the **subject**, use *who* or *what* in place of the subject, and statement word order: ***wh- word** (= **subject**) + **verb***

SUBJECT
Someone saw you.

Who saw you?

SUBJECT
Something happened.

What happened?

b. For questions about the **object**, use *who* or *what* and this word order:
wh- word** + **auxiliary** + **subject** + **verb

OBJECT
You saw someone.

Who did you see?

OBJECT
He said something.

What did he say?

REMEMBER: An **auxiliary** verb is a verb such as ***do*** (*does, did*), ***have*** (*has, had*), ***can***, or ***will***. ***Be*** can be an auxiliary too.

• ***Who* will** she defend?
• ***What* is** he doing?

USAGE NOTE: In **very formal** English, we sometimes use ***whom*** instead of *who* in questions about the **object**.

MORE COMMON
Who did you see?

VERY FORMAL
Whom did you see?

3 To ask more **detailed information** about people and things, use:
• ***which*** + **noun** (to ask about a choice)
• ***whose*** + **noun** (to ask about possessions)
• ***how many*** + **noun** (to ask about quantities)

a. For questions about the **subject**, use this word order: ***wh- word** + **noun** + **verb***

b. For questions about the **object**, use this order:
wh- word** + **noun** + **auxiliary** + **subject** + **verb

• ***Which* witness** told the truth?
• ***Whose* lawyer** do you believe?
• ***How many* people** saw the trial?

• ***Which* defendant answered** best?

• ***Which* defendant did you trust** more?

(continued on next page)

4	To ask about **place**, **reason**, and **time**, use **where**, **why**, and **when**, and this word order: **wh- word + auxiliary + subject + verb**	• **Where will** she go? • **Why does** she want to defend him? • **When did** she arrive?
5	When the main verb is a form of **be** (*am, is, are, was, were*) use: • **wh- word + be** OR • **wh- word + noun + be**	• **Who is** the first witness? • **Where are** the witnesses? • **How many witnesses are** there?

STEP 3 FOCUSED PRACTICE

EXERCISE 1: Discover the Grammar

Match the questions and answers.

   _f_   **1.** Who did you see?

   _a_   **2.** Who saw you?

   _d_   **3.** What hit her?

   _b_   **4.** What did she hit?

   _c_   **5.** Which man did you give the money to?

   _e_   **6.** Which man gave you the money?

a. His wife saw me.

b. She hit a car.

c. I gave the money to Harry.

d. A car hit her.

e. Harry gave me the money.

f. I saw the defendant.

EXERCISE 2: Questions

(Grammar Notes 1–5)

Complete the cross-examination. Write the lawyer's questions. Use the words in parentheses and make any necessary changes.

1. LAWYER: _What time did you return home?_
               (what time / you / return home)
  WITNESS: I returned home just before midnight.

2. LAWYER: _____
               (how / you / get home)
  WITNESS: Someone gave me a ride. I was in a hurry.

3. LAWYER: _____
               (who / give / you / a ride)
  WITNESS: A friend from work.

4. LAWYER: _____
               (what / happen / next)
  WITNESS: I opened my door and saw someone on my living room floor.

5. LAWYER: _____
               (who / you / see)
  WITNESS: Deborah Collins.

6. LAWYER: For the record, _____.
(who / be / Deborah Collins)

WITNESS: She's my wife's boss. I mean, she *was* my wife's boss. She's dead now.

7. LAWYER: _____
(what / you / do)

WITNESS: I called the police.

8. LAWYER: _____
(when / the police / arrive)

WITNESS: In about 10 minutes.

9. LAWYER: _____
(what / they / ask you)

WITNESS: They asked me to describe the crime scene.

10. LAWYER: _____
(how many police officers / come)

WITNESS: I don't remember. Why?

LAWYER: I'm asking the questions here. Please just answer.

EXERCISE 3: Questions

(Grammar Notes 1–5)

Read the answers. Then ask questions about the underlined words or phrases.

1. Court begins <u>at 9:00 A.M.</u>

   When does court begin?

2. <u>Something horrible</u> happened.

   _____

3. <u>Five</u> witnesses described the crime.

   _____

4. The witness indicated <u>Harry Adams</u>.

   _____

5. <u>The witness</u> indicated Harry Adams.

   _____

6. The district attorney questioned <u>the restaurant manager</u>.

   Who did _____

7. The manager looked <u>frightened</u>.

   How did the manager look like?

(continued on next page)

8. <u>The judge</u> spoke to the jury.

Who spoke

9. The verdict was "<u>guilty</u>."

What was the verdict?

10. The jury found Adams guilty <u>because he didn't have an alibi</u>.

Why

11. The trial lasted <u>two weeks</u>.

12. Adams paid his lawyer <u>$2,000</u>.

EXERCISE 4: Editing

Read a reporter's notes. There are nine mistakes in the use of **wh-** *questions. The first mistake is already corrected. Find and correct eight more.*

Questions

did Jones go
Where ~~Jones went~~ on January 15?

Who went with him?

What time he return home?

Who he called?

How much money he had with him?

Whom saw him at the station the next day?

How did he look?

Why he was in a hurry?

How many suitcases did he have?

When the witness call the police?

What did happen next?

What his alibi was?

EXERCISE 5: Listening

A | *Someone is on the phone with a friend. There is a bad connection. Listen to the statements. Then listen again and circle the letter of the question the friend needs to ask in order to get the correct information.*

1. **a.** Who did you see at the restaurant?
   b. Who saw you at the restaurant?

2. **a.** Which car did the truck hit?
   b. Which car hit the truck?

3. **a.** When did it happen?
   b. Why did it happen?

4. **a.** Whose mother did you call?
   b. Whose mother called you?

5. **a.** Who did you report it to?
   b. Who reported it?

6. **a.** How many people heard the shouts?
   b. How many shouts did you hear?

7. **a.** Who saw the man?
   b. Who did the man see?

8. **a.** Why do you have to hang up?
   b. When do you have to hang up?

B | *Listen to the short conversations and answer the question in each one.*

1. the teacher

2. _____

3. _____

4. _____

5. _____

6. _____

7. _____

8. _____

EXERCISE 6: Pronunciation

A | *Read and listen to the Pronunciation Note.*

Pronunciation Note

In *wh-* **questions**, the voice usually **falls at the end**.

EXAMPLE: Where do you live?

But sometimes, when we **don't understand someone**, we use *wh-* questions to ask the person to repeat the information. We **stress the *wh-* word** and the voice **rises at the end**.

EXAMPLE: **A:** I live in Massachusetts.

  B: Where do you live?
  A: In Massachusetts.

B | *Listen to the questions. Check (✓) if the person is asking for **information** or for **repetition**.*

	Information ↗	Repetition ↗
1. Where did he go?	☐	☑
2. What did he do next?	☐	☐
3. What was in the box?	☐	☐
4. When did the woman leave?	☐	☐
5. How much did it cost?	☐	☐
6. Who called you?	☐	☐
7. Why did you leave?	☐	☐
8. Who saw you?	☐	☐

C | *Listen again and repeat the questions.*

EXERCISE 7: Role Play: On the Witness Stand

Work with a partner. Look at the court transcript on page 58 again. Read it aloud. Then continue the lawyer's questioning of the witness. Ask at least six more questions.

> **EXAMPLE:** **LAWYER:** When did the woman leave?
> **WITNESS:** She was still there when we heard his car speed away.
> **LAWYER:** What happened next?

EXERCISE 8: Game: To Tell the Truth

A | *Work in groups of three. Each student tells the group an interesting fact about his or her life. The fact can only be true for this student.*

> **EXAMPLE:** **A:** I play three musical instruments.
> **B:** I speak four languages.
> **C:** I have five pets.

B | *The group chooses a fact and goes to the front of the class. Each student states the same fact, but remember: Only one student is telling the truth.*

> **EXAMPLE:**

C | *The class asks the three students* **wh-** *questions to find out who is telling the truth.*

EXAMPLE: THEA: Ed, which four languages do you speak?
        ED: I speak Russian, French, Spanish, and English.

        LEV: Ed, where did you learn Russian?
        ED: I was born in Russia.

        MEI: Ed, who taught you French?
        ED: My grandmother is French. I learned it from her.

        JOSÉ: Ed, how do you say "witness" in Spanish?
        ED: . . .

EXERCISE 9: Writing

A | *Work with a partner. Think of something exciting or interesting that you once saw. Tell your partner. Then write a list of questions and interview your partner to get more information. Use* **wh-** *questions. Take notes and write up the interview.*

EXAMPLE: **A:** I once saw a bad car accident.
        B: Where did it happen?
        A: On the highway.
        B: How many cars were in the accident?
        A: There was one car and a truck.
        B: What did you do?
        A: I . . .

B | *Check your work. Use the Editing Checklist.*

Editing Checklist

Did you use . . . ?
- [ ] the correct **wh-** words
- [ ] the correct word order
- [ ] auxiliary verbs in questions about the object
- [ ] auxiliary verbs in questions beginning with **when**, **where**, and **why**

A | *Match the questions and answers.*

_____ **1.** Where did Feng go Wednesday night?

_____ **2.** When was the movie over?

_____ **3.** How long was it?

_____ **4.** Which movie did he see?

_____ **5.** How many people went?

_____ **6.** Who went with him?

_____ **7.** Whose car did they use?

_____ **8.** Why did they choose that movie?

a. *Date Night.*

b. Because it got great reviews.

c. Xavier's.

d. At 11:00.

e. Laurel and Xavier.

f. Two and a half hours.

g. Three.

h. To the movies.

B | *Circle the correct words to complete the sentences.*

1. Where does Shari <u>work / works</u> now?

2. How <u>did she / she did</u> find that job?

3. Who <u>did tell / told</u> Shari about it?

4. Why <u>she left / did she leave</u> her old job?

5. When did she <u>start / started</u> to work there?

6. Who <u>is her boss / her boss is</u>?

7. What <u>did / does</u> she do at her new job?

C | *Find and correct five mistakes.*

A: What did you did with my math book? I can't find it.

B: Nothing. Where you saw it last?

A: In the living room. I was watching *Lost* on TV. What Zack's phone number?

B: I'm not sure. Why you want to know?

A: He took the class last year. I'll call him. Maybe he still has his book.

B: Good idea. What time does he gets out of work?

From Grammar to Writing

COMBINING SENTENCES WITH TIME WORDS

You can often improve your writing by combining two short sentences into one longer sentence that connects the two ideas. The two sentences can be combined by using **time words** such as *while*, *when*, *as soon as*, *before*, *after*, or *until*. The new, longer sentence is made up of a main clause and a time clause.

EXAMPLE: I was shopping. I saw the perfect dress for her. →

TIME CLAUSE   MAIN CLAUSE
While I was shopping**,** I saw the perfect dress for her.

MAIN CLAUSE   TIME CLAUSE
I saw the perfect dress for her **while** I was shopping.

The time clause can come first or second. When it comes first, a **comma** separates the two clauses.

1 | *Read the paragraph. Underline all the sentences that are combined with a time word.*
Circle the time words.

> I always exchange holiday presents with my girlfriend, Shao Fen. Last year, (while) I was shopping for her, I saw an umbrella in her favorite color. As soon as I saw it, I thought of her. I bought the umbrella and a scarf in the same color. When Shao Fen opened the present, she looked really upset. She didn't say anything, and she didn't look at me. I felt hurt and confused by her reaction. Later she explained that in Chinese, the word for "umbrella" sounds like the word for "separation." When she saw the umbrella, she misunderstood. She thought I wanted to end the relationship. After I heard that, I was very upset! When we both felt calmer, we talked about our misunderstanding. At the end, we laughed about it, and I think we're better friends because of it. I discovered something new about Shao Fen's culture. Now I want to learn more about cross-cultural communication.

2 | *Look at the student's paragraph. Combine the pairs of underlined sentences with time words such as **when**, **while**, **as soon as**, **before**, and **after**. Use your own paper.*

> I usually keep my wallet in my back pocket when I go out. <u>Two weeks ago, I was walking on a crowded street. I felt something.</u> I was in a hurry, so I didn't pay any attention to it at the time. <u>I got home. I noticed that my wallet was missing.</u> I got frightened. It didn't have much money in it, but my credit card and my driver's license were there. <u>I was thinking about the situation. My brother came home.</u> He told me to report it to the police, just for the record, in case someone found the wallet. <u>I called the police. They weren't very encouraging.</u> They said that wallets often get "picked" from back pockets. They didn't think I would get it back. Now I'm a lot more careful. <u>I go out. I put my wallet in my front pocket.</u>

> EXAMPLE: Two weeks ago, **while** I was walking on a crowded street, I felt something.

3 | *Before you write . . .*

1. We often say, "Learn from your mistakes." Think about a misunderstanding or a mistake that you experienced or observed. How did your behavior or thinking change because of your experience?

2. Describe the experience to a partner. Listen to your partner's experience.

3. Ask and answer questions about your experiences, for example: *When did it happen? Why did you . . . ? Where were you when . . . ? How did you feel? What do you do now . . . ?*

4 | *Write a draft of your story. Follow the model below. Remember to use some of the time words and include information that your partner asked about.*

as soon as	before	until	when	while

I (or My friend) always / often / usually / never _____

_____

_____ .

Last week / Yesterday / In 2010, _____

_____

_____

_____ .

Now, _____

_____ .

5 | *Exchange stories with a different partner. Complete the chart.*

1. The writer used time words to connect ideas.   **Yes** ☐   **No** ☐

2. What I liked in the story:

   _____

   _____

   _____

3. Questions I'd like the writer to answer in the story:

   Who _____?

   What _____?

   When _____?

   Where _____?

   How _____?

   (Your own question) _____?

6 | *Work with your partner. Discuss each other's chart from Exercise 5. Then rewrite your own paragraph and make any necessary changes.*

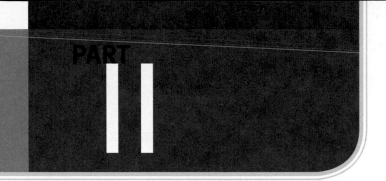

The Future

STEP 1 GRAMMAR IN CONTEXT

Before You Read

Look at the photo. Discuss the questions.

1. Where do you think the first space tourists will travel?
2. Why do people want to travel into space?
   Would you like to?

Read

Read the transcript of a radio program about space tourism.

SPACE TOURISTS: NOT JUST SCIENCE FICTION[1]

ROHAN: Good evening, and welcome to *The Future Today*. I'm Enid Rohan, and tonight Dr. Richard Starr, president of YourSpace, Inc., **is going to talk** to us about space tourism. Dr. Starr, **is** this really **going to happen**?

STARR: Yes, it **is**, Enid. We're already building the space planes. And we're selling tickets and planning our first trips now. In fact, our training program for passengers **is starting** next January.

ROHAN: Where **will** these tours **go**? **Will** they **travel** to the Moon? Mars?

STARR: **No**, they **won't**. The first space tourists **aren't going to go** that far. They**'re** only **going to travel** about 100 kilometers, or 62 miles above the Earth. That's the edge of space. A trip **will last** about three hours.

ROHAN: But the tickets cost $200,000! Who**'s going to pay** that much for just three hours?

STARR: A lot of people. It**'s going to be** an incredible trip. Come and see! We**'ll save** one of our best seats for you.

ROHAN: What **will** a trip **be** like?

STARR: First of all, you**'ll experience** zero gravity[2]—and let me tell you, it's an amazing feeling. And you**'ll get** a bird's-eye view of the Earth from space. You **won't believe** your eyes! You**'re going to think** about the Earth in a whole new way. Besides, tickets **won't** always **be** so expensive. Costs **are going to fall** a lot.

ROHAN: **Will** I **need** a spacesuit?

STARR: No, you **won't**. That **will be** one of the great things about this trip. No spacesuits and no seat belts except for takeoff and landing. The cabins **will be** large, so passengers **will float** freely during the trip.

ROHAN: Sounds great. I think I**'ll ask** my boss to send me on a trip. Maybe I**'ll** even **do** a show from space! So tell me, when **does** the first flight **leave**?

STARR: It **leaves** on January 1, two years from now. But you **won't be** on that one—our first three flights are already sold out!

---

[1] *science fiction:* stories about the future, often about space travel and scientific discoveries

[2] *gravity:* the force that makes things fall to the ground. (In *zero gravity*, things do not stay on the ground.)

After You Read

A | Vocabulary: *Complete the sentences with the words from the box.*

edge	experience	float	incredible	sold out	takeoff

1. There are no more tickets for the space tour. It's _____.

2. We live at the _____ of a forest. Sometimes bears come into our yard!

3. Sy took _____ photos on his trip to Antarctica. He saw some strange and wonderful sights.

4. As a space tourist, you'll _____ a lot of feelings—amazement, excitement, fear, and much more.

5. I was only scared at _____—when the space plane left the ground. After that, I felt OK.

6. What did I do on vacation? I lay on the beach and watched the clouds _____ by.

B | Comprehension: *Based on the information in the reading, which of the statements are true right **Now**? Which will be true only in the **Future**? Check (✓) the correct boxes.*

	Now	Future
1. Companies are building space planes.	*N* ☐	☐
2. Tourists are buying tickets.	*N* ☐	☐
3. A training program for passengers is starting.	*F* ☐	☐
4. Space tours travel about 100km (62 miles) above the Earth.	*F* ☐	☐
5. Tickets are very expensive.	*N* ☐	☐
6. The first flight is ready to leave.	*F* ☐	☐

The edge of space

BE GOING TO FOR THE FUTURE

Statements				
Subject	*Be*	*(Not) Going to*	Base Form of Verb	
I	am			
You	are			
He She It	is	(not) going to	leave	soon.
We You They	are			

Yes / No Questions				
Be	Subject	*Going to*	Base Form of Verb	
Am	I			
Are	you			
Is	he she it	going to	leave	soon?
Are	we you they			

Short Answers						
Affirmative			Negative			
	you	are.		you're		
	I	am.		I'm		
Yes,	he she it	is.	No,	he's she's it's	not.	
	you we they	are.		you're we're they're		

Wh- Questions				
Wh- Word	*Be*	Subject	*Going to*	Base Form of Verb
When Why	are	you	going to	leave?

WILL FOR THE FUTURE

Statements			
Subject	***Will (not)***	**Base Form of Verb**	
I You He She It We You They	**will (not)**	**leave**	soon.

Yes / No Questions			
Will	**Subject**	**Base Form of Verb**	
Will	I you he she it we you they	**leave**	soon?

Short Answers					
Affirmative			**Negative**		
Yes,	you I he she it you we they	**will.**	**No,**	you I he she it you we they	**won't.**

Wh- Questions			
***Wh-* Word**	***Will***	**Subject**	**Base Form of Verb**
When	**will**	you	**leave**?

PRESENT PROGRESSIVE FOR THE FUTURE

Statements		
Subject + *Be*	**(Not) + Base Form +** *-ing*	
We**'re**	**(not) leaving**	soon.
It**'s**		

SIMPLE PRESENT FOR THE FUTURE

Statements		
Subject		**Verb**
We	**leave**	Monday at 6:45 A.M.
It	**leaves**	

GRAMMAR NOTES

1
There are several ways to talk about the **future**. You can use:

- *be going to*
- *will*
- **present progressive**
- **simple present**

Now

Past ——————|———————X————→ **Future**

                     meeting

USAGE NOTE: Sometimes only one form of the future is appropriate, but in many cases more than one form is possible.

- They**'re going to have** a meeting.
- I think I**'ll go**.
- It**'s taking** place next week.
- It **starts** at 9:00 A.M. on Monday.

2
To talk about **facts** or things you are certain will happen in the future, use:

- *be going to*

OR

- *will*

- The sun **is going to rise** at 6:43 tomorrow.

OR

- The sun **will rise** at 6:43 tomorrow.

3
To make **predictions** about things you are quite sure will happen in the future, use:

- *be going to*

OR

- *will*

BE CAREFUL! Use *be going to* (NOT *will*) when something that you <u>see right now</u> makes you almost certain an event is going to happen.

- I think a lot of people **are going to travel** to space.

OR

- I think a lot of people **will travel** to space.

A: Look at those dark clouds!
B: It**'s going to rain**.
   NOT: It~~'ll~~ rain.

4
To talk about future **plans** or things you have already decided, use:

- *be going to*

OR

- **present progressive**

USAGE NOTE: We often use the **present progressive** for plans that are <u>already arranged</u>.

- I**'m going to fly** to Chicago next week.

OR

- I**'m flying** to Chicago next week.
  NOT: I~~'ll fly~~ to Chicago next week.

- I**'m flying** to Chicago next week. I already have a ticket.

5	For **quick decisions** (made as you are speaking), or to make **offers** or **promises**, use *will*.	**QUICK DECISION:** **A:** The Space Show is opening next week. **B:** Sounds interesting. I think I**'ll go**. **OFFER AND PROMISE:** **A:** I'd like to go too, but I don't have a ride. **B:** I**'ll drive** you. But I'd like to leave by 7:00. **A:** No problem. I**'ll be** ready.
6	To talk about **scheduled future events** (timetables, programs, schedules), use the **simple present**. We often use **verbs** such as *start*, *leave*, *end*, and *begin* this way.	• The shuttle **leaves** at 9:00 A.M. • The conference **starts** tomorrow morning.

REFERENCE NOTES

For **contractions** of *I am*, *you are*, *I will*, *you will*, etc., see Appendix 26, page A-12.
For a complete presentation of **present progressive** and **simple present** forms, see Unit 1, page 4.
Will can also be used for **making a request**; see Unit 15 on page 205.

STEP 3 FOCUSED PRACTICE

EXERCISE 1: Discover the Grammar

A | *Read the transcript of an interview with a future space tourist. There are thirteen forms of the future. The first form is already circled. Find and circle twelve more.*

OUT OF THIS WORLD

ROHAN: This is Enid Rohan, reporting from Spaceport America. Lyn Filipov is in the training program here for a flight with YourSpace, Inc. She's going to fly to the edge of space very soon. So, Lyn, which flight are you taking?

FILIPOV: The one that leaves on March 30. The earlier ones were all sold out.

ROHAN: What's the training like?

FILIPOV: Well, at 100 kilometers—that's 62 miles—above the Earth, there won't be any gravity, so we're practicing moving around in zero-g. It's an incredible feeling—like floating in water, or flying. You feel really free.

ROHAN: Aren't you even a little scared?

FILIPOV: Right now, I can't wait to go. I'm pretty sure I'll be terrified on takeoff, but it'll be worth it. Totally.

(*continued on next page*)

OUT OF THIS WORLD

ROHAN: How can you afford this? Are you an Internet millionaire?

FILIPOV: No, I'm not. Actually, I won a big lottery. When I saw my winning numbers, my first thought was, "I'll buy a ticket for a space tour."

ROHAN: What an amazing story! But you're very young. How does your family feel about this?

FILIPOV: I'm not *that* young. I'll be 23 next month. But my parents are nervous, of course. My mother is really afraid I'm going to love space travel and I'll want to keep doing it. And my younger brother is jealous.

ROHAN: What do you say to make them feel better?

FILIPOV: I tell my mother, "Listen, Mom, this is a once-in-a-lifetime thing. I won't make a habit of space travel, I promise." My brother? He wants a career in space travel, so he's going to study a lot harder from now on. That's what he says, anyway.

ROHAN: Have a great time, Lyn. And let us know what it was like.

FILIPOV: Thanks. I'll send you photos.

B | *Complete the chart. List the thirteen future verb forms. Then check (✓) the correct column for each form.*

	Facts	Predictions	Plans	Quick Decisions	Offers and Promises	Schedules
1. 's going to fly			✓			
2.						
3.						
4.						
5.						
6.						
7.						
8.						
9.						
10.						
11.						
12.						
13.						

EXERCISE 2: *Will* for Facts and Predictions

(Grammar Notes 2–3)

*It is the year 2020, and an international group of space tourists are getting ready for their space flight. Part of the training program includes a Question and Answer (Q & A) session with astronaut William R. Pogue. Complete the questions and answers. Use the verbs in parentheses with **will** or **won't**.*

It'll Be Great!

Q: _____Will_____ it _____take_____ a long time to get used to zero gravity?
                          1. (take)

A: No, ____it won't____. Every day you _____ more comfortable, and after three
          2.   **3. (feel)**

   days you _____ used to being in space.
              4. (become)

★ ★ ★

Q: _____ I _____ sick?
                        5. (feel)

A: Yes, you might feel sick for a little while. But it _____ long.
                                                            6. (last)

★ ★ ★

Q: I love to read. How _____ I _____ my book open to the right page?
                                              7. (keep)

A: Actually, reading a book in space can be quite a problem. You _____ strong
                                                                        8. (need)

   clips to hold the book open. It can be a little frustrating at first, but after a while you

   _____ used to it.
        9. (get)

★ ★ ★

Q: _____ I _____ the same?
                        10. (look)

A: Actually, you _____ the same at all. Your face and eyes _____ puffy.
                      11. (look)   **12. (get)**

   The first time you look in a mirror, you probably _____ yourself.
                                                        13. (recognize)

★ ★ ★

Q: _____ I _____ in my sleep?
                        14. (float)

A: Yes, if you are not tied down. And then you should be careful because you _____
                                                                                    15. (bump)

   into things all night long. Trust me. You can get hurt!

★ ★ ★

Q: I like salt and pepper on my food. Can I still use them in zero gravity?

A: Yes, you _____ still _____ salt and pepper, but not like you do on
                                    16. (have)

   Earth. You _____ small, squeezable bottles with salt water and pepper water so
              17. (use)

   the grains don't float away. You just squeeze it on your food. Don't worry about it.

   It _____ great!
        18. (be)

EXERCISE 3: *Be going to* for Prediction

(Grammar Note 3)

Look at the pictures. They show events from a day in the life of Professor Starr. Write predictions or guesses. Use the words from the box and a form of **be going to** *or* **not be going to**. *Choose between affirmative and negative.*

answer the phone	get out of bed	give a speech	have dinner	~~take a trip~~
drive	get very wet	go to sleep	rain	watch TV

1. <u>He's going to take a trip.</u>

2. _____

3. _____

4. _____

5. _____

6. _____

7. _____

8. _____

9. _____   10. _____

EXERCISE 4: Present Progressive for Plans

(Grammar Note 4)

Write about Professor Starr's plans for next week. Use the information from his calendar and the present progressive.

	Monday	**Tuesday**	**Wednesday**	**Thursday**	**Friday**	**Saturday**
A.M.	Teach my economics class	Take the train to Tokyo	Do the interview for <u>The Space Show</u>	Work on the Space Future website	Go to an exercise class	Answer emails from the Space Future website
P.M.		Meet friends from England for dinner	Answer questions from the online chat	↓	Fly to New York for the Space Transportation Conference	Write a speech for the next space travel conference

1. On Monday morning *he's teaching his economics class* _____.

2. On Tuesday morning _____.

3. On Tuesday evening _____.

4. On Wednesday morning _____.

5. On Wednesday afternoon _____.

6. All day Thursday _____.

7. On Friday morning _____.

8. On Friday evening _____.

9. On Saturday morning _____.

10. On Saturday afternoon _____.

EXERCISE 5: Simple Present for Schedules

(Grammar Note 6)

It is June 2050. You and a friend are planning a trip to the Moon. Your friend just got the schedule, and you are deciding which shuttle to take. Use the words in parentheses to ask questions, and look at the schedule to write the answers. Use the simple present.

2050 SHUTTLE SERVICE TO THE MOON
Fall Schedule

All times given in Earth's Eastern Standard Time

SEPTEMBER		OCTOBER		NOVEMBER	
Leave Earth	Arrive Moon	Leave Earth	Arrive Moon	Leave Earth	Arrive Moon
9/4 7:00 A.M.	9/7 6:00 P.M.	10/15 4:00 A.M.	10/18 3:00 P.M.	11/4 1:00 P.M.	11/8 12:00 A.M.
9/20 10:00 A.M.	9/23 9:00 P.M.	10/27 11:00 A.M.	10/30 10:00 P.M.	11/19 6:00 P.M.	11/23 5:00 A.M.

1. (when / the shuttle / fly to the Moon this fall)

   A: *When does the shuttle fly to the Moon this fall?*

   B: *It flies to the Moon in September, October, and November.*

2. (how many / shuttle flights / leave this fall)

   A: _____

   B: _____

3. (how often / the shuttle / depart for the Moon each month)

   A: _____

   B: _____

4. (when / the earliest morning flight / leave Earth)

   A: _____

   B: _____

5. (what time / the latest shuttle / leave Earth)

   A: _____

   B: _____

EXERCISE 6: Forms of the Future

(Grammar Notes 1–6)

Two people are having a cup of coffee and planning their trip to the Space Conference. Read their conversation and circle the most appropriate future forms.

JASON: I just heard the weather report. It's raining / (It's going to rain) tomorrow.
                    1.

ARIEL: Oh no. I hate driving in the rain. And it's a long drive to the conference.

JASON: Wait! I have an idea. (We'll take) / We're going to take the train instead!
                    2.

ARIEL: Good idea! Do you have a train schedule?

JASON: Yes. Here's one. There's a train that will leave / (leaves) at 7:00 A.M.
                    3.

ARIEL: What about lunch? Oh, I know. (I'll make) / I'm making some sandwiches for us.
                    4.

JASON: OK. You know, it's a long trip. What are we doing / (are we going) to do all those hours?
                    5.

ARIEL: Don't worry. (We'll think) / We're thinking of something.
                    6.

JASON: Maybe (I'll bring) / I'm bringing my laptop, and we can watch a movie.
                    7.

ARIEL: Great. Hey, Jason, your cup will fall / ('s going to fall)! It's right at the edge of the table.
                    8.

JASON: Got it! You know, we have to get up really early. I think (I'm going) / I'll go home now.
                    9.

ARIEL: OK. (I'm seeing) / I'll see you tomorrow. Good night.
                    10.

EXERCISE 7: Editing

Read the student's report on space travel. There are eleven mistakes in the use of the future. The first mistake is already corrected. Find and correct ten more.

    Both astronauts and space tourists will ~~traveling~~ *travel* in space, but tourists *are* going to have a much different experience. Space tourists *are* is going to travel for fun, not for work. So, they *won't* willn't have to worry about many of the technical problems that astronauts worry about. For example, space tourists will *won't* need not to figure out how to use tools without gravity. And they *aren't* isn't going to go outside the spaceship to make repairs. For the most part, space tourists will just *go* going to see the sights and have a good time.

    Still, there will be similarities. Regular activities *will* be the same for astronauts and space tourists. For example, eating, washing, and sleeping will turned into exciting challenges for everyone in space. And on long trips, everyone is going to doing exercises to stay fit in zero gravity. And both astronauts and space tourists *are* will going to have many new adventures!

EXERCISE 8: Listening

A | *Listen to six short conversations. Decide if the people are talking about something happening* **Now** *or in the* **Future**. *Then listen again and check (✓) the correct column.*

	Now	Future
1.	☐	✓
2.	✓	☐
3.	✓	☐
4.	✓	☐
5.	✓	☐
6.	✓	☐

B | *Read the statements. Then listen again to the conversations and check (✓)* **True** *or* **False** *about each conversation. Correct the false statements.*

	True	False
1. The woman ~~plans to go out with friends~~. *doesn't have any special plans*	☐	✓
2. The woman doesn't think the photos are very good.	☐	✓
3. Professor Starr won't take the call.	✓	☐
4. The lecture is about traveling to Mars.	☐	✓
5. The man isn't going to meet his parents at the airport.	✓	☐
6. The train to Boston left five minutes ago.	☐	✓

EXERCISE 9: Pronunciation

A | *Read and listen to the Pronunciation Note.*

Pronunciation Note

In **conversation**, we often pronounce *will* "ll" after consonants.

EXAMPLE: The trip **will** last three hours.   →   "The trip'**ll** last three hours."

We also often pronounce *going to* "gonna."

EXAMPLE: I'm **going to** be 23 soon.   →   "I'm **gonna** be 23 soon."

But do NOT use "gonna" in **writing**. Use *going to*.

B | *Listen to the conversation. Notice the pronunciation of* **going to** *and* **will.**

A: I think I'm **going to** go to the park tomorrow.

B: That **will** be nice. Are you **going to** go in the morning?

A: Yeah. The park **will** be crowded in the afternoon. Want to come?

B: Yeah, I do. There's **going to** be an art show there tomorrow.

A: Maybe Jane **will** have some things in the show. She takes incredible photos.

B: Oh, wait! I think my parents are **going to** be here tomorrow.

A: OK. Maybe we**'ll** do something together next weekend.

C | *Listen again to the conversation and repeat each statement or question. Then practice the conversation with a partner.*

EXERCISE 10: Making Plans

A | *Complete your weekend schedule. If you have no plans, write* **free.**

	Saturday	Sunday
12:00 P.M.		
1:00 P.M.		
2:00 P.M.		
3:00 P.M.		
4:00 P.M.		
5:00 P.M.		
6:00 P.M.		
7:00 P.M.		
8:00 P.M.		
9:00 P.M.		

B | *Now work with a partner. Ask questions to decide on a time when you are both free to do something together.*

EXAMPLE: **A:** What are you doing Saturday afternoon? Do you want to go to the movies?
            B: I'm going to go to the library. How about Saturday night? Are you doing anything?

EXERCISE 11: Reaching Agreement

Work with your partner from Exercise 10. Look at the weekend schedule of events. Then look at your schedules from Exercise 10. Decide which events to attend and when.

○○○ Riverside

WEEKEND EVENTS IN RIVERSIDE
June 20 and 21

EVENTS	WHERE AND WHEN
Art in the Park Painting, photography, jewelry, and more! Support our local artists.	River Park, all day Saturday and Sunday
International Food Festival Moussaka, pad thai, spaetzle—you'll find plenty of interesting tastes here. International music and dance too.	Conference Center, Saturday 1:00 P.M.–7:00 P.M.
Walking Event 5 kilometers for Jay Street Clinic. Join us and help the city's only free clinic.	Start at River Park, Sunday 11:00 A.M. End at the clinic, 10 W. Jay St.
Zero G Experience space travel in this new film. On the big, big IMAX screen, it'll feel like you're really there.	Science Museum, starts Sunday Show times: 10:00 A.M. and 3:00 P.M.
Dancing with the Stars Free concert, with plenty of room for dancing. Bring a picnic and your own chairs.	Brown's Beach, Saturday 7:00 P.M.–Midnight

EXAMPLE: **A:** What are you doing Sunday? Do you want to go to see the space travel movie, *Zero G*?

B: Hmm. Maybe. What else is happening on Sunday?

EXERCISE 12: Writing

A | *Write a paragraph about your life five years from now. Answer the following questions. Include plans, predictions, and facts.*

- Where will you live?
- What kind of job will you have?
- What transportation will you use?

EXAMPLE: Most of my family lives in Los Angeles, so I'm probably going to live there too. I'm graduating from college in two years, and I'm going to look for a job in space travel. I'll probably drive an electric car because I'm sure gas will get more expensive. I'll be 25 in five years, so I think I'll probably be married. Maybe I'll even have a child.

B | *Check your work. Use the Editing Checklist.*

Editing Checklist

Did you use . . . ?
- [ ] *will* and *be going to* for predictions and facts
- [ ] *be going to* and the present progressive for plans

A | *Circle the correct words to complete the sentences.*

1. We 'll go / **'re going** to a concert on Saturday. I already have the tickets.

2. You can give me that envelope. I **'ll** / 'm going to mail it for you on the way to school.

3. Look out! That vase will / **is going to** fall off the shelf!

4. Take your umbrella. It 'll / **'s going to** rain.

5. Sara gives / **is giving** a party tomorrow night.

B | *Complete the sentences about the future with the correct form of the verbs in parentheses.*

1. It's almost June. What __are going__ we __doing (are going to do__ this summer?
   (do)

2. Don't eat so much. You __are going/will__ sick tomorrow.
   (feel)

3. The package __is going to /will__ in a few days.
   (arrive)

4. That driver __is going to get__ a speeding ticket. The police are right behind him.
   (get)

5. Bye. I __'ll__ you tomorrow.
   (see)

6. Look at Tommy's face. I think he __'s going to cry__ .
   (cry)

7. What time __is/will/does__ the movie __start / starting__ ?
   (start)

8. __Will/going to__ Mahmoud __call__ back this afternoon?
   (call)

9. Don't worry. He __won't/isn't going__ to call you.
   (not forget)

10. Bye. I __'ll speak__ to you next week.
    (speak)

C | *Find and correct five mistakes.*

1. When will Ed gets home tomorrow?

2. The movie starts at 7:30, so I think I go.

3. Do you want to go with me, or are you study tonight?

4. What you are going to do next weekend?

5. I'm going be home all day.

Future Time Clauses
SETTING GOALS

STEP 1 GRAMMAR IN CONTEXT

Before You Read

Look at the picture. Discuss the questions.

1. What is the girl thinking?
2. What are some typical goals that people have?
3. What will people do to reach those goals?

Read

Read the article about setting goals.

GO FOR IT! What are your dreams for the future?

Will you have your degree **when you're 22**? Will you start your own business **before you turn 40**? We all have dreams, but they'll remain just dreams **until we change them to goals**. Here's how.

PUT YOUR DREAMS ON PAPER. After you write a dream down, it will start to become a goal. Your path will be a lot clearer. For example, Latoya Jones wrote this:

> **Before I turn 30,** I'm going to be a successful businessperson.

Now her dream is starting to become her goal.

LIST YOUR REASONS. When things get difficult, you can read this list to yourself and it will help you to go on. This is what Latoya put at the top of her list:

> My parents will be proud of me **when I'm a successful businessperson**.

WRITE DOWN AN ACTION PLAN. What are you planning to do to achieve your goal? This is Latoya's action plan:

> I'm going to go to business school **as soon as I save enough money to pay for it**.
>
> **When I graduate,** I'll get a job with a big company.
>
> **After I get some experience**, I'll find a better job.

TAKE YOUR FIRST STEPS TODAY. Here are the first steps Latoya is going to take:

> **Before I apply to schools,** I'm going to download some online[1] catalogs.
>
> I'll prepare carefully for interviews **after I apply**.
>
> I won't decide on a school **until I visit several of them**.

You can do exactly what Latoya did to achieve your own goals. Keep this article in a safe place. **When you decide to start,** you'll know what to do. Remember, the longest journey starts with the first step!

---
[1] *online:* on the Internet

After You Read

A | Vocabulary: *Circle the letter of the word or phrase that best completes each sentence.*

1. When you **achieve** something, you get it _____.
   a. as a gift
   b. after hard work
   c. from your family

2. Sam got a college **catalog** because he wanted to _____.
   a. pay his bill
   b. look at a homework assignment
   c. find information about classes

3. Melissa got a **degree** when she _____.
   a. mailed her college applications
   b. graduated from college
   c. listened to the weather report

4. When you **download** something from the Internet, you _____.
   a. put it on your computer
   b. throw it away
   c. email it

5. A **goal** is _____.
   a. not very important to you
   b. something you plan and work for
   c. a person who gives you advice

6. At a college **interview**, you _____.
   a. meet with someone from the school
   b. go on a tour of the college
   c. take a language test

B | Comprehension: *For each pair of sentences (**a** or **b**), check (✓) the action that comes first.*

Latoya's action plan:

1. _____ **a.** She will download school catalogs.   _____ **b.** She will apply to schools.

2. _____ **a.** She will save money.   _____ **b.** She will go to business school.

3. _____ **a.** She will get a job with a big company.   _____ **b.** She will graduate.

FUTURE TIME CLAUSES

Statements				
Main Clause			**Time Clause**	
I **will** I **am going to**				I **graduate**.
She **will** She **is going to**	**get** a job	**when**	she **graduates**.	
They **will** They **are going to**				they **graduate**.

Yes / No Questions				
Main Clause			**Time Clause**	
Will you	**get** a job	**when**	you **graduate**?	
Are you **going to**				

Short Answers					
Affirmative			**Negative**		
Yes,	I	**will**. **am**.	No,	I	**won't**. **'m not**.

Wh- Questions				
Main Clause			**Time Clause**	
Where	**will** you **are** you **going to**	**get** a job	**when**	you **graduate**?

GRAMMAR NOTES

1 Use **future time clauses** to show the time relationship between <u>two future events</u>.

The verb in the **main clause** is in the **future**. The verb in the **time clause** is in the **present**.

BE CAREFUL! Do NOT use *be going to* or *will* in a future time clause.

The **time clause** can come at the <u>beginning</u> or at the <u>end</u> of the sentence. The meaning is the same.

Use a **comma** after the time clause when it comes at the <u>beginning</u>. Do NOT use a comma when it comes at the end.

- She'll find a job **when** she graduates.

   MAIN CLAUSE   TIME CLAUSE
- He**'s going to move** *after* he **graduates**.
  (First he'll graduate. Then he'll move.)

   MAIN CLAUSE   TIME CLAUSE
- We**'ll miss** him *when* he **leaves**.
  (First he'll leave. Then we'll miss him.)

Not: after he ~~is going to graduate~~.
Not: when he ~~will leave~~.

- *Before* she applies, she'll visit schools.
  OR
- She'll visit schools *before* she applies.

Not: She'll visit school before she applies.

(continued on next page)

2 Future time clauses begin with **time expressions** that show the <u>order of events</u>.

a. **When**, **after**, and **as soon as** introduce the <u>first</u> event.

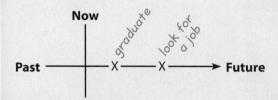

- **When** I graduate, I'll look for a job.
- I'll look for a job **after** I graduate.
  (First I'll graduate. Then I'll look for a job.)

- **As soon as** I graduate, I'll look for a job.
  (First I'll graduate. Immediately after that, I'll look for a job.)

b. **Before** introduces the <u>second</u> event.

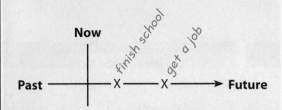

- **Before** I get a job, I'll finish school.
  (First I'll finish school. Then I'll get a job.)

c. **Until** also introduces the <u>second</u> event. It means "only up to the time" of the second event.

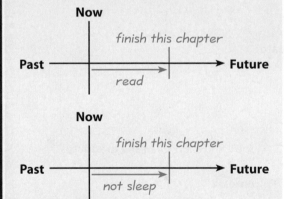

- I'll read **until** I finish this chapter.
  (I'll keep reading, but only up to the time that I finish this chapter. Then I'll stop.)

- I won't sleep **until** I finish this chapter.
  (I'll stay awake, but only up to the time that I finish this chapter. Then I'll go to sleep.)

d. **While** introduces an event that will happen <u>at the same time</u> as another event.

You can use either the **simple present** or **present progressive** with an action verb after *while*.

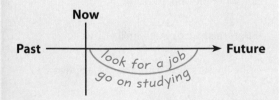

- **While** I look for a job, I'll go on studying.
  OR
- **While** I'm looking for a job, I'll go on studying.
  (I'll look for a job and study at the same time.)

EXERCISE 1: Discover the Grammar

Read the numbered sentence. Then circle the letter of the two sentences that have a similar meaning.

1. Amber will open her own business when she finishes school.

    a. Amber will open her own business. Then she'll finish school.

    (b.) Amber will finish school. Then she'll open her own business.

2. Denzell won't quit until he finds another job.

    a. Denzell will find another job. Then he'll quit.

    b. Denzell will quit. Then he'll find another job.

3. Jake will retire as soon as he turns 60.

    a. Jake will retire. Then he'll turn 60.

    b. Jake will turn 60. Then he'll retire.

4. After the Morrisons sell their house, they'll move to Florida.

    a. The Morrisons will sell their house. Then they'll move to Florida.

    b. The Morrisons will move to Florida. Then they'll sell their house.

5. Marisa will call you when she gets home.

    a. Marisa will call you. Then she'll get home.

    b. Marisa will get home. Then she'll call you.

6. Dimitri is going to live with his parents until he gets married.

    a. Dimitri is going to get married. Then he'll live with his parents.

    b. Dimitri will live with his parents. Then he'll get married.

7. While Li-jing is in school, she'll work part-time.

    a. Li-jing will finish school. Then she'll get a part-time job.

    b. Li-jing will go to school. At the same time she'll have a part-time job.

8. Marta will have her degree before she turns 21.

    a. Marta will get her degree. Then she'll turn 21.

    b. Marta will turn 21. Then she'll get her degree.

9. Adel and Farah won't buy a house until their son is two years old.

    a. They'll buy a house. Then their son will turn two.

    b. Their son will turn two. Then they'll buy a house.

10. Ina will live in Paris while she studies French cooking.

    a. First she'll study French cooking. Then she'll move to Paris.

    b. She'll study French cooking. At the same time, she'll live in Paris.

EXERCISE 2: Simple Present or Future

(Grammar Note 1–2)

Complete the student's worksheet. Use the correct form of the verbs in parentheses.

GOAL PLANNING WORKSHEET

A. What is your most important goal?

- I _____*'ll get*_____ a job after I _____*graduate*_____.
  1. (get)   2. (graduate)

B. List the reasons you want to achieve this goal.

- When I _____ a job, I _____ more money.
  3. (get)   4. (have)
- When I _____ enough money, I _____ a used car.
  5. (save)   6. (buy)
- I _____ happier when I _____ employed.
  7. (feel)   8. (be)
- I _____ new skills while I _____.
  9. (learn)   10. (work)

C. What is your action plan?

- Every morning when I _____, I _____ online for
  11. (get up)   12. (check)
  employment ads.

- When I _____ to my friends, I _____ them if they know
  13. (talk)   14. (ask)
  of any jobs.

- I _____ information about résumé writing before I _____
  15. (download)   16. (write)
  a new résumé.

- While I _____ to find a job, I _____ my
  17. (try)   18. (improve)
  computer skills.

- Before I _____ on an interview, I _____ how to
  19. (go)   20. (know)
  use Excel and PowerPoint.

D. What are the steps you will take right away?

- Before I _____ anything else, I _____ a list of people to
  21. (do)   22. (write)
  contact for help.

- As soon as I _____ all the people on my list, I _____ on
  23. (contact)   24. (work)
  fixing up my résumé.

EXERCISE 3: Order of Events

(Grammar Notes 1–2)

Combine the pairs of sentences. Use the future and the simple present or present progressive form of the verb. Decide which sentence goes first. Remember to use commas when necessary.

1. Sandy and Jeff will get married. Then Sandy will graduate.

   _____*Sandy and Jeff will get married*_____ before _____*Sandy graduates*_____ .

2. Jeff is going to get a raise. Then they are going to move to a larger apartment.

   As soon as _____ .

3. They're going to move to a larger apartment. Then they're going to have a baby.

   After _____ .

4. They'll have their first child. Then Sandy will get a part-time job.

   _____ after _____ .

5. Sandy will work part-time. Then their child will be two years old.

   _____ until _____ .

6. Jeff will go to school. At the same time, Sandy will work full-time.

   _____ while _____ .

7. Jeff and Sandy will achieve their goals. Then they'll feel very proud.

   When _____ .

EXERCISE 4: Editing

Read the journal entry. There are ten mistakes in the use of future time clauses. The first mistake is already corrected. Find and correct nine more. Remember to look at punctuation!

> Graduation is next month! I need to make some plans now because when exams
>
> ~~will~~ start, I don't have any free time. What am I going to do when I'll finish school?
>   *start*
>
> My roommate is going to take a vacation before she'll look for a job. I can't do that
>
> because I need to earn some money soon. I think that after I'll graduate I'm going to
>
> take a desktop publishing class. As soon as I learn the software I look for a job with a
>
> business publisher. It's hard to find full-time jobs, though. Part-time jobs are easier to find.
>
> Maybe I'll take a part-time job after I find a good full-time one. Or maybe I'll take a
>
> workshop in making decisions, before I do anything!

EXERCISE 5: Listening

A | *A woman is calling Jobs Are Us Employment Agency. Read the list of steps she will take to get a job. Then listen to her conversation. Listen again and number the steps in order.*

The woman is going to:

_____ **a.** speak to a job counselor

_____ **b.** have an interview at the agency

__1__ **c.** send a résumé

_____ **d.** receive more job training

_____ **e.** go to companies

_____ **f.** take a skills test

B | *Read the statements. Then listen again to the call and circle the correct information.*

1. The agency is going to hire the woman / help the woman find a job.

2. The woman's goal is to work for her college / a company.

3. The woman has a college degree / a lot of work experience.

4. The man thinks she's going to need more training / experience before she goes on interviews.

5. The man will send the woman his résumé / a brochure.

EXERCISE 6: Pronunciation

A | *Read and listen to the Pronunciation Note.*

Pronunciation Note
When the **time clause comes first**, the voice often **falls at the end of the time clause**. It falls **more** at the end of the **second clause**. EXAMPLE: *When* I finish the homework, I'm going to have lunch.

B | *Listen to the short conversations and notice the intonation in the answers.*

1. **A:** When are you going to call Dan?

    B: After I do my homework, I'll call him.

2. **A:** Are you going to look for a full-time job?

    B: No. Until I graduate, I'm only going to work part-time.

3. **A:** Are we going to read something new now?

    B: As soon as we take the test, we'll begin a new chapter.

4. **A:** How is Marta doing in her new job?

    B: Great. Before she's 30, she'll open her own business.

5. **A:** Philippe's new house is far from work. How will he get there?

    B: After he moves, he's going to buy a car.

C | *Listen again to the conversations and repeat the answers. Then practice the conversations with a partner.*

EXERCISE 7: What About You?

A | *Complete the sentences with your own information.*

1. I'm going to continue studying English until _____.

2. While I'm in this class, _____.

3. When I finish this class, _____.

4. I'll stay in this country until _____.

5. As soon as _____, I'll _____.

6. I'm not going to _____ until _____.

7. I'm going to feel a lot better after _____.

8. Before _____, _____.

B | *Work in small groups and compare your answers with those of your classmates. How many different answers are there? Remember that all sentences refer to future time.*

EXAMPLE: **A:** I'm going to study English until I pass the TOEFL exam. What about you?
B: I'm going to continue studying until I get a job.
C: Me too!

EXERCISE 8: Game: What's Next?

Work in a group and form a circle. One person says a sentence with a future time clause. Use your imagination—your sentences don't have to be true! The next person begins a new sentence using information from the main clause. Continue around the circle as long as you can.

EXAMPLE:

EXERCISE 9: Writing

A | *Complete the worksheet for yourself. Use future time clauses.*

GOAL PLANNING WORKSHEET

A. What is your most important goal?

1. _____

B. List three reasons you want to achieve this goal.

1. _____

2. _____

3. _____

C. What are the first three steps of your action plan?

1. _____

2. _____

3. _____

B | *Check your work. Use the Editing Checklist.*

Editing Checklist

Did you use . . . ?
- ☐ sentences with future time clauses
- ☐ the present in the time clauses
- ☐ the future in the main clauses
- ☐ a comma when the time clause comes first

Check your answers on page UR-2.

Do you need to review anything?

A | *Circle the correct words to complete the sentences.*

1. What are you going to do after you <u>will graduate / graduate</u>?

2. We won't start a new chapter until we <u>finished / finish</u> this one.

3. <u>When / Until</u> Jorge gets a raise, he's going to buy a new car.

4. <u>Is / Will</u> Andrea find a job by the time she graduates?

5. Where will you live while you're <u>learning / going to learn</u> English?

6. We won't start the test <u>until / when</u> the teacher arrives. She has the tests.

7. <u>Will you / Are you</u> going to take another class after you finish this one?

B | *Complete the sentences with the correct form of the verbs in parentheses.*

1. Yuri is going to take night classes while he _____ full time.
   (work)

2. Until he buys a new computer, he _____ for online courses.
   (not register)

3. When he takes online courses, he _____ more time at home.
   (spend)

4. He'll help his daughter with her homework while he _____ for his
   (study)
   own courses.

5. He _____ for a new job before he graduates.
   (not look)

6. By the time he _____, he's going to have a lot of work experience.
   (graduate)

7. Before he starts his new job, he _____ a vacation.
   (take)

C | *Find and correct six mistakes. Remember to look at punctuation.*

A: Are you going to call Phil when we'll finish dinner?

B: No, I'm too tired. I'm just going to watch TV after I go to sleep.

A: Before I wash the dishes, I'm going answer some emails.

B: I'll help you, as soon as I'll drink my coffee.

A: No rush. I have a lot of emails. I won't be ready to clean up until you'll finish.

From Grammar to Writing
SHOWING THE ORDER OF EVENTS

When you write about your future plans and goals, use sentences with future time clauses to show the relationship between two future events. Use **time words** (*as soon as*, *after*, *before*, *by the time*, *when*, *while*, and *until*) to introduce the time clause. The time words show the order of the events.

EXAMPLE: First I'll go to the gym. Then I'll call my friend. →

SECOND EVENT   FIRST EVENT
I'll call my friend **after** I go to the gym.

FIRST EVENT   SECOND EVENT
After I go to the gym, I'll call my friend.

The time clause can come first or second. When it comes first, a **comma** separates the two clauses.

1 | *Read the blog post about weekend plans. Underline the future time clauses. Circle the time words in the future time clauses.*

The Weekend: Plan Ahead for a Good One!

It's Sunday night, and once again, I'm wondering, *Where did the weekend go?* So from now on, (before) the weekend arrives, I'm going to make a plan. My goal: have some fun *and* get the chores done. Here's how I'll achieve that goal next weekend. First, after I finish this blog post, I'm going to buy movie tickets for Saturday night online. Next, no more sleeping late on Saturday! As soon as the alarm clock rings, I'm going to jump out of bed. Then I'll clean the apartment. (And this time, I'll keep working until I finish.) Finally, coffee! While I have my first cup, I'll talk to my friends about the film festival that night. After coffee, it'll be time do the grocery shopping. This will be incredible—I'll actually get to the farmers market before the good stuff is sold out. After that, I'll just relax until it's time to go out. On Sunday, my sister and her family are coming to lunch. No problem! By the time they get here, I'll be ready. In fact, I probably won't even start cooking until I finish my workout at the gym. Is this a plan or an impossible dream? When next Sunday night rolls around,[1] I'll let you know!

---

[1]*roll around:* to arrive

2 | *Look at the pairs of events from Gary's plans. What will happen first? Number the events in each pair:* **1** *for first event;* **2** *for second event; write* **1** *for both events when they happen at the same time.*

a. __2__ the weekend arrives   __1__ I make a plan

b. _____ the alarm clock rings   _____ I jump out of bed

c. _____ I have my first cup of coffee   _____ I talk to my friends

d. _____ get to the farmers market   _____ the good stuff is sold out

e. _____ my sister and her family get here   _____ I'm ready

f. _____ I start to cook   _____ I finish my workout

g. _____ next Sunday rolls around   _____ I let my readers know

3 | *Before you write . . .*

1. Think about the coming weekend. What are some necessary chores? Will you do something for fun? Where will you go? What friends or family members will you see?

2. Talk about your plans with a partner. Listen to your partner's plans. Ask and answer questions about your plans, for example: *What's the most important thing? What will you do after that? Where are you going to . . . ? Who will . . . ?*

3. Complete the timeline with the things you plan to do this weekend.

    EXAMPLE:

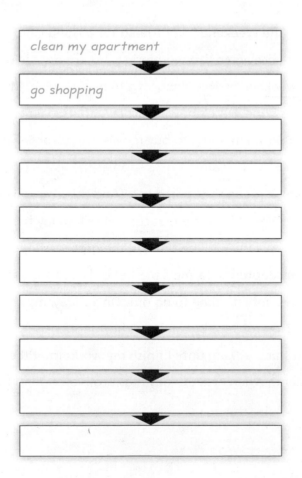

4 | *Write a first draft of a blog post about your weekend plans. Use the blog in Exercise 1 as a model and your timeline to organize your ideas. Include information that your partner asked about. Remember to use the present in future time clauses.*

EXAMPLE: Tomorrow is Saturday, and my friends are coming to dinner. My apartment is a mess, but I have a plan! As soon as I get up Saturday morning, I'm going to clean the apartment. When I finish, I'll . . .

5 | *Exchange drafts with a different partner. Complete the chart.*

1. The writer used future time clauses   **Yes** ☐   **No** ☐

2. Check (✓) the time words and phrases the writer used to connect the time clauses:

   ☐ *after*   ☐ *as soon as*   ☐ *before*   ☐ *by the time*   ☐ *when*   ☐ *while*   ☐ *until*

3. What I found most interesting in the paragraph:

   _____

   _____

   _____

4. Questions I'd like the writer to answer in the story:

   Who _____?

   When _____?

   Why _____?

   (Your own questions) _____?

   _____?

   _____?

6 | *Work with your partner. Discuss each other's charts from Exercise 5. Then rewrite your own paragraph and make any necessary changes.*

PRESENT PERFECT

Present Perfect: *Since* and *For*

CAREERS

Before You Read

Look at Bob Burnquist's sports card. Discuss the questions.

1. What are his interests?
2. What are your interests?
3. What is Bob's motto[1]?
4. Do you have a motto? What is it?

Read

Read the article about a champion skateboarder.

by Mariana Andrade

When he was only 11 years old, Bob Burnquist's life changed dramatically. A skate park opened just three blocks from his house in São Paulo, Brazil. Bob got his very first skateboard and started skating. He**'s been** a skater **since then**.

At first he did it just for fun, but soon he turned pro.[3] His first big international contest was in Canada in 1995. Bob won. **Since then** he **has taken** home many more first-place prizes and gold medals. He **has** also **earned** enough money to support himself while doing what he loves most. In 2002 he was voted "King of Skate" in a California contest.

Bob **has lived** in California **since 1995**, but he frequently returns to Brazil. He**'s had** dual citizenship (Brazil and the United States) **for many years**. Does he consider himself American? Bob says, "I'm American, South American. . . . A citizen of the world."

The skateboard isn't the only board he uses. Bob also enjoys snowboarding and surfing. **Since he moved to California**, he **has been** close to snow-topped mountains and the beach. His backyard and, of course, the streets provide opportunity for skating. As he once said, "If you snowboard, surf, and skate, you pretty much cover the whole earth."

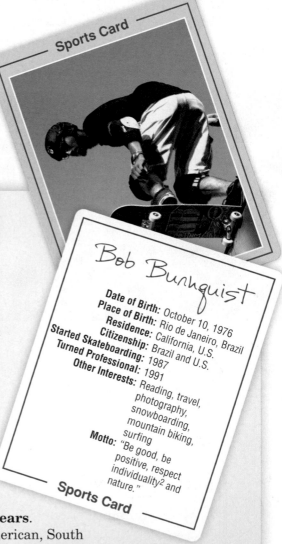

Sports Card

Bob Burnquist

Date of Birth: October 10, 1976
Place of Birth: Rio de Janeiro, Brazil
Residence: California, U.S.
Citizenship: Brazil and U.S.
Started Skateboarding: 1987
Turned Professional: 1991
Other Interests: Reading, travel, photography, snowboarding, mountain biking, surfing
Motto: "Be good, be positive, respect individuality[2] and nature."

Sports Card

---

[1] ***motto:*** a short statement of your life goals or beliefs
[2] ***individuality:*** the way people are different from each other
[3] ***turn pro:*** to become a professional (do a sport for money)

After You Read

A | Vocabulary: *Circle the letter of the word or phrase closest in meaning to the words in* **blue.**

1. Bob's life changed **dramatically**.
   a. slowly and a little
   b. dangerously
   c. quickly and a lot

2. He earned enough money to **support himself**.
   a. pay for skating lessons
   b. pay for his own food, clothing, and home
   c. buy an expensive skateboard

3. Does Bob **consider himself** American?
   a. want to be
   b. like being
   c. think he is

4. The streets provide **opportunity** for skating.
   a. some dangers
   b. good chances
   c. a lot of contests

5. Bob's **residence** is in California.
   a. home
   b. office
   c. family

6. Bob always says, "**Be positive.**"
   a. Be 100 percent certain.
   b. Believe good things will happen.
   c. Be strong.

B | Comprehension: *Check (✓)* **True** *or* **False.** *Correct the false statements.*

	True	False
1. Bob Burnquist doesn't skate anymore.	☐	☐
2. He has won only one first-place prize since 1995.	☐	☐
3. Bob moved to California in 1995.	☐	☐
4. Bob is a citizen of many countries.	☐	☐
5. He lives close to the beach.	☐	☐

PRESENT PERFECT WITH *SINCE* AND *FOR*

Statements				
Subject	*Have (not)*	Past Participle		*Since / For*
I You* We They	**have (not)**	**been**	here	**since** 1995. **for** a long time.
He She It	**has (not)**	**lived**		

You is both singular and plural.

Contractions	
Affirmative	Negative
I have = **I've** you have = **you've** we have = **we've** they have = **they've** he has = **he's** she has = **she's** it has = **it's**	have not = **haven't** has not = **hasn't**

Yes / No Questions				
Have	Subject	Past Participle		*Since / For*
Have	I you we they	**been**	here	**since** 1995? **for** a long time?
Has	he she it	**lived**		

Short Answers					
Affirmative			Negative		
Yes,	you I / we you they	**have.**	**No,**	you I / we you they	**haven't.**
	he she it	**has.**		he she it	**hasn't.**

Wh- Questions				
Wh- Word	*Have*	Subject	Past Participle	
How long	**have**	I you we they	**been**	here?
	has	he she it	**lived**	

Short Answers
Since 1995. **For** many years.

GRAMMAR NOTES

1 Use the **present perfect** with *since* or *for* to talk about something that <u>began</u> in the past and <u>continues</u> into the present (and may continue into the future).

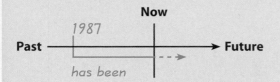

- Bob **has been** a skater *since* 1987.
  (He became a skater in 1987, and he is still a skater.)

- He **has been** a skater *for* many years.
  (He became a skater many years ago, and he is still a skater.)

2 Use *since* + **point in time** (*since yesterday, since 5:00, since Monday, since 1995, since then*) to show <u>when</u> something started.

- He **has won** many contests *since 1995*.
- *Since then* he **has become** famous.

Since can also introduce a **time clause**. Use a **comma** after the clause with *since* when it comes <u>first</u>.

- He **has loved** sports *since he was a child*.
- *Since he turned pro,* he **hasn't taken** a vacation.

Use *for* + **length of time** (*for 10 minutes, for two weeks, for years, for a long time*) to show <u>how long</u> something has lasted.

- Bob **has owned** a restaurant *for years*.
- He **hasn't broken** a board *for a long time*.

Expressions with *since* or *for* can go at the <u>beginning or end</u> of the sentence.

- *Since then* he has become famous. OR
- He has become famous *since then*.

3 The present perfect is formed with *have* + **past participle**.

- He **has lived** there for years.
- They **have been** partners since 1998.

a. The **past participle** of **regular verbs** is formed by adding *-d* or *-ed* to the base form of the verb. It is the same as the regular simple past form of the verb.

BE CAREFUL! There are often **spelling changes** when you add *-ed* to the verb.

b. Many common verbs are **irregular**. Their past participle is NOT formed by adding *-d* or *-ed*.

Here is a list of many of the **irregular verbs** used in this unit. It shows both the simple past and the past participle of each verb. Notice that most irregular verbs have a past participle form that is different from the simple past form.

BASE FORM	SIMPLE PAST	PAST PARTICIPLE
love	love**d**	love**d**
want	want**ed**	want**ed**
marry	marr**ied**	marr**ied**
stop	stop**ped**	stop**ped**
be	was	**been**
become	became	**become**
go	went	**gone**
have	had	**had**
meet	met	**met**
take	took	**taken**
wear	wore	**worn**
win	won	**won**
write	wrote	**written**

REFERENCE NOTE
For a more complete list of **irregular verbs**, see Appendix 1 on page A-1.

EXERCISE 1: Discover the Grammar

Read the information about Caterina and Roque. Then circle the letter of the sentence (a or b) that best describes the situation.

1. Caterina has been a skater since 2003.

   (a.) She is still a skater.

   b. She is not a skater anymore.

2. She has lived in the same apartment for five years.

   a. She lived in a different apartment six years ago.

   b. She moved two years ago.

3. Caterina and Roque have been married for five years.

   a. They are not married now.

   b. They got married five years ago.

4. They haven't been on a vacation since 2006.

   a. They are on a vacation now.

   b. They were on a vacation in 2006.

5. Caterina hasn't won a contest for two years.

   a. She won a championship two years ago.

   b. She didn't win a championship two years ago.

6. She has stayed positive about her career since she won her last contest.

   a. She expects to win more contests.

   b. She isn't hopeful anymore.

EXERCISE 2: *Since* or *For*   *(Grammar Note 2)*

*Complete the sentences about Brazilian sportswriter Mariana Andrade. Use **since** or **for**.*

1. Mariana Andrade has lived in São Paulo _____*since*_____ 1995.

2. She has supported herself as a sportswriter _____ four years.

3. _____ June she has written several articles about skateboarding.

4. This sport has been very popular in Brazil _____ many years.

5. Mariana has met Burnquist twice _____ she started her job.

6. She loves to skate, but she hasn't had much opportunity _____ a long time.

7. She has been married to Alvaro, another skater, _____ 2003.

EXERCISE 3: Forms of the Present Perfect

(Grammar Note 3)

Complete the article about Roque Guterres. Use the correct form of the verbs in parentheses.

Roque Guterres _____ has loved _____ skating since he was a little boy. He
                          1. (love)

began skating when he was 10, and he _____ since that time. Roque
                                              2. (not stop)

_____ a professional skater now for several years. He and Caterina
            3. (be)

_____ in Rio since they got married. They _____
            4. (live)   **5. (have)**

the same one-bedroom apartment for five years. They _____ a vacation for
                                                              6. (not take)

many years, but they _____ to several skating contests since Roque turned
                              7. (go)

pro. Roque _____ in four international contests since last year.
                    8. (skate)

He _____ two second-place prizes since then. Since he was a child,
            9. (win)

he _____ to be a pro. "Ever since my dream came true," says Guterres,
            10. (want)

"I _____ myself a lucky man."
            11. (consider)

EXERCISE 4: Forms of the Present Perfect with *Since* or *For*

(Grammar Notes 2–3)

Complete the sentences. Use the present perfect form of the verbs in parentheses and **since**
or **for**.

Skateboarding _____ has been _____ popular _____ for _____ more than 50
                        1. (be)   **2.**

years. People all over the world love the sport.

Skateboards _____ around _____ a long
                    3. (be)   **4.**

time. In the 1930s, the first ones were simple wooden boxes on metal wheels. They

_____ dramatically _____ then!
            5. (change)   **6.**

The first skateboarding contest took place in California in 1963. _____ then,
                                                                                    7.

thousands of contests _____ place all over the world.
                              8. (take)

In 1976, the first outdoor skate park opened in Florida. _____ then, hundreds of
                                                                        9.

parks _____ in countries around the world.
            10. (open)

Skateboarding can be dangerous. _____ the 1960s, hundreds of thousands of
                                          11.

people around the world _____ to hospital emergency rooms because
                                  12. (go)

of injuries.

(continued on next page)

When he was seven years old, Jon Comer lost his right foot as a result of a car accident. But

that didn't stop him. _____ then he _____ one of the
                            13.   14. (become)

best-known professional skateboarders in the world, thanks to his great skill and very

positive attitude.

Tony Hawk _____ professionally _____ many years,
                  15. (not compete)   16.

but he is still the most famous and successful skateboarder in the world.

EXERCISE 5: Questions, Statements, and Short Answers

(Grammar Notes 1–3)

A | *Amy Lu is applying for a job as a college sports instructor. Look at her online résumé and the interviewer's notes. The year is 2011.*

Amy Lu
525 Ahina St
Honolulu, HI 96816

INTERVIEWED
09/18/11

Education:
2003   Certificate (American College of Sports Medicine)
2000   M.A. Physical Education (University of Texas)   moved to
                                                         Honolulu in
                                                         2001

Employment:
2002–present   part-time physical education teacher (high school)
2000–present   sports trainer (private)
                        teaches tennis, swimming

Skills:
speak English, Portuguese, and Chinese
martial arts   got black belt in tae kwon do
                  2 mos. ago

Other Interests:
travel, sports photography, skateboarding, surfing

Awards:
2003   Teacher of the Year Award
2000   First Prize in Sunburn Classic Skate Contest

Memberships:
2003–present   member of National Education Association (NEA)

B | *John Sakaino is interviewing Amy Lu for a job as a college sports instructor. Complete his questions. Use the words in parentheses.*

1. (how long / live in Honolulu)

   JOHN: How long have you lived in Honolulu?

   AMY: I've lived in Honolulu for 15 years. OR I've lived in Honolulu since 2001.

2. (how long / have your M.A. degree)

   JOHN: _____

   AMY: _____

3. (have any more training / since / you get your M.A.)

   JOHN: _____

   AMY: _____

4. (how long / be a physical education teacher)

   JOHN: _____

   AMY: _____

5. (how long / work as a sports trainer)

   JOHN: _____

   AMY: _____

6. (how long / have a black belt in tae kwon do)

   JOHN: _____

   AMY: _____

7. (win any awards since then)

   JOHN: I see you won a medal in skateboarding. _____

   AMY: _____. I won the Teacher of the Year Award in 2003.

8. (how long / be a member of NEA)

   JOHN: _____

   AMY: _____

C | *Imagine you are Amy Lu. Answer the questions. Use the information in her résumé and use contractions when possible.*

EXERCISE 6: Editing

*Read the posts to an online skateboard message board. There are ten mistakes in the use of the present perfect with **since** and **for**. The first mistake is already corrected. Find and correct nine more.*

The Skateboarding Board
Tell us your skating stories here!

I've had
~~I have~~ my skateboard for two years. For me, it's much more than just a sport. It's a form of transportation. It's much faster than walking!

Jennifer, U.S.

I've been a skater since five years. Since December I won two contests. I'd love to turn pro one day and support myself skating.

Paulo, Brazil

Help! I've broken three boards for January!!! Is this normal? How long you have had your board?

Sang-Ook, South Korea

Broken boards?! That's nothing! Consider yourself lucky! I've break my wrist twice since I started skating!

Marta, Mexico

Last year, my board hit a rock while I was skating in the street. I fell and hit my head and had to go to the emergency room. I always worn a helmet since then!

Megan, Australia

I live in California since 2006. My first love is surfing, but when there aren't any waves, I jump on my skateboard and take to the streets! My motto is "Make the best of what you have!"

Ming, U.S.

Wow! Yesterday, my friend gave me a copy of the video "OP King of Skate." I've watch it three times since then. The Burnquist part is awesome!

Todd, Canada

At last! A skate park opened near my home last week. Since then I gone every day. It's a lot more fun than skating in the streets!

Sylvie, France

EXERCISE 7: Listening

A | *Read the statements. Then listen to the interview. Listen again and circle the correct information.*

1. Eliana is a <u>professional athlete</u> / <u>college student</u> / <u>sports announcer</u>.

2. She wants to work for a <u>college / radio station / sports team</u>.

3. She lives in <u>Tampa / L.A. / São Paulo</u>.

4. She works <u>full time / part time / for a TV station</u>.

5. She writes articles about <u>sports / L.A. / job interviews</u>.

6. She considers herself <u>a sports writer / an athlete / a sports announcer</u>.

B | *Listen again to the interview and complete the interviewer's notes. Use **since** and **for**.*

WSPR Radio
_____

Eliana Serrano   Interviewed Sept. 9

Eliana has been an athlete ___for 15 years_____.
                                        1.

She's been an announcer _____.
                                        2.

She's lived in L.A. _____.
                                        3.

She's worked part time at WABC _____.
                                        4.

She's written sports articles _____.
                                        5.

She's considered herself an announcer _____.
                                        6.

EXERCISE 8: Pronunciation

A | *Read and listen to the Pronunciation Note.*

Pronunciation Note
In **yes/no questions**, the voice usually **rises** at the end of the question.
In **wh- questions**, the voice usually **falls** at the end of the question.
EXAMPLES: Are you a student?   **Where** do you go to school?

B | *Listen to the short conversations. Notice how the voice rises or falls at the end of the questions. Draw arrows going up (⬈) or down (⬊).*

1. **A:** How long have you been a student?
   B: Since 2008.

2. **A:** Have you worked since you moved here?
   B: Yes, I have.

3. **A:** How many jobs have you had since then?
   B: I've had two jobs since I moved here.

4. **A:** Have you been at your job for a long time?
   B: No, I haven't.

5. **A:** How long have you lived here?
   B: For three years.

C | *Listen again and repeat each question. Then practice the conversations with a partner.*

EXERCISE 9: Role Play: A Job Interview

A | *Chin Ho Cho and Clara Reston are applying for a job as a college music teacher. Look at their résumés. Work with a partner and write five or more interview questions. Begin your questions with* **How long, How many,** *and* **Have you . . . since?**

Chin Ho Cho

Education:
2000   M.A. in Music Education
        (Boston University)

Teaching Experience:
2000–present The Juilliard School

Courses Taught:
Voice and Piano
History of Music
Symphonies of Beethoven
20th Century Jazz

Publications:
"Introducing Computers into Music Class"
(*The Journal of Music*, 2002)

Awards:
Teacher of the Year, 2002
Winner of University of Maryland Piano
  Competition, 2009

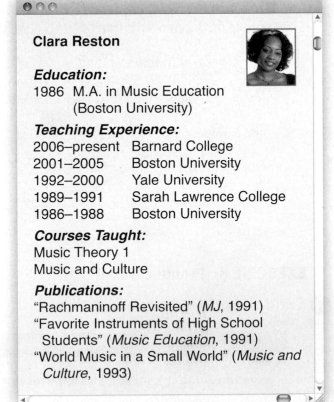

Clara Reston

Education:
1986 M.A. in Music Education
        (Boston University)

Teaching Experience:
2006–present   Barnard College
2001–2005   Boston University
1992–2000   Yale University
1989–1991   Sarah Lawrence College
1986–1988   Boston University

Courses Taught:
Music Theory 1
Music and Culture

Publications:
"Rachmaninoff Revisited" (*MJ*, 1991)
"Favorite Instruments of High School
  Students" (*Music Education*, 1991)
"World Music in a Small World" (*Music and
  Culture*, 1993)

EXAMPLE: How long have you been a music teacher?

B | *Work with your partner. Role-play two interviews (one for Chin Ho Cho and one for Clara Reston). Take turns being the interviewer.*

> EXAMPLE: **A:** How long have you been a music teacher, Chin Ho?
> **B:** I've been a music teacher since 2000.

C | *Work in small groups. Decide who to hire for the job and why. Remember to use **since** and **for**.*

> EXAMPLE: **A:** Chin Ho Cho has had the same job since he got his M.A. degree.
> **B:** Clara Reston has a lot of experience. She's been a teacher since 1986.
> **C:** Chin has taught . . .

EXERCISE 10: Writing

A | *Write a paragraph about someone's accomplishments. It can be someone famous or someone you know. Use the present perfect with **since** or **for**.*

> EXAMPLE: Amy Lu has been a high school physical education teacher and a private sports trainer for many years. She has received two awards since 2000, one for teaching and the other for skateboarding. She has been a member of the National Education Association since 2003. Amy has many interests. She speaks three languages. She has also been a student of martial arts for a long time, and she has had her black belt in tae kwon do for two months.

B | *Check your work. Use the Editing Checklist.*

Editing Checklist

Did you use . . . ?
- [ ] *since* and *for*
- [ ] *have* + the correct past participle

Check your answers on page UR-2.

Do you need to review anything?

A | Complete the sentences with **since** or **for**.

1. Sara has lived in San Francisco _____ 10 years.

2. She has wanted to be a tennis player _____ she was a little girl.

3. She's been a professional player _____ several years.

4. Sara has had the same trainer _____ a long time.

5. _____ 2010 she has won several competitions.

6. _____ the past few weeks, she has had a wrist injury.

7. _____ then she hasn't been able to practice.

B | Complete the sentences with the present perfect form of the verbs in parentheses.

1. I _____ a skateboarder for many years.
   (be)

2. Since 2010 I _____ any skating accidents.
   (not have)

3. My brother _____ the sport since he was a little boy.
   (love)

4. Together we _____ in many competitions.
   (compete)

5. He _____ several competitions since last year.
   (win)

6. We _____ each other for a few months.
   (not see)

C | Find and correct seven mistakes.

1. Marta and Tomás lived here since they got married in 1998.

2. Tomás has been a professional tennis player since he has come to this country.

3. He has won several competitions for then.

4. Since I have known Tomás, he had three different coaches.

5. I haven't see Marta for several weeks.

6. She have been in Brazil since April 1.

7. I've wanted to visit Brazil since years, but I haven't had any vacation time since I got

   this new job.

Present Perfect: *Already, Yet,* and *Still*
PARTY PLANNING

STEP 1 GRAMMAR IN CONTEXT

Before You Read

Look at the title of the article. Discuss the questions.

1. How do you feel about parties?
2. Which do you prefer: giving a party or going to one? Why?

Read

Read the article about how to plan a party.

It's Party Time!

It's almost the end of the year, and you**'ve already been** to several parties, but you **haven't given** one **yet**. You're a little nervous, but you decide it's time to take the plunge.[1]

First things first: **Have** you **chosen** the date **yet**? What about the time?

OK. You**'ve already chosen** the date and the time and **mailed** the invitations. But you **still haven't decided** on the menu, and now your party is just one week away! Don't panic!

We spoke to Patty Cake, a professional party planner. She says, "It *is* very important to be organized, but remember: You don't need a whole new set of skills. Think about your everyday life. You**'ve already done** many of the things you need to do for a party. You know how to shop for food, put it on plates, and introduce friends to one another. Now, all you need to do is just bring your many skills together."

Still need help? Party planners, like Patty Cake, can offer specific advice. She says, "We**'ve already helped** hundreds of people plan successful parties—big and small. If you **haven't used** a party-planning service **yet**, you should give it a try." And you don't have to spend a lot of money. Free advice is available on the Internet. There you will also find handy[2] lists where you can check off things you**'ve already done** (and see the things you **haven't done yet**!). So, take a deep breath, relax, and enjoy the party!

---

[1] ***take the plunge:*** to do an activity that seems difficult or frightening
[2] ***handy:*** useful; easy to use

After You Read

A | Vocabulary: *Complete the sentences with the words from the box.*

available	organized	professional	specific	successful

1. OK. The drinks are on the table over there. Extra chairs are in the bedroom. The cake is in the refrigerator. I'll take it out at 8:00 P.M. That's it! I think I'm quite _____.

2. I can meet you for lunch any day this week to discuss plans for your party. You can also call me anytime—day or night. As you can see, I'm pretty _____.

3. Marta has a Ph.D. in economics, and she's already written three books. Her latest book is on the bestseller list! She's really _____.

4. Please bring two 10-ounce bags of Crispy Chips. The ones in the blue bag—they're low in fat, but not low in salt. You'll find them at Shopwise in aisle 6. I know I'm being very _____, but I want to be sure you get the right ones!

5. Jake offered to paint the apartment, but I prefer to hire _____ painters. They have training, job experience, and insurance if something goes wrong!

B | Comprehension: *Reread the article. Check (✓) the correct answers.*

The party giver . . .

☐ **1.** went to several parties

☐ **2.** gave a party

☐ **3.** chose a date for the party

☐ **4.** chose the time

☐ **5.** sent invitations

☐ **6.** decided on a menu

A party invitation

PRESENT PERFECT: *ALREADY, YET,* AND *STILL*

Affirmative Statements: *Already*

Subject	*Have*	*Already*	Past Participle		*Already*
They	have	already	mailed	the invitations.	
She	has		chosen	the menu.	
They	have		mailed	the invitations	already.
She	has		chosen	the menu	

Negative Statements: *Yet*

Subject	*Have not*	Past Participle		*Yet*
They	haven't	mailed	them	yet.
She	hasn't	chosen	it	

Negative Statements: *Still*

Subject	*Still*	*Have not*	Past Participle	
They	still	haven't	mailed	them.
She		hasn't	chosen	it.

Yes / No Questions: *Yet*

Have	Subject	Past Participle		*Yet*
Have	they	mailed	them	yet?
Has	she	chosen	it	

Short Answers

Affirmative			Negative	
Yes,	they **have**.	No,	they **haven't**.	
	she **has**.		she **hasn't**.	
			not **yet**.	

GRAMMAR NOTES

1 Use the **present perfect** with *already*, *yet*, or *still* to talk about things that happened or did not happen at an <u>indefinite</u> (not exact) time in the past.

a. Use *already* in **affirmative statements** to talk about something that has happened before now.

- I've *already* mailed the invitations.
- Jenna **has** *already* **met** Carlos.

b. Use *yet* in **negative statements** to talk about something that has not happened before now (in the near past).

A: Jenna **has***n't* **called** *yet*.
B: Oh, I'm sure we'll hear from her later.

c. You can also use *still* in **negative statements**. *Still* has a similar meaning to *not yet*, but it shows that the speaker is <u>surprised</u> or <u>unhappy</u> with the situation.

- I *still* **haven't mailed** the invitations! *(I haven't mailed the invitations yet, and I really need to do it!)*

d. Use *yet* in **questions** to ask if something has happened before now. Notice the different possible ways of giving **negative answers**.

A: **Have** you **bought** the soda *yet*?
B: No, I haven't. OR No, *not yet*. OR *Not yet*.

(continued on next page)

2 **USAGE NOTES:**

a. We sometimes use *already* in **questions** to express <u>surprise</u> that something has happened <u>sooner than expected</u>.

- **Has** Carlos **arrived** *already*? The party doesn't start until 8:00!

b. In American English, we sometimes use the **simple past** with *already* and *yet*.

- Jenna **has** *already* **left**. OR
- Jenna *already* **left**.

BE CAREFUL! When we use *already*, *yet*, or *still* + **present perfect** we do <u>NOT</u> use past time expressions.

- We've *already* **met** Carlos.
  NOT: We've already met Carlos last month.

3 *Already* usually goes <u>between</u> *have* and the past participle. It can also go at the <u>end</u> of the clause.

- I've *already* **baked** the cake. OR
- I've **baked** the cake *already*.

Yet usually goes at the <u>end</u> of the clause.

- They **haven't arrived** *yet*.

Still goes <u>before</u> *haven't*.

- They *still* **haven't arrived**.

REFERENCE NOTES

For a list of **irregular past participles**, see Appendix 1 on page A-1.
For more about the **indefinite past**, see Unit 10 on page 134.

STEP 3 FOCUSED PRACTICE

EXERCISE 1: Discover the Grammar

Read the first statement. Then decide if the second statement is **True (T)** *or* **False (F).**

1. I've already given many parties.
___F___ This will be my first party.

2. I haven't baked the cake yet.
_____ I plan to bake a cake.

3. Has Bev arrived yet?
_____ I'm surprised that Bev is here.

4. Tom and Lisa still haven't arrived.
_____ I expect them to arrive.

5. Has Jenna left already?
_____ I'm surprised that Jenna left.

6. Have you had a cup of tea yet?
_____ I don't know if you had a cup of tea.

7. Carlos has already met my sister.
_____ I need to introduce Carlos to her.

8. I still haven't called Mehmet.
_____ I don't plan to call him.

9. Has Tom bought the chips yet?
_____ I think Tom is going to bring the chips.

10. I still haven't talked to the party planner.
_____ I should call her.

11. Have you taken any photos yet?
_____ I saw you take some photos.

12. Is it 9:00 already?
_____ I thought it was later than 9:00.

EXERCISE 2: Questions, Statements, and Short Answers   *(Grammar Notes 1–3)*

Complete the conversations. Use the present perfect form of the verbs in parentheses with **already** *or* **yet** *and short answers. Use contractions when possible. Go to Appendix 1 on page A-1 for help with irregular verbs.*

1. **A:** This is a great party. Marta made the cake. She's a professional baker. _____*Have*_____

    you _____*tried*_____ it _____*yet*_____?
    <u>(try)</u>

    B: _____*No*_____, I _____*haven't*_____. But I'm going to have a piece now.

2. **A:** Jenna, I'd like you to meet my friend Carlos.

    B: We _____ _____ _____. Marta introduced us.
    <u>(meet)</u>

3. **A:** Would you like another cup of coffee?

    B: No, thanks. I _____ _____ _____ three cups!
    <u>(have)</u>

4. **A:** _____ Jenna _____ _____? It's still early!
    <u>(leave)</u>

    B: _____, she _____. She's in the kitchen.

5. **A:** _____ you _____ Tarantino's new movie _____?
    <u>(see)</u>

    B: _____, I _____. It's great. What about you?

    A: I _____ _____ it _____, but I want to.
    <u>(see)</u>

6. **A:** This was a great party. I'm giving my own party next week. I _____

    _____ _____ the whole thing, but I'm still nervous about it.
    <u>(plan)</u>

    B: Don't worry. If you organize it well, the rest will take care of itself!

EXERCISE 3: Affirmative and Negative Statements

(Grammar Note 3)

*Read Fabrizio's party-planning checklist. Write statements about the things that he **has already done** and the things that he **hasn't done yet** (or the things that he **still hasn't done!**). Use contractions when possible. Go to Appendix 1 on page A-1 for help with irregular verbs.*

Things to Do

✓	pick a date
	choose a time!!
✓	find a location
✓	write a guest list
✓	buy invitations
	send invitations!!
	ask friends to help
	plan the menu!!
✓	pick out music
	shop for food
	clean the house
✓	borrow some chairs

1. *He's already picked a date.*

2. *He hasn't chosen a time yet.* OR *He still hasn't chosen a time.*

3. _____

4. _____

5. _____

6. _____

7. _____

8. _____

9. _____

10. _____

11. _____

12. _____

EXERCISE 4: Editing

Read the online bulletin board. There are nine mistakes in the use of the present perfect with **already** and **yet**. The first mistake is already corrected. Find and correct eight more.

Ask the Party Planner!

Doug asked: Help! My party is next week, and I ~~already~~ *still* haven't figured out the food! I'm not at all organized. I've yet wasted three days worrying, and I still don't have any ideas. What should I do?

The Party Planner's Advice: Don't panic! Your guests haven't started arriving already, so there's still time. Ask everyone to bring something! (You've already invite people, right?) Or order pizza. I haven't met anyone already who doesn't like pizza.

• •

Rosa asked: I'd like to find a "theme" for my next birthday party. I've already have a pasta party (10 kinds of pasta!), and I've already gave a movie party (everyone dressed up as a movie character). Both were very successful, but I haven't still decided what to do this time. Any ideas?

The Party Planner's Advice: Sure. Has you tried this one yet? Ask each guest to bring a baby photo of himself or herself. Collect the photos. People try to match the photos with the guests! Your guests will love it!

STEP 4 COMMUNICATION PRACTICE

EXERCISE 5: Listening   #44 Track

A | *Some friends are planning a party. Look at their "To Do" list. Then listen to their conversation. Listen again and check (✓) the things they've already done.*

To Do

✓ 1. choose a date
2. find a place
3. invite people
4. borrow extra chairs

5. figure out food
6. buy soda
7. find someone to help set up
8. select music

B | Listen again to the conversation and answer the questions. Check (✓) all the correct answers.

Who...?	the man	the woman	Jason	Ella
1. is nervous about the party	✓	☐	☐	☐
2. has already invited everyone	☐	☐	☐	☐
3. has already agreed to have the party at his/her place	☐	☐	☐	☐
4. has already borrowed extra chairs	☐	☐	☐	☐
5. asks about food and drinks	☐	☐	☐	☐
6. hasn't decided on the food yet	☐	☐	☐	☐
7. offers to pick up soda	☐	☐	☐	☐
8. is available to help set up	☐	☐	☐	☐
9. sounds pretty organized	☐	☐	☐	☐
10. has already taken care of the music	☐	☐	☐	☐

EXERCISE 6: Pronunciation

A | Read and listen to the Pronunciation Note.

Pronunciation Note
In **conversation**, we almost always use **contractions of *have*** when the verbs are in the present perfect.
EXAMPLES: He **has** already left. → "**He's** already left." She **has not** called yet. → "She **hasn't** called yet." **We have** already seen him. → "**We've** already seen him." I still **have not** mailed the invitations. → "I still **haven't** mailed the invitations."

B | Listen to the short conversations and notice the contractions with have.

1. **A:** Who have you called?
   B: **I've** already called Jason.

2. **A:** Is he coming to the party?
   B: He still **hasn't** decided.

3. **A:** Can you come?
   B: Sorry. **We've** already made plans.

4. **A:** When is it?
   B: They **haven't** chosen a date yet.

5. **A:** Should I buy soda?
   B: **She's** already bought the soda.

6. **A:** Where is it?
   B: **He's** already put it away.

7. **A:** Do you have a question?
   B: **You've** already answered it.

8. **A:** Are they coming?
   B: **They've** already said yes.

C | Listen again to the conversations and repeat the answers. Then practice the conversations with a partner.

EXERCISE 7: Information Gap: Chores

Work in pairs (A and B). **Student A,** *follow the instructions on this page.* **Student B,** *turn to page 131 and follow the instructions there.*

1. Look at the picture of the Meiers' dining room and at Gisela's "To Do" list. Cross out the chores that Gisela has already done.

2. Answer your partner's questions about Gisela's chores.

   EXAMPLE: **B:** Has Gisela vacuumed the carpet yet?
   A: No, she hasn't. OR No, not yet.

3. Look at Helmut's "To Do" list. Ask your partner questions to find out which chores Helmut has already done. Cross out those chores.

   EXAMPLE: **A:** Has Helmut bought a memory card yet?
   B: Yes, he has. OR Yes, he's already gotten one.

Now compare lists with your partner. Are they the same?

EXERCISE 8: What About You?

*Write a list of things that you planned or wanted to do by this time (for example, find a new job, paint the apartment). Include things that you **have already done** and things that you **haven't done yet**. Exchange lists with a classmate and ask and answer questions about the items on the lists.*

EXAMPLE: **A:** Have you found a new job yet?
B: No, not yet. I'm still looking. OR Yes, I have.
What about you? Have you . . . ?

EXERCISE 9: Writing

A | *Think about a goal you are working on at the moment.*

EXAMPLES: organizing a party, finding a job, finding a new apartment, finding a college, getting a driver's license

B | *Write a list of things people do to reach this goal.*

EXAMPLE: Finding a new apartment
 • choose a neighborhood
 • find information about the neighborhood
 • read newspaper and online ads
 • look at apartments

C | *Write two paragraphs. Describe things you **have already done** and things you **haven't done yet** to reach your goal.*

EXAMPLE: I would like to find a new apartment. I've already chosen a neighborhood, but I haven't researched it yet . . .

D | *Check your work. Use the Editing Checklist.*

Editing Checklist

Did you use the . . . ?
☐ present perfect with *already*
☐ present perfect with *still*
☐ present perfect with *yet*
☐ correct word order

1. Look at the picture of the Meiers' kitchen and at Helmut's "To Do" list. Cross out the chores that Helmut has already done.

2. Look at Gisela's "To Do" list. Ask your partner questions to find out which chores Gisela has already done. Cross out those chores.

   EXAMPLE: **B:** Has Gisela vacuumed the carpet yet?
   A: No, she hasn't. OR No, not yet.

3. Answer your partner's questions about Helmut's chores.

   EXAMPLE: **A:** Has Helmut bought a memory card yet?
   B: Yes, he has. OR Yes, he's already gotten one.

Now compare lists with your partner. Are they the same?

Check your answers on page UR-3.

Do you need to review anything?

A | Circle the correct words to complete the sentences.

1. I've started planning your graduation party last night / already.

2. We still / yet haven't chosen a restaurant for the party. I'm getting nervous.

3. I met Nita yesterday, but I haven't met her boyfriend already / yet.

4. Did / Has Marla left already? The party just started!

5. Have you told / tell your friends about the party?

6. No, not told / yet.

B | Complete the conversations with the present perfect form of the verbs in parentheses and **already, still,** or **yet.**

- ANN: Ed _____ _____ _____! Amazing!
  1. (graduate / already)

  BEN: I know, but don't relax yet. We _____ _____ _____ the party.
  2. (have / still)

- ANN: _____ they _____ the food _____? Should I begin to worry?
  3. (deliver / yet)

  BEN: It just arrived. But Ed _____ _____ _____ the tables.
  4. (set / still)

  ANN: Well, he _____ _____ _____. I'll help him finish.
  5. (start / already)

- BEN: Some of Ed's friends _____ _____ _____.
  6. (arrive / still)

  ANN: I know . . . I don't think his new girlfriend _____ _____ _____.
  7. (arrive / yet)

  ED: Mom and Dad, _____ you _____ Christy _____?
  8. (meet / yet)

C | Find and correct six mistakes.

A: I can't believe it's the 10th already. And we still didn't finished planning.

B: We haven't checked the guest list for a while. Who hasn't replies yet?

A: Sally hasn't called about the invitation already. I wonder if she's coming.

B: Maybe she just forgot. Have you called yet her?

A: I've already call her a couple of times. She hasn't still called back.

STEP 1 GRAMMAR IN CONTEXT

Before You Read

Look at the title of the article and at the photos. Discuss the questions.

1. What do you think the article is about?
2. Would you like to do the things in the photos? Why or why not?

Read

Read the article about unusual vacations.

Been There? Done That? Maybe it's time for something new . . . (or maybe not!)

by Rosa García

Today's world is getting smaller. People are traveling the globe[1] in record numbers.[2] They**'ve been** to Rome. They**'ve visited** Greece. They**'ve seen** the ancient pyramids of Egypt. They**'ve gone** skiing in the Swiss Alps. Now, they're looking for new places to see and new things to do. They want adventure. *Travel Today* **has just come out** with its annual survey. As part of the survey, the magazine asks its readers the following question: "What would you like to do that you**'ve never done** before?"

Here are some of their answers:

I**'ve made** several trips to Egypt, but I**'ve never ridden** a camel. I**'ve always wanted** to do that.

Moving along.
Camel ride in the desert

Hot-air ballooning! My boyfriend **has tried** this several times, but I**'ve never done** it.

Up, up, and away!
Hot-air ballooning over Turkey

I**'ve ice skated** and I**'ve climbed** mountains, but I**'ve never been** ice climbing. That's something I'd definitely like to try!

Work or play?
Ice climbing in the U.S.

---

[1] *globe:* the world
[2] *in record numbers:* much more than in the past

(*continued on next page*)

Riding a camel, hot-air ballooning, ice climbing . . . These are just a few activities that travelers can choose from today. All you need is time, money (a lot of it!), and a sense of adventure.[3] But you don't have to go to a faraway place in an unusual type of transportation to have a great vacation! **Have** you **ever spent** the day walking in the woods, **heard** the sound of the wind, or **watched** the sun set over the ocean? These can be wonderful adventures too! And a lot more affordable!

[3] *sense of adventure:* the ability to enjoy new things

After You Read

A | Vocabulary: *Look at the reading. Find a word or phrase with a similar meaning to . . .*

1. very old   _____

2. exciting, unusual experience   _____

3. every year   _____

4. questionnaire   _____

5. way of traveling someplace   _____

6. cheaper   _____

B | Comprehension: *Which activities have the readers of* Travel Today *tried? Check (✓) them.*

☐ **1.** skiing in the Alps   ☐ **3.** hot-air ballooning   ☐ **5.** mountain climbing

☐ **2.** riding a camel   ☐ **4.** ice-skating   ☐ **6.** ice climbing

STEP 2 GRAMMAR PRESENTATION

PRESENT PERFECT: INDEFINITE PAST

Statements			
Subject	*Have (not)*	**Past Participle**	
They	**have (not)**	visited	Egypt.
She	**has (not)**	been	there.

Statements with Adverbs					
Subject	*Have (not)*	**Adverb**	**Past Participle**		**Adverb**
They	**have**	*never*	visited	Egypt.	
		just			
She	**has**	*recently*	been	there.	
They	**have (not)**		visited	Egypt	*twice.*
					lately.
She	**has (not)**		been	there	*recently.*

Yes / No Questions				
Have	**Subject**	**(Ever)**	**Past Participle**	
Have	they	(ever)	**visited**	Egypt?
Has	she		**been**	there?

Short Answers			
Affirmative		**Negative**	
Yes,	they **have**.	No,	they **haven't**.
	she **has**.		she **hasn't**.
			never.

Wh- Questions				
Wh- Word	**Have**	**Subject**	**Past Participle**	
How often	**have**	they	**visited**	Egypt?
	has	she	**been**	there?

GRAMMAR NOTES

1 Use the **present perfect** to talk about things that happened at an **indefinite (not exact) time** in the past.

Use the present perfect when you <u>don't know</u> when something happened or when the specific time is <u>not important</u>.

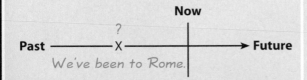

Use the present perfect (not the simple past) to show that the result of the action or state is **important in the present**. The present perfect always has some connection to the present.

USAGE NOTE: For many speakers **been to** and **gone to** have different meanings.

- They**'ve traveled** to Egypt.
  (You don't know the exact time.)

- We**'ve been** to Rome.
  (The exact time isn't important.)

- The hotel **has closed**.
  (So we can't stay there now.)

- He**'s been to** France.
  (At some point in the past, he visited France, but he's not there now.)

- He**'s gone to** France.
  (He's in France now.)

(continued on next page)

2 We can also use the **present perfect** with **adverbs** to talk about the **indefinite past**.

   a. Use adverbs like *twice* or *often* to talk about <u>repeated actions</u> at some indefinite time in the <u>past</u>.

- They**'ve seen** the Pyramids *twice*.
- We**'ve** *often* **stayed** at that hotel.

   b. Use *always* and *never* for actions or states that <u>continue to the present</u>.

- I**'ve** *always* **wanted** to go to Rome, but I**'ve** *never* **gone**.

   c. Use *ever* to ask questions. It means at <u>any time before now</u>. Use *never* for <u>negative answers</u>.

- **A: Have** you *ever* **been** to Rome?
- **B: No**, I**'ve** *never* **been** there. OR **No**, *never*.

   d. Use *just*, *lately*, and *recently* to stress that something happened in the <u>very recent</u> (but still indefinite) <u>past</u>.
- *just* = a very short time before now
- *lately* and *recently* = in the near past

- I**'ve** *just* **gotten** back from China.
- They **haven't been** there *lately*.
- He**'s** *recently* **flown** a lot.

USAGE NOTE: In American English, we often use *just* and *recently* with the <u>simple past</u>. You can't use *lately* with the simple past.

- I**'ve** *just* **returned** OR I *just* **returned**.
- NOT: I returned ~~lately~~.

BE CAREFUL! Do <u>NOT use the present perfect</u> with adverbs that refer to a definite past time.

- I **got** back *yesterday*.
- NOT: ~~I've gotten~~ back yesterday.

3 Notice the **word order** in sentences with the **present perfect** and **adverbs**:

   a. Adverbs such as *twice* and expressions such as *many times* usually go at the <u>end of the sentence</u>.

- She**'s been** there *twice*.
- I**'ve been** there *many times*.

   b. Adverbs of frequency such as *always*, *often*, and *never* usually go <u>before the past participle</u>.

- I**'ve** *always* **wanted** to stay there.
- We**'ve** *often* **talked** about it.

   c. • *Just* goes <u>before</u> the past participle.
- *Lately* goes at the <u>end</u> of the sentence.
- *Recently* can go <u>before</u> the past participle or at the <u>end</u> of the sentence.

- I**'ve** *just* **had** dinner.
- I **haven't flown** *lately*.
- He**'s** *recently* **flown** a lot. OR He**'s flown** a lot *recently*.

REFERENCE NOTES

For a list of **irregular past participles**, see Appendix 1 on page A-1.
For a complete presentation of all the **present perfect forms**, see Unit 8 on page 110.
For **present perfect** with *already*, *yet*, and *still*, see Unit 9 on page 123.

EXERCISE 1: Discover the Grammar

Read the first statement. Then decide if the second statement is **True (T)** *or* **False (F)**. *If there isn't enough information in the first statement to know the answer, put a question mark* **(?)** *on the line.*

1. Adventure vacations have become very popular.

___T___   They are popular now.

___?___   **2.** I've been to Italy twice.

      I was there two years ago.

___F___   **3.** I have never been to the Himalayas.

      I went to the Himalayas a long time ago.

___T___   **4.** I've just returned from China.

      I was in China a short time ago.

___F___   **5.** Greg asks you, "Have you ever been to Costa Rica?"

      Greg wants to know when you were in Costa Rica.

___F___   **6.** Marta asks you, "Have you read any good travel books lately?"

      Marta wants to know about a travel book you read last year.

___T___   **7.** We have visited Egypt several times.

      This is not our first visit to Egypt.

___?___   **8.** I've been on an African safari.[1]

      I'm on a safari now.

---

[1] *safari:* a trip through the country areas of Africa in order to watch wild animals

EXERCISE 2: Statements and Questions

(Grammar Notes 1–2)

Complete the interview between Travel Today (**TT**) *and travel writer* Rosa García (**RG**). *Use the present perfect form of the verbs in parentheses. Use contractions when possible.*

TT: As a travel writer, you ___'ve visited___ many places. Any favorites?

                            1. (visit)

RG: Thailand. It's a beautiful, amazing country. I _____ there five times.

                                                        2. (be)

TT: What _____ your most unusual travel experience?

                           3. (be)

RG: My *most* unusual? I _____ so many! I _____ near sharks

                                4. (have)   **5. (swim)**

      (in a cage, of course!), I _____ dinner next to a very active volcano,

                                         6. (eat)

      I _____ in an ice hotel in Finland . . .

                  7. (sleep)

(continued on next page)

TT: The world _____ a lot smaller. There are fewer and fewer "undiscovered" places.
               8. (become)

     _____ you ever _____ a really great place and decided not to tell your
                    9. (find)

     readers about it?

RG: No, never. I _____ about doing that a few times, but I _____ never
               10. (think)

     _____ a place secret. I _____ always _____ about it.
         11. (keep)   **12. (write)**

TT: Where _____ you _____ recently?
                  13. (be)

RG: I _____ just _____ from a hot-air ballooning trip in Australia. It was really
           14. (return)

     fantastic. In fact, ballooning is my new favorite form of transportation!

TT: Where are you going next?

RG: On an African safari! I _____ never _____ on one, and I'm really excited.
                       15. (be)

     I _____ always _____ to do that.
               16. (want)

TT: Good luck! I look forward to your African safari article.

EXERCISE 3: Affirmative and Negative Statements   *(Grammar Notes 1–3)*

*Look at the survey. Then write sentences about things Andy **has done** and things he **hasn't done**. Use contractions when possible.*

Travel Time Survey

Name: ___*Andy Cheng*___

Have you ever done the following activities?
Check (✓) the ones you have done.

1. rent a car   ☐
2. rent a motorcycle   ☑
3. ride a camel   ☐
4. go up in a hot-air balloon   ☑
5. have some really unusual food   ☑
6. see ancient pyramids   ☐
7. sail a boat on the Nile River   ☑
8. swim with dolphins in the ocean   ☑
9. be on a safari   ☐
10. fly around the world   ☐

1. He hasn't rented a car. OR He's never rented a car.

2. He's rented a motorcycle.

3.

4.

5.

6.

7.

8.

9.

10.

EXERCISE 4: Word Order

(Grammar Note 3)

Complete the conversation. Put the words in parentheses in the correct order. Use the present perfect form of the verbs. Include short answers. Use contractions when possible.

EVAN: Hot-air ballooning! What's it like? _____ *I've never done this* _____ before!
1. (I / do this / never)

ANDY: You'll love it. _____,
2. (I / a few times / go up)

but _____.
3. (not do / it / lately / I)

EVAN: _____?
4. (you / a lot / travel)

ANDY: Yes, _____. I'm a travel writer, so it's part of my job.
5.

EVAN: That's great! _____ on a safari?
6. (you / be / ever)

ANDY: No, _____, but _____.
7.   8. (want / to go / always / I)

EVAN: Me too. _____.
9. (I / several times / to Africa / be)

In fact, _____ back from a trip there.
10. (I / get / just)

But _____ on a safari.
11. (never / I / be)

ANDY: Look. _____
12. (they / finish / just)

getting the balloon ready. It's time to go up!

EXERCISE 5: Statements

(Grammar Notes 1–2)

Look at some of Rosa's things. Write sentences using the present perfect form of the verbs from the box. Use adverbs when possible.

| ~~be~~ | ride | see | stay | travel | write |

1. *She's been to Egypt twice.*

2. _____

3. _____

4. _____

5. _____

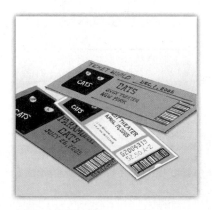

6. _____

EXERCISE 6: Editing

Read the comments found on a hot-air ballooning website. There are twelve mistakes in the use of the present perfect and adverbs. The first mistake is already corrected. Find and correct eleven more.

upandaway.com

have
We ~~has~~ received many comments from our clients. We'd like to share some with you.

Comments

been
I have always be afraid of heights. But after I saw the beautiful photos on your website,

has
I knew I had to go hot-air ballooning! This have been one of the best experiences of my

life. Thank you!

Britta Kessler, Germany

4
We've returned just from a fantastic vacation. I've told all my friends about your

company.

James Hudson, Canada

I've always wanted to go up in a hot-air balloon. I was not disappointed!

Antonio Vega, Mexico

I have (5)
I just seen some new photos posted on the website! Awesome!

Bill Hampton, USA

gone (6)
I've never went hot-air ballooning, but after visiting your wonderful website, I've

decided to sign up!

Amalia Lopes, Brazil

written (7)
We gave our parents a balloon trip as an anniversary gift. They've just wrote to say it

never (8)
was fantastic. They've ever been very adventurous, but now they want to go rafting!

Pat Calahan, Ireland

9
You have ever seen the face of a kid on a hot-air balloon ride? The cost of the ride: a lot.

That look on her face: priceless!

Lydia Hassan, New Zealand

12 broke   *10*
I broken my leg last month, so I haven't lately been able to do sports—boring! Your

mountain balloon trip has just gave me a lift—in more than one way!

given (11)

May Roa, Philippines

EXERCISE 7: Listening

A | *Read the statements. Then listen to the conversation. Listen again and circle the correct information.*

1. The woman is <u>on vacation</u> / <u>at a travel agency</u>.
2. She goes on vacation <u>once</u> / <u>twice</u> a year. *— annual*
3. She <u>has</u> / <u>hasn't</u> done a lot of adventure traveling.
4. This year she wants to do something she <u>has</u> / <u>hasn't</u> done before.
5. She thinks two of the vacations sound too <u>dangerous</u> / <u>expensive</u>.
6. The last vacation possibility the man mentions <u>is</u> / <u>is not</u> very expensive.

B | *Look at the choices. Then listen again to the conversation and check (✓) the activities Olivia's done before. Circle the number of the best vacation choice for her.*

1. ☐

2. ☐

3. ☐

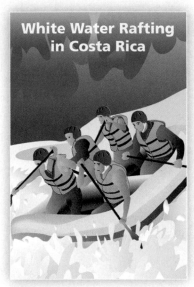

4. ☐

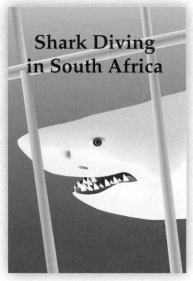

5. ☐

6. ☐

EXERCISE 8: Pronunciation

A | *Read and listen to the Pronunciation Note.*

Pronunciation Note

After a noun, we often pronounce:

- **have** like the word *"of"*

- **has** like "s," "z," or "iz."

EXAMPLES:

The **books have** arrived.	→	"The **books of** arrived."
The **book has** arrived.	→	"The **book's** arrived."
My **sister has** gone on vacation.	→	"My **sister'z** gone on vacation."
The **bus has** been late a lot.	→	"The **bus'iz** been late a lot."

B | *Listen to the short conversations and notice the pronunciation of* **have** *and* **has**.

1. **A:** My **friends have** just returned from their trip.
   B: Oh, did they have a good time?

2. **A:** The **plane has** just landed.
   B: It was a good flight.

3. **A:** The **book has** arrived.
   B: Great! I can't wait to read it.

4. **A:** The **hotels have** recently closed.
   B: Too bad. We'll have to find new ones.

5. **A:** Our **boss has** left for vacation.
   B: When will she be back?

6. **A:** The **survey has** just come out.
   B: Oh, what does it say?

7. **A:** These **countries have** become very popular.
   B: I know. I'd love to visit them.

8. **A:** The **trip has** become more affordable.
   B: Well, maybe we can go more often now.

9. **A:** I think **class has** started.
   B: Let's go in.

C | *Listen again to the conversations and repeat the first statement in each one. Then practice the conversations with a partner.*

EXERCISE 9: Find Someone Who . . .

A | *Ask your classmates questions. Find out how many people have ever done any of the following things. Add four more activities. When someone answers* **yes,** *ask more questions. Get the stories behind the answers.*

- ride a horse
- take a long car trip
- climb a mountain
- eat something unusual
- be on a boat
- go camping

- see ancient Roman ruins
- hear a mariachi band
- _____
- _____
- _____
- _____

> **EXAMPLE:** **A:** Have you ever ridden a horse?
> **B:** Yes, I have. A couple of times.
> **A:** Did you enjoy it? Did anything exciting happen?

B | *Share your answers and stories with the class.*

> **EXAMPLES:** Two people have ridden a horse. Miguel has ridden twice. Once when he . . .
> No students have . . .

EXERCISE 10: Writing

A | *Read the quote. Then write a paragraph that answers the questions.*

"My favorite thing is to go where I've never been."
Diane Arbus (1923–1971, photographer, U.S.)

What does Arbus mean? Do you feel the same way? Where have you been? Would you like to go there again? Where have you never been that you would like to go?

> **EXAMPLE:** I've read the quote by Diane Arbus. I think it means . . .

B | *Check your work. Use the Editing Checklist.*

Editing Checklist

Did you use the . . . ?
- ☐ present perfect without adverbs of time
- ☐ present perfect with adverbs of time such as *twice, always, never, just, recently, lately*
- ☐ correct word order

UNIT 10 Review

Check your answers on page UR-3.
Do you need to review anything?

A | Circle the correct words to complete the sentences.

1. Have you <u>twice / ever</u> been to Egypt?

2. I've <u>just / lately</u> returned from Cairo.

3. I've <u>was / been</u> there twice, and I'm returning next summer.

4. <u>Has / Have</u> Jon ever ridden a camel?

5. I haven't read any good travel books <u>lately / never</u>.

6. One of my classmates <u>is / has</u> recommended a good book.

B | Complete the sentences with the present perfect form of the correct verbs from the box.

be	give	read	see	show	take	want

1. _____ you ever _____ the pyramids?

2. I _____ never _____ to Egypt.

3. Elena _____ just _____ an interesting book about ancient Egypt.

4. She _____ _____ it to me to read.

5. I _____ always _____ to ride a camel.

6. My brother _____ _____ several trips there.

7. He _____ recently _____ me his photos.

C | Find and correct seven mistakes.

1. I've lately traveled a lot.

2. We've returned just from an African safari.

3. I've never have so much fun before.

4. Have you been ever on a safari?

5. No, but I've recently went hot-air ballooning.

6. My wife and I has decided to go next summer.

7. I've saw a lot of great photos on a hot-air ballooning website.

Unit 10 Review: Present Perfect: Indefinite Past **145**

Present Perfect and Simple Past
LONG-DISTANCE RELATIONSHIPS

Before You Read

Look at the picture and read the title of the article. Discuss the questions.

1. What do you think a "long-distance marriage" is?
2. Where are the two people living?
3. What are some reasons married people might live apart?

Read

Read the excerpt from an article in Modern Day *magazine.*

LIFESTYLES

An Ocean Apart

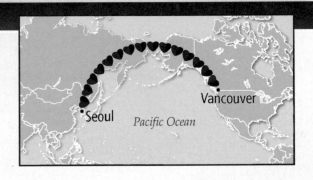

Seoul   *Pacific Ocean*   Vancouver

He lives in South Korea. She lives in Canada. But Lee Shinjeng and Park Sunmi **have been** married for four years. So why are they living apart? The couple has a "long-distance marriage." And they are not alone. Many couples around the world **have found** this arrangement to be a temporary solution in difficult economic[1] times.

When they **got** married, both Shinjeng and Sunmi **had** very good jobs. Then, two weeks after the wedding, Sunmi, a professional violinist, **lost** hers. After looking for a job for almost a year, she **got** an offer in Vancouver, Canada. Sunmi **didn't want** to leave Seoul, but she **felt** she **couldn't turn** it **down**. So she **moved**, and her husband, an engineer at a large company in Seoul, **didn't**. How **has** this **worked out**? It **hasn't been** easy. With airfares being so high, the couple **has not been** able to afford many trips to see each other. Last year they **saw** each other just three times (twice when Sunmi was performing abroad), and so far this year, they**'ve** only **seen** each other once.

The marriage, however, remains strong. How do they stay emotionally close when they are geographically so far away? Sunmi says, "Thanks to email, instant messages, text messages, and cell phones, we**'ve managed** to be in touch several times a day—not easy with the 17-hour time difference! At 6:00 A.M. I**'ve** just **prepared** breakfast and am getting ready to start my day, but for Shinjeng it's 11:00 P.M. and he**'s** already **had** dinner and is getting ready for bed." **Has** all this trouble **been** worth it? "Yes!" says the couple in unison[2]. "We both have jobs that we really like," says Shinjeng. "Besides, we really need the money."

"But," adds Sunmi, "we're really looking forward to the day we can be together again."

---

[1] *economic:* about business and money
[2] *in unison:* at the same time

After You Read

A | Vocabulary: *Circle the letter of the word or phrase closest in meaning to the word in* **blue.**

1. How do they like the new **arrangement**?
   - **a.** choice
   - **b.** way of doing something
   - **c.** art show

2. Sometimes they think their problem has no **solution**.
   - **a.** answer
   - **b.** reason
   - **c.** cause

3. They don't like living **apart**.
   - **a.** in different places
   - **b.** together
   - **c.** in an apartment

4. She **managed** to get a new job.
   - **a.** tried
   - **b.** wanted
   - **c.** was able

5. She couldn't **turn down** the offer.
   - **a.** say no to
   - **b.** say yes to
   - **c.** think about

6. It's a **temporary** job.
   - **a.** well-paying
   - **b.** short-time
   - **c.** long-distance

B | Comprehension: *Check (✓)* **True** *or* **False.** *Correct the false statements.*

	True	False
1. Shinjeng and Sunmi plan to get married.	☐	☐
2. They are now living together in South Korea.	☐	☐
3. Their jobs are very important to them.	☐	☐
4. They take a lot of trips together.	☐	☐
5. The couple has a close relationship.	☐	☐

PRESENT PERFECT AND SIMPLE PAST

Present Perfect
She **has been** here since 2008.
They**'ve lived** here for 20 years.
We**'ve spoken** once today.
He **hasn't flown** this month.
Has she **called** him today?

Simple Past
She **was** in South Korea in 2007.
They **lived** there for 10 years.
We **spoke** twice yesterday.
She **didn't fly** last month.
Did she **call** him yesterday?

GRAMMAR NOTES

1 Use the **present perfect** to talk about things that started in the past, <u>continue up to the present</u>, and may continue into the future.

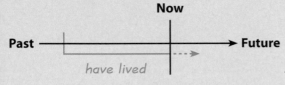

Use the **simple past** to talk about things that happened in the past and have <u>no connection to the present</u>.

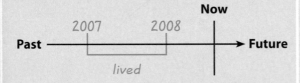

- They **have lived** apart *for the past three years*. (*They started living apart three years ago and are still living apart.*)

- They **lived** together *for one year*. (*They lived together until 2008. They no longer live together.*)

2 Use the **present perfect** to talk about things that happened at an <u>indefinite time</u> in the past.

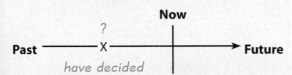

Use the **simple past** to talk about things that happened at a <u>specific time</u> in the past. The exact time is known and sometimes stated.

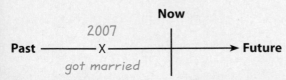

BE CAREFUL! Do <u>NOT use the present perfect</u> with a specific point in time. The only exception is with *since*.

- They **have decided** to live apart. (*We don't know exactly when the decision was made, or the time of the decision is not important.*)

- They **got married** *in 2007*.

- I **lived** in Seoul *in 2007*. NOT: ~~I've lived~~ in Seoul in 2007.
- I**'ve lived** in Seoul *since 2007*.

3 Use the **present perfect** to talk about things that have happened in a time period that is <u>not finished</u>, such as *today, this morning, this month, this year*.

Use the **simple past** to talk about things that happened in a time period that is <u>finished</u>, such as *yesterday, last month, last year*.

BE CAREFUL! Some time expressions such as *this morning*, *this month*, or *this year* can refer to an <u>unfinished or finished</u> time period. Use the present perfect if the time period is unfinished. Use the simple past if the time period is finished.

- He**'s called** three times *today*.
  (Today isn't finished, and it's possible that he'll call again.)

- He **called** three times *yesterday*.
  (Yesterday is finished.)

- It's 10:00 A.M. She**'s had** three cups of coffee *this morning*.
  (The morning isn't finished.)

- It's 1:00 P.M. She **had** three cups of coffee *this morning*.
  (The morning is finished.)

REFERENCE NOTES

For the **simple past**, see Unit 2.
For the **present perfect** with *since* and *for*, see Unit 8.
For the **present perfect** for **indefinite past**, see Unit 10.
For a list of **irregular verbs**, see Appendix 1 on page A-1.

STEP 3 FOCUSED PRACTICE

EXERCISE 1: Discover the Grammar

*Read the information about Sunmi and Shinjeng. Then circle the letter of the sentence (**a** or **b**) that best describes the situation.*

1. It's 2011. Sunmi moved to Vancouver in 2008. She still lives there.
   a. She lived in Vancouver for three years.
   b. She's lived in Vancouver for three years.

2. Last year Sunmi and Shinjeng enjoyed their vacation in Paris.
   a. They had a good time.
   b. They've had a good time.

3. Sunmi is telling her friend about her present job. Her friend asks,
   a. "How long were you there?"
   b. "How long have you been there?"

4. Shinjeng is telling Sunmi that the weather in Seoul has been too hot for the past five days.
   a. The weather is uncomfortable now.
   b. The weather is comfortable now.

(continued on next page)

5. Sunmi studied the piano for 10 years, but she doesn't play anymore.

    a. She has played the piano for 10 years.

    b. She played the piano for 10 years.

6. Shinjeng is an engineer. He is interviewing for an engineering job in Vancouver. He says,

    a. "I was an engineer for five years."

    b. "I've been an engineer for five years."

7. This year the couple has met once in Los Angeles. They'll meet in Paris.

    a. They've seen each other only once this year.

    b. They saw each other only once this year.

8. Sunmi's mother visited her once in Vancouver. When she got home, she wrote,

    a. "It was a great visit."

    b. "It has been a great visit."

9. Shinjeng and Sunmi haven't emailed each other this week.

    a. Shinjeng's computer was broken.

    b. Shinjeng's computer has been broken.

EXERCISE 2: Present Perfect or Simple Past

(Grammar Notes 1–3)

Complete the postings to an online board for people in long-distance relationships. Circle the correct verb forms.

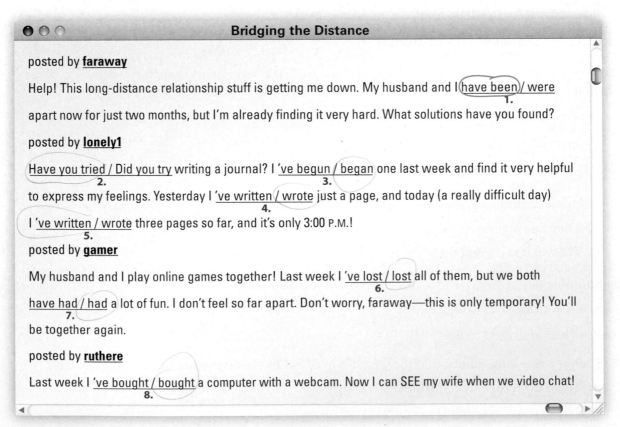

Bridging the Distance

posted by **faraway**

Help! This long-distance relationship stuff is getting me down. My husband and I (have been) / were
1.
apart now for just two months, but I'm already finding it very hard. What solutions have you found?

posted by **lonely1**

Have you tried / Did you try writing a journal? I 've begun / began one last week and find it very helpful
2.   **3.**
to express my feelings. Yesterday I 've written / wrote just a page, and today (a really difficult day)
4.
I 've written / wrote three pages so far, and it's only 3:00 P.M.!
5.
posted by **gamer**

My husband and I play online games together! Last week I 've lost / lost all of them, but we both
6.
have had / had a lot of fun. I don't feel so far apart. Don't worry, faraway—this is only temporary! You'll
7.
be together again.

posted by **ruthere**

Last week I 've bought / bought a computer with a webcam. Now I can SEE my wife when we video chat!
8.

posted by **greenbay**

My wife and I (have been) / were married for 10 years, but last year I 've had to / (had to) relocate
9.   10.
because of my job. My wife couldn't come, so we have a phone date every night. It's true: Absence

makes the heart grow fonder.

posted by **singleman**

Forget about it! I 've learned / learned from experience. This long-distance stuff is for the birds!
11.
I 've tried / tried it a few years ago, and it 's been / was awful. It's true what they say: Out of sight,
12.   13.
out of mind.

posted by **lilypad**

Last night I 've called / called my husband while I was having dinner. Luckily, we're in the same time
14.
zone, so he was having dinner too. We 've stayed / (stayed) on the phone, and it 's felt / (felt) like we were
15.   16.
eating together! But, to be honest, we 've been / were apart for too long, and I'll be happy when we
17.
can REALLY be together again.

EXERCISE 3: Present Perfect or Simple Past Statements *(Grammar Notes 1–3)*

*Complete the entry in Sunmi's journal. Use the present perfect or simple past form of the
verbs in parentheses.*

Thursday, September 28

This is my first journal entry. Yesterday, I _____ found _____ a website for couples
1. (find)
living apart. A few hours ago, someone ____ posted ____ a suggestion. They said that
2. (post)
keeping a journal can really help. So, here goes!

It's 8:00 P.M. It 's been _____ a hard day, and it's not over yet. I still have to
3. (be)
practice that new violin concerto. I ____ began ____ working on it a few days ago, but
4. (begin)
I have learned ____ only about half of it so far. And we begin rehearsing tomorrow. Work
5. (learn)
has been ____ difficult lately. I 've worked ____ late every night this week.
6. (be)   7. (work)
I feel exhausted, and I did not get ____ much sleep last night. And of course, I miss
8. (not get)
Shinjeng. Even though I ____ saw ____ him last month, it seems like a long time ago.
9. (see)
This long-distance relationship is beginning to get me down. We 've lived ____ apart
10. (live)
for too long. Oh, there's the phone. I hope it's him!

EXERCISE 4: Present Perfect or Simple Past Contrast

(Grammar Notes 1–2)

Shinjeng and Sunmi met in 2005. Since then, Shinjeng has changed. Write sentences describing how he has changed. Use the words in the lists.

In 2005	Since then
1. have / long hair	wear / his hair very short
2. wear / a beard and moustache	be / clean shaven
3. be / thin	gain / weight
4. wear / blue glasses	have / contact lenses
5. be / a student	become / an engineer
6. live / with his parents	buy / an apartment
7. be / single	get / married

1. _In 2005 he had long hair._

   Since then, he has worn his hair very short.

2. _____

   _____

3. _____

   _____

4. _____

   _____

5. _____

   _____

6. _____

   _____

7. _____

   _____

EXERCISE 5: *Wh-* Questions

(Grammar Notes 1–3)

Read the magazine article on page 146 again. Imagine that you wrote the article. You asked Shinjeng questions to get your information. What were they? Write questions. Use the words in parentheses. Choose between the present perfect and simple past.

1. (how long / be married)

    You: *How long have you been married?*

    Shinjeng: Four years.

2. (when / get married)

    You: _____

    Shinjeng: In 2007.

3. (when / your wife / lose her job)

    You: _____

    Shinjeng: Two weeks after our wedding.

4. (when / she / get a new job offer)

    You: _____

    Shinjeng: About a year later.

5. (how long / you / live apart)

    You: _____

    Shinjeng: For three years.

6. (how often / see each other last year)

    You: _____

    Shinjeng: Just three times.

7. (how often / see each other this year)

    You: _____

    Shinjeng: Only once so far.

8. (how / you / manage to stay close)

    You: _____

    Shinjeng: Through email, instant messages, text messages, and the cell phone.

EXERCISE 6: Editing

Read Sunmi's blog post. There are twelve mistakes in the use of the present perfect and the simple past. The first mistake is already corrected. Find and correct eleven more.

Long-Distance Relationships

I'm Not Alone!

Wednesday, September 7.20.11

I've just finished reading an interesting article about Felicia Mabuza-Suttle. Actually, ~~I read~~ *I've read* several

articles about her this year. She's a well-known international businesswoman, and up until 2004 she has

been a talk-show host in South Africa. Guess what! We have something in common! Although they now

live together, she and her husband have had a "long-distance marriage" for more than 15 years! She lived

in Johannesburg, South Africa; he lived in Atlanta, Georgia. Just like me and my husband, that's a whole

ocean apart! They have met in the 1970s. In the first 10 years of their marriage,

they have lived in more than 10 cities. Then, in the early 1990s, she has returned to

South Africa to help her country. In 2003, she has gone back to the States, and she

and her husband lived there together since then. So, it looks like things have

worked out for them! That's encouraging! She still makes several trips back to

South Africa every year—this year she was there twice so far. Here's a photo of her:

I love Vancouver and my job, but I really miss my husband. We didn't manage to see each other that

much since I left Seoul. I have been much happier when we have lived together. I know the situation is

temporary, but I hope, like Mabuza-Suttle and her husband, we can find a way to be together again soon.

Posted by Park Sunmi at 10:54 PM   0 Comments

STEP 4 COMMUNICATION PRACTICE

EXERCISE 7: Listening

A | *A student working for the school newspaper is interviewing two college professors. Read the list. Then listen to the interview. Listen again and check (✓) the items that are now true.*

The professors _____.

☑ **1.** are married
☐ **2.** live in different cities
☐ **3.** are at the same university

☐ **4.** live in Boston
☐ **5.** are in Madison
☐ **6.** have a house

B | *Read the statements. Listen again to the interview and circle the correct information.*

1. The couple has been married for two / (ten) years.

2. For a long time, they couldn't find a job / an apartment in the same city.

3. Now they work at the same company / university.

4. They have lived / lived in Boston for six years.

5. They have lived / lived in Madison for almost a year.

6. They have finally been able to buy a car / house.

7. They no longer need to drive / fly to see each other on weekends.

EXERCISE 8: Pronunciation

A | *Read and listen to the Pronunciation Note.*

> **Pronunciation Note**
>
> The **simple past** form and the **past participle** of **regular verbs** are the same.
> They both end in **-ed**.
>
> **EXAMPLE:**   visit   visit**ed**   have visit**ed**
>
> The **-ed** ending has **three** different pronunciations:
>
> **EXAMPLE:**   /t/   /d/   /ɪd/ (this ending adds a syllable to the word: *visit-ed*)
>
>   hop**ed**   liv**ed**   visit**ed**

B | *Listen to the short conversations. Notice the pronunciation of the simple past forms and past participles. Check (✓) the correct pronunciation of the ending.*

		/t/	/d/	/ɪd/
1.	**A:** Have you **visited** Dino this month?	☐	☐	☐
	B: Yes, I **visited** him last weekend.	☐	☐	☐
2.	**A:** Have you **tried** out your webcam?	☐	☐	☐
	B: Yes, we **tried** it out last night.	☐	☐	☐
3.	**A:** Have you ever **lived** abroad?	☐	☐	☐
	B: I **lived** in Turkey for two years.	☐	☐	☐
4.	**A:** Have you ever **wanted** to move?	☐	☐	☐
	B: I **wanted** to move to Mexico right after college.	☐	☐	☐
5.	**A:** Have you **finished** your homework?	☐	☐	☐
	B: I **finished** hours ago.	☐	☐	☐
6.	**A:** Has Sunmi **practiced** the violin today?	☐	☐	☐
	B: She **practiced** for two hours this morning.	☐	☐	☐

C | *Listen again. Practice the conversations with a partner.*

EXERCISE 9: Compare and Contrast

Work in pairs. Look at Sunmi's records from last year and this year. It's now the end of August. Compare what she did last year with what she's done this year. You can use the verbs from the box.

attend	give	go	have	perform	practice	see	study

LAST YEAR					
January	**February**	**March**	**April**	**May**	**June**
• concert in N.Y. • L.A. – violin workshop	• L.A. – violin workshop • 1 seminar	• concert in N.Y.	• attend lecture	• 10 vacation days	• 2 concerts – Ottawa • 1 concert – Toronto
July	**August**	**September**	**October**	**November**	**December**
• Sue's wedding	• music conference – Seoul ♥ Shinjeng	• Mom's visit • attend lecture	• concert in Toronto	• <u>Modern Day</u> interview	• 10 vacation days ♥ Shinjeng

THIS YEAR					
January	**February**	**March**	**April**	**May**	**June**
• concert in San Francisco	• concert in N.Y. • attend lecture	• Nan's wedding	• concert in Toronto	• concert in Paris ♥ Shinjeng	• 5 vacation days • 1 seminar
July	**August**	**September**	**October**	**November**	**December**
• Barry's wedding	• music conference • attend lecture				

EXAMPLE: **A:** Last year she performed in New York twice.
             B: So far this year she's only performed there once.

EXERCISE 10: Interview

A | *Many people have long-distance relationships with a friend or family member. Work with a partner. Interview each other about a long-distance relationship that your partner is in. Use the words to ask questions. Remember to use the present perfect and the simple past.*

- Who / have / this relationship with?
- How long / know / this person?
- Who / move away?
- Why / move away?
- When / last see each other?

- How often / be in contact / this year?
- How often / be in contact / last year?
- How / manage / to stay close?
- be / difficult?
- miss each other?

> **EXAMPLE:** **A:** Who have you had a long distance-relationship with?
> **B:** I've been in a long-distance relationship with my best friend for five years. She lives in Mexico.

B | *Continue the interview with questions of your own.*

EXERCISE 11: Writing

A | *Write two paragraphs about a long-distance relationship that you have or someone you know has. Use the present perfect and simple past.*

> **EXAMPLE:** My classmate's family lives more than halfway around the world from him, but he has managed to stay in close contact with them. Last month, he flew home to see them. They had a great time, and . . .

B | *Check your work. Use the Editing Checklist.*

Editing Checklist

Did you use the . . . ?
- ☐ present perfect for things that started in the past and continue up to the present
- ☐ simple past for things that happened in the past and have no connection to the present
- ☐ present perfect for things that happened at an indefinite time in the past
- ☐ simple past for things that happened at a specific time in the past
- ☐ present perfect for things that have happened in a time period that is not finished
- ☐ simple past for things that happened in a time period that is finished

A | *Imagine you are interviewing Ken. Write questions with the words in parentheses. Use the present perfect or the simple past.*

Ken moves to Vancouver		gets engineering degree	starts first professional job	marries Tina	loses job	moves to Singapore to work	Tina joins him in Singapore
2005	2006	2007	2008	2009	2010	2011	July, this year

1. _____
   (when / move to Vancouver)

2. _____
   (how long / be an engineer)

3. _____
   (work / in Vancouver for a long time)

4. _____
   (when / get married)

5. _____
   (how many years / live in Singapore)

6. _____
   (your wife / live in Singapore long)

B | *Complete the paragraph with the present perfect or the simple past form of the verbs in parentheses.*

I _____ in Singapore for a month, and it still feels special to see Ken every
        1. (be)

day. There's so much to do! We _____ five apartments last week, and so far this
                                2. (see)

evening we _____ three places off our list. Maybe we'll actually decide on one
            3. (cross)

before we fall asleep! I still _____ very much of the city, but this morning we
                               4. (not see)

_____ a boat tour. It _____ great! Ken _____ some
    5. (take)   **6. (be)**   **7. (learn)**

Chinese already, so he _____ lunch for us. I _____ much Chinese in
                        8. (order)   **9. (not learn)**

Vancouver, but I'll learn fast.

C | *Find and correct five mistakes.*

Tina and Ken lived apart for a while, but then Tina found a job in Singapore. She has moved

there last month. Here are some of their thoughts:

KEN: I'm so glad Tina is finally here. Last year has been the hardest time of my life.

TINA: Before I got here, I didn't understood Ken's experiences. But I was in culture shock since

I arrive, and I'm learning a new job too! Now I know what a rough time Ken had at first.

UNIT 12 Present Perfect Progressive and Present Perfect

CLIMATE CHANGE

STEP 1 GRAMMAR IN CONTEXT

Before You Read

Look at the picture. Discuss the questions.

1. What is happening to the Earth?
2. Why does the Earth have a thermometer in it?
3. Look at the title. What is a hot topic?

Read

 Read the article about climate change.

Global Warming[1]: A Hot Topic

By Dr. Jane Owen

The Earth's climate **has changed** many times. Warm oceans covered the Earth for millions of years. Then those oceans turned to ice for millions more. If the climate **has been changing** for five billion years, why is global warming such a hot topic today? What are people arguing about?

Almost everyone agrees that the Earth **has been getting** hotter. But not everyone agrees about the cause. Most climate experts think that human activities **have added** to global warming. The coal and oil we burn for energy **have been sending** more and more gases into the air around the Earth. The gases keep the heat in the atmosphere[2] and also cause air pollution. These experts believe humans can slow global warming.

Others say global warming is mostly the result of natural causes, such as changes in the sun. They don't believe that human activities can make things better or worse.

Human or natural, the effects of global warming **have been** powerful. Here are just two examples:

• In the Arctic,[3] ice **has been melting** quickly. As a result, polar bears and other animals **have become** endangered species.[4] Arctic towns and villages are also in danger as sea levels rise.

• In parts of Africa, rainfall **has decreased**. Water and food **have become** very scarce. Both people and animals **have been suffering** badly.

Does it really matter what causes global warming? Yes! If we **have been** part of the cause, then we can be part of the solution. Recently, people **have been developing** ways to use clean solar energy. In addition, they **have been designing** homes and cars that use less energy. Will it help? Maybe. Is it worth a try? You decide—it's your world too!

---

[1] *global warming:* the continuing increase in the Earth's temperatures (including air and oceans) since the 1950s
[2] *atmosphere:* the air that surrounds the Earth
[3] *the Arctic:* the most northern part of the Earth
[4] *endangered species:* a type of animal or plant that may not continue to exist

After You Read

A | Vocabulary: *Match the words with their definitions.*

_____ **1.** expert   **a.** power that makes machines work

_____ **2.** climate   **b.** to create a drawing that shows how to build something

_____ **3.** develop   **c.** someone with special knowledge of a subject

_____ **4.** energy   **d.** the typical weather in an area

_____ **5.** design   **e.** something unhealthy in the air or water

_____ **6.** pollution   **f.** to work on a new idea or product to make it successful

B | Comprehension: *Circle the letter of the word or phrase that best completes each sentence.*

1. In the past, the Earth's climate was always _____.

     a. cooler

     b. hotter

     c. changing

2. Most experts think the Earth is now _____ than before.

     a. cooler

     b. hotter

     c. no different

3. Some people think that one cause of global warming is _____.

     a. humans

     b. polar bears

     c. ice

4. Other people think that our activities are making _____.

     a. the sun hotter

     b. the Earth cooler

     c. almost no difference

5. One idea for slowing global warming is for us to _____.

     a. protect endangered animals

     b. use clean energy

     c. move to the Arctic

PRESENT PERFECT PROGRESSIVE AND PRESENT PERFECT

Present Perfect Progressive

Statements				
Subject	*Have (not)*	*Been*	Base Form of Verb + *-ing*	*(Since / For)*
I You* We They	**have (not)**	**been**	**working**	(**since** 2009). (**for** years).
He She It	**has (not)**			

*You is both singular and plural.

Yes / No Questions				
Have	Subject	*Been*	Base Form of Verb + *-ing*	*(Since / For)*
Have	you	**been**	**working**	(**since** 2009)? (**for** years)?
Has	she			

Short Answers				
Affirmative		Negative		
Yes,	I / we	**have.**	**No,**	I / we	**haven't.**
	she	**has.**		she	**hasn't.**

Wh- Questions				
Wh- Word	*Have*	Subject	*Been*	Base Form of Verb + *-ing*
How long	**have**	you	**been**	**working**?
	has	she		

Present Perfect Progressive and Present Perfect

Present Perfect Progressive	Present Perfect
They **have been living** here for many years.	They **have lived** here for many years.
I**'ve been reading** this book since Monday.	I**'ve read** two books about solar energy.
Dr. Owen **has been writing** articles since 2000.	Dr. Owen **has written** many articles.
She**'s been working** in Kenya for a year.	She**'s worked** in many countries.

GRAMMAR NOTES

1

We often use the **present perfect progressive** to show that something is <u>unfinished</u>. It started in the past and is still continuing. The focus is on the <u>continuation</u> of the action.

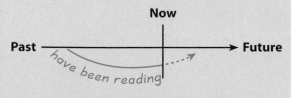

We often use the **present perfect** to show that something is <u>finished</u>. The focus is on the <u>result</u> of the action.

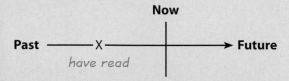

USAGE NOTE: We also use the **present perfect progressive** for <u>finished</u> actions that ended in the <u>very recent past</u>. You can often still see the results of the action.

BE CAREFUL! We usually do NOT use **non-action verbs**, such as *be*, *have*, and *know* in the **progressive**.

- I**'ve been reading** a book about solar energy.
  (*I'm still reading it.*)

- She**'s been writing** an article.
  (*She's still writing it.*)

- I**'ve read** a book about solar energy.
  (*I finished the book.*)

- She**'s written** an article.
  (*She finished the article.*)

- Look! The streets are wet. It**'s been raining**.
  (*It stopped raining very recently.*)
  NOT: It's ~~rained~~.

- She**'s had** the same job since 2000.
  NOT: She's ~~been having~~ the same job since 2000.

2

We often use the **present perfect progressive** to talk about **how long** something has been happening.

We often use the **present perfect** to talk about:
- **how much** someone has done
- **how many things** someone has done
- **how many times** someone has done something

- I**'ve been reading** books about wind energy **for two months**.

- I**'ve read** *a lot* about it.
- She**'s written** *three* articles.
- I**'ve read** that book *twice*.

3 Sometimes you can use either the **present perfect progressive** or the **present perfect**. The meaning is basically the same. This is especially true with verbs such as *live*, *study*, *teach*, and *work* with for or since.

USAGE NOTES:
a. We often use the **present perfect progressive** to show that something is <u>temporary</u>.

b. We often use the **present perfect** to show that something is <u>permanent</u>.

• Jane is a climate expert. She**'s been studying** global warming **for** 10 years.
OR
• Jane is a climate expert. She**'s studied** global warming **for** 10 years.
(*In both cases, she is still studying it.*)

• They**'ve been living** here *since* 1995, but they are moving next month.

• They**'ve lived** here *since* they were children. They've always lived here.

REFERENCE NOTES
For a list of **non-action verbs**, see Appendix 2 on page A-2.
For use of the **present perfect** with *since* and *for*, see Unit 8 on page 110.
For use of the **present perfect** for the **indefinite past**, see Unit 10 on page 134.

STEP 3 FOCUSED PRACTICE

EXERCISE 1: Discover the Grammar

Read the sentences. Then check (✓) the correct box to show if the action is finished or unfinished.

	Finished	Unfinished
1. Professor Owen has been reading a book about global warming.	☐	☑
2. She's read a book about global warming.	☐	☐
3. She's written a magazine article about air pollution.	☐	☐
4. She's been waiting for some supplies.	☐	☐
5. They've lived in Ontario since 2002.	☐	☐
6. They've been living in Ontario since 2002.	☐	☐
7. We've been developing plans with the leaders of many countries.	☐	☐
8. We've developed these plans with many leaders.	☐	☐
9. Look out the window, it's been raining.	☐	☐
10. Look. Someone has watered the plants.	☐	☐

EXERCISE 2: Present Perfect Progressive or Present Perfect   *(Grammar Notes 1–3)*

Complete the statements. Circle the correct form of the verbs. In some cases, both forms are correct.

1. Professor Owen is working on two articles for the next issue of *Green Earth* magazine. She has written / (has been writing) these articles since Monday.

2. *Green Earth* magazine has published / has been publishing its third annual report on the environment. It is an excellent report.

3. Professor Owen has discussed / has been discussing global warming many times.

4. She has spoken / has been speaking at our school many times about climate change.

5. Congress has created / has been creating a new study group to find solutions to climate change. The group has already developed some interesting ideas.

6. The new group has a lot of work to do. Lately, the members have studied / have been studying the use of solar energy for homes. They're learning about pollution from buildings.

7. Professor Owen was late for a meeting with the members of Congress. When she arrived the chairperson said, "At last, you're here. We 've waited / 've been waiting for you."

8. Professor Owen has lived / has been living in Kenya for the last two years, but she will return to the United States in January.

9. She has worked / has been working with environmentalists in Kenya and Tanzania.

10. Kenyans have planted / have been planting 30 million trees since the 1970s.

EXERCISE 3: Present Perfect Progressive   *(Grammar Note 1–2)*

A | *Look at the two pictures of Professor Jane Owen.*

B | *Complete the sentences describing what has been happening in the pictures. Use the present perfect progressive form of the verbs in parentheses. Choose between affirmative and negative.*

1. She ___'s been working___ in her office.
   (work)

2. She _____ to climate experts.
   (talk)

3. She _____ a book.
   (write)

4. She _____ the newspaper.
   (read)

5. She _____ coffee.
   (drink)

6. She _____ tea.
   (drink)

7. She _____ her sandwich.
   (eat)

8. She _____ TV.
   (watch)

9. She _____ hard.
   (work)

10. It _____ all day.
    (rain)

EXERCISE 4: Statements

Complete Jane Owen's blog about the Solar Decathlon, a competition for the best solar houses (houses that get all their energy from the sun). Use the present perfect progressive or the present perfect form of the verbs in parentheses.

```
 ○ ○ ○                            Greenmail
```

The house designed by the team from Spain.

A beautiful solar village ____has appeared____ in the
1. (appear)
middle of Washington, D.C. Sorry, the houses aren't for
sale. Universities in Canada, Europe, and the United
States _____ them here for an
2. (bring)
international competition of solar houses. Universities

_____ in this competition since 2004. For all the contests, talented students
3. (participate)

_____ the houses, and they _____ them as well! Over the years,
4. (design)   5. (build)

the homes _____ more energy efficient *and* more beautiful. This year, students
6. (get)

from Canada _____ energy solutions for very cold climates. The team from Spain
7. (find)

_____ a roof that moves to follow the sun. German designers _____
8. (design)   9. (develop)

a home that owners can control over the Internet. (If you forget to turn off the stove, you can do it

online!) This year, 20 houses _____ the competition. I _____
10. (enter)   11. (visit)

the houses since I got here, and I _____ also _____ to many of
12. (talk)

the student designers. So far, what I hear most often is, "I could *totally* live in this house!" I agree.

Check next week's blog for the winners.

EXERCISE 5: Questions and Answers

(Grammar Note 2)

Professor Owen is interviewing one of the student designers at the Solar Decathlon. Use the words in parentheses to write Dr. Owen's questions. Use her notes to complete the student's answers. Choose between the present perfect progressive and the present perfect.

started project two years ago

cost—$250,000

house tours—all afternoon

visitors this week—so far about 30,000

interest in solar energy—started 3 years ago

total energy production today—more than the house needs!

the team's third competition

one prize for lighting design

1. (how long / your team / work / on this project)

   OWEN: *How long has your team been working on this project?*

   STUDENT: *We've been working on this project for two years.*

2. (how much money / the team / spend / on the house)

   OWEN: _____

   STUDENT: _____

3. (how long / you / lead tours / today)

   OWEN: _____

   STUDENT: _____

4. (how many people / visit / this week)

   OWEN: _____

   STUDENT: _____

5. (how long / you / be / interested in solar energy)

   OWEN: _____

   STUDENT: _____

6. (how much energy/ the house / produced today)

OWEN: _____

STUDENT: _____

7. (how many competitions / your team / entered)

OWEN: _____

STUDENT: _____

8. (how many prizes / your team / win)

OWEN: _____

STUDENT: _____

EXERCISE 6: Editing

Read the student's email. There are eight mistakes in the use of the present perfect progressive and the present perfect. The first mistake is already corrected. Find and correct seven more.

Hi guys,

            written
Sorry I haven't ~~wrote~~ sooner. I haven't been having any free time since we arrived in Madrid for

the solar house competition. (Our house got here before us!) I'm really excited and also really

tired. Since we arrived, we've been lived on pizza and coffee. I haven't sleeping more than a few

hours since … well, I can't remember when. Our team has been working day and night for the

last two weeks, and today the house looks wonderful. I'm so proud—we've designed a home

that's beautiful AND reduces pollution. We're finally ready for the judges, so I've spent most of

the day looking at other teams' houses. I've been visiting 10 houses today. They are so interesting

and creative! For the last hour, I've just been hanging out in a café with some people from the

other teams. I've already been drinking three cups of coffee—it's delicious, but really strong!

We been practicing our Spanish with the Madrid team. I still don't understand too much, but our

teammate Eloy Ruiz is from Puerto Rico, and he's been helped me out a lot. Wish us luck and

check your email for photos of the house.

Katie

EXERCISE 7: Listening

A | *You're going to listen to five short conversations. Before you listen, look at the pairs of pictures. Each pair shows two different versions of a recent activity. Work with a partner and describe what has happened and what has been happening in each picture.*

1.

a.

b.

EXAMPLE: In this picture, they've planted one tree.   Here they've planted two.

2.

a.

b.

3.

a.

b.

4.

a.

b.

5.

a.

b.

C | Look at the pictures again. Complete the sentences with the correct verb form for the pictures you chose in Part B. Then listen again to the conversations and check your work.

1. They _____'ve planted_____ some trees in front of the new library.

2. We _____ this pizza.

3. It _____ a lot since we spoke, but today we _____ on it.

4. We just sent the house, and I _____ all my stuff.

5. Well, for one thing, she _____ a book about global warming.

EXERCISE 8: Pronunciation

A | Read and listen to the Pronunciation Note.

Pronunciation Note
In **affirmative sentences**, we usually **stress** the **main verb**, but NOT the auxiliary verb such as *have* or *has*. EXAMPLES: I've been **working** in the library. I've **finished** my report. In **negative sentences**, we **stress** both the **main verb** and the **auxiliary verb**. EXAMPLES: He **hasn't** been **calling** lately. We **haven't seen** him very often either.

B | Listen to the short conversations and complete the answers with the verb forms that you hear. Use contractions.

1. **A:** *Avatar* is playing at the college theater.

   B: Oh, I _____ it.

2. **A:** I didn't see Emma yesterday.

   B: She _____ Mondays.

3. **A:** I just handed in my research paper. What about you?

   B: Well, I _____ it.

4. **A:** There's a new student in our class.

   B: I _____ about her.

5. **A:** Did you decide on a vacation?

   B: We _____ about it.

C | Listen again and repeat the responses. Then practice the conversations with a partner.

EXERCISE 9: Find Someone Who...

A | *Interview your classmates. Ask questions with the present perfect progressive or present perfect. Find someone who has recently . . .*

- been enjoying this weather
- been working hard
- changed jobs
- seen a good movie

- moved
- been learning a new hobby or skill
- talked to an interesting person
- taken a trip

> EXAMPLE: **A:** Hi Eloy. What have you been doing lately? Have you been enjoying this weather?
> **B:** Oh, yeah. I've been spending a lot of time outside.

B | *Then ask more questions. Keep the conversation going!*

> EXAMPLE: **A:** Oh, what have you been doing?
> **B:** I've been riding my bike in the park and going for long walks.

EXERCISE 10: Picture Discussion

Work with a partner. Discuss the picture. Think about the questions. Then compare your ideas with those of another pair of students.

- What does the picture show?
- What does it mean?
- Is it a strong message? Why or why not?
- Do you agree with the message?

> EXAMPLE: **A:** In this picture, there's a polar bear . . .
> **B:** I think it means . . .

EXERCISE 11: Discussion

Have a discussion in small groups. What changes have you made or experienced recently? Use the present perfect progressive and the present perfect to talk about them.

Have you changed . . . ?

- your opinions about society or the environment
- the way you look or dress
- the people you hang out with
- your hobbies or interests
- your goals
- *(other)* _____

> EXAMPLE: **A:** Recently, I've gotten more interested in the environment. I've been recycling paper and other things. I've also been walking or riding my bike more.
> **B:** I've just started a job, so I've been wearing business clothes instead of jeans.
> **C:** You look good, Ben! For myself, I've been . . .

EXERCISE 12: Writing

A | *Write an email to friends or family about what you've been doing lately. You can use ideas from Exercises 9 and 11.*

EXAMPLE: Hi Everyone,
  A new semester has started, and I've been pretty busy lately. I've been working really hard on a science project. We're learning how to check the water quality in the lake. I've gotten more interested in the environment because of this project, so I've been riding my bicycle almost everywhere—it's great exercise *and* good for the environment. Oh, and I've just finished a very interesting book about global warming. Life hasn't been all work, though. I've also been hanging out with some interesting new friends . . .

B | *Check your work. Use the Editing Checklist.*

Editing Checklist

Did you use the . . . ?
- ☐ present perfect progressive for things that are unfinished
- ☐ present perfect for things that are finished
- ☐ present perfect progressive to talk about how long something has been happening
- ☐ present perfect to talk about how much, how many, and how many times something has happened

---

A | Circle the correct words to complete the sentences.

1. Professor Ortiz <u>has written / has been writing</u> 10 articles on global warming.

2. Today she <u>has been choosing / has chosen</u> the title for a new article: *It's Melting!*

3. I <u>'ve read / 've been reading</u> one of her books. I'll give it to you when I'm finished.

4. My sister <u>has read / has been reading</u> it twice already.

5. I wanted to finish it today, but I <u>'ve had / 've been having</u> a headache all day.

6. I <u>'ve taken / 've been taking</u> two aspirins for it.

B | Complete the conversations with the present perfect progressive or present perfect form of the verbs in parentheses.

- **A:** How long _____ you _____ in Dallas?
  1. (live)

  B: I _____ here for more than 10 years. What about you?
  2. (be)

  A: I moved here last month. I _____ it a lot.
  3. (enjoy)

- **A:** _____ you _____ any books by Peter Robinson?
  4. (read)

  B: Yes. In fact, I'm reading one now.

  A: Really? How many books _____ he _____?
  5. (write)

- **A:** Why are your books all over the place? I _____ to clean up!
  6. (try)

  B: I _____ for my exam.
  7. (study)

- **A:** How long _____ Vilma _____ a student here?
  8. (be)

  B: This is her third semester.

  A: _____ she _____ her major?
  9. (choose)

C | Find and correct five mistakes.

1. Janet hasn't been writing a word since she sat down at her computer.

2. Since I've known Dan, he's been having five different jobs.

3. I've drunk coffee all morning. I think I've been having at least 10 cups!

4. We've been lived here for several years, but we're moving next month.

From Grammar to Writing
THE TOPIC SENTENCE AND PARAGRAPH UNITY

A **paragraph** is a group of sentences about **one main idea**. Writers often state the main idea in one sentence, called the **topic sentence**. The topic sentence is often near the beginning of the paragraph.

1

A | *Read the personal statement for a job application. First cross out any sentences that do not belong in the paragraph. (Later you will choose a topic sentence.)*

Please describe your work experience.

_____
(topic sentence)

While I was in high school, I worked as a server at Darby's during the summer and on weekends. ~~Summers here are very hot and humid.~~ I worked with many different kinds of customers, and I learned to be polite even with difficult people. They serve excellent food at Darby's. Because I was successful as a server, I received a promotion after one year. Since high school, I have been working for Steak Hut as the night manager. I have developed management skills because I supervise six employees. One of them is a good friend of mine. I have also learned to order supplies and to plan menus. Sometimes I am very tired after a night's work.

B | *Now choose one of the sentences as the topic sentence and write it as the first sentence of the paragraph.*

- I feel that a high school education is necessary for anyone looking for a job.

- My restaurant experience has prepared me for a position with your company.

- Eating at both Darby's and Steak Hut in Greenville is very enjoyable.

- I prefer planning menus to any other task in the restaurant business.

2 | *You can use a cluster diagram to develop and organize your ideas. Complete the cluster diagram for the paragraph in Exercise 1.*

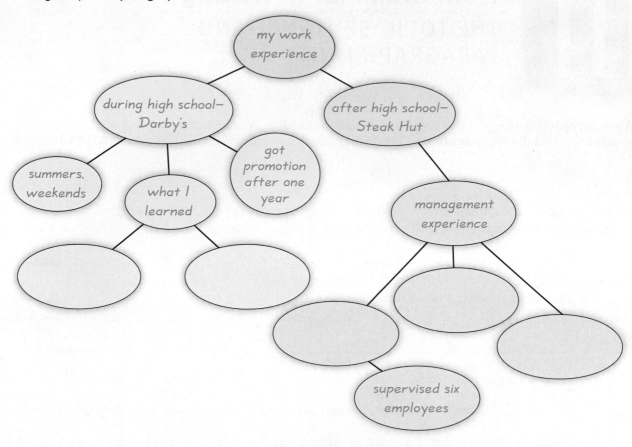

3 | *Before you write . . .*

1. On a separate piece of paper, make a cluster diagram for your accomplishments. Do not include a topic sentence.

2. Work with a small group. Look at each other's diagrams and develop a topic sentence for each one.

3. Ask and answer questions to develop more information about your accomplishments.

4 | *Write a personal statement about your accomplishments. Use your diagram as an outline.*

MODALS AND SIMILAR EXPRESSIONS

"Got your e-mail, thanks."

Before You Read

Look at the article. Discuss the questions.

1. What are the people in the photo doing?
2. Look at the title of the article. Guess the main point.

Read

Read the article about a dance company.

Born to Dance

by V. Gupta

"Who made up the rule that you **can** only **dance** on your two feet?" asks Mary Verdi-Fletcher, president and founding director[1] of Dancing Wheels. She is also one of its main dancers. Verdi-Fletcher was born with a medical condition called spina bifida.[2] As a result, by the age of 12, she **wasn't able to stand** or **walk**. But that didn't stop her from dancing. People said, "You **can't walk**; how **can** you **be** a dancer?" Verdi-Fletcher, however, *knew* it was possible to dance in a wheelchair because, as she says, "Dance is an emotion that comes from within."

When she entered her first dance competition, the audience was confused. "She's in a wheelchair. How **can** she **dance**?" But at the end of the performance, they stood and applauded. Not only **could** she **dance**, but she **could hypnotize**[3] an audience with her talent. When the artistic director of the Cleveland Ballet first saw her, he thought, "*That* is a dancer. . . . You **can't take** your eyes off her."

Dancing Wheels was the first integrated dance company in the United States with both "sit-down dancers" and "stand-up dancers." The group presents a new definition of dance. It also changes the perception of what people **can** or **cannot do**. "Through our dance," says Verdi-Fletcher, "we want to show that anything is possible and achievable. . . . People need to see they **can achieve** their dreams and aspirations—but not without a lot of hard work and dedication."

[1] *founding director:* someone who starts a company or business
[2] *spina bifida:* a condition in which the bones of the spine do not develop in a normal way
[3] *hypnotize:* to be so interesting that people cannot think about or look at anything else

After You Read

A | Vocabulary: *Circle the letter of the word or phrase that best completes each sentence.*

1. A **confused** person _____.
   a. isn't able to dance
   b. doesn't understand something
   c. won't applaud

2. A person with **talent** _____.
   a. works hard
   b. talks a lot
   c. has natural ability

3. An **integrated** group is one with _____ members.
   a. a lot of
   b. different kinds of
   c. very interesting

4. Dancing Wheels changed my **perception** of dance. In other words, the group changed my _____ of dance.
   a. enjoyment
   b. ideas
   c. performance

5. If you have a lot of **aspirations**, you have _____.
   a. strong desires to do something
   b. serious health problems
   c. interests that you enjoy

6. Someone with **dedication** _____.
   a. dances very well
   b. often changes his or her mind
   c. continues to work hard

B | Comprehension: *Read each statement. Circle the correct information.*

1. Verdi-Fletcher shows that people <u>can / can't</u> dance in a wheelchair.

2. She is a <u>"sit-down" / "stand-up"</u> dancer.

3. She is also the director of <u>The Cleveland Ballet / Dancing Wheels</u>.

4. She believes that the ability to dance comes from <u>inside / outside</u> a person.

5. At the end of her first dance competition, the audience <u>loved / was confused by</u> her performance.

6. Verdi-Fletcher believes it is <u>easy / difficult</u> to reach your life goals.

ABILITY: *CAN* AND *COULD*

Statements			
Subject	**Can / Could (not)**	**Base Form of Verb**	
I You He She We You They	can (not)	dance	now.
	could (not)		last year.

Contractions		
cannot OR can not	=	can't
could not	=	couldn't

Yes / No Questions		
Can / Could	**Subject**	**Base Form of Verb**
Can	I you he she we you they	dance?
Could		

Short Answers					
Affirmative			**Negative**		
Yes,	you I he she you we they	can.	No,	you I he she you we they	can't.
		could.			couldn't.

Wh- Questions			
Wh- Word	**Can / Could**	**Subject**	**Base Form of Verb**
How well	can	she	dance?
	could	you	

ABILITY: *BE ABLE TO*

Statements			
Subject	**Be**	**(Not) Able to**	**Base Form of Verb**
I	am		
You	are		
He She	is	(not) able to	practice.
We You They	are		

Yes / No Questions				Short Answers							
Be	**Subject**	**Able to**	**Base Form of Verb**	Affirmative			Negative				
Is	she	able to	practice?	Yes,	she	**is.**	No,	she	**isn't.**		
Are	you				I	**am.**		I'm	**not.**		

Wh- Questions				
Wh- Word	**Be**	**Subject**	**Able to**	**Base Form of Verb**
When	**is**	she	able to	practice?
How often	**are**	you		

GRAMMAR NOTES

1 Use **can**, **could**, or a form of **be able to** to talk about natural or learned **ability**.

- She **can dance**, but she **can't sing**.
- We **could ride** bikes, but we **couldn't drive**.
- Soon, you**'ll be able to write** to me in English.

2 **Can** and **could** are **modals**. Like all modals:

- They are followed by the <u>base form</u> of a verb: **modal + base form of verb**

  - Mary **can dance**.
    NOT: Mary can ~~to~~ dance.

- They have the <u>same form for all subjects</u>. (They do NOT use *-s* for the third-person singular.)

  - I **can** dance, and she **can** dance too.
    NOT: She ~~cans~~ dance.

- They form the negative with *not*. (They do NOT use *do*.)

  - She **can't** sing.
    NOT: She ~~doesn't can~~ sing.

- They go before the subject in questions. (They do NOT use *do*.)

  - **Can** Antonio dance too?
    NOT: ~~Does~~ can Antonio dance too?

Be able to is an expression **similar to a modal**, but it isn't a real modal: it has <u>different forms</u> (*am, is, are; was, were; will be*).

- **Was** she **able to dance** when she was young?
- **Will** he **be able to learn** the tango by Monday?

(continued on next page)

3	Use *can* or sometimes *am/is/are able to* for **present ability**.	• She **can speak** English, but she **can't speak** French.
	a. *Can* is much <u>more common</u> than *be able to* in everyday speech about present ability.	MORE COMMON: **Can** you **speak** French? LESS COMMON: **Are** you **able to speak** French?
	b. We use *be able to* when the ability to do something comes after a lot of <u>hard work</u>.	• French was difficult for me, but now I**'m able to have** a conversation because I spent a year studying in France.
4	Use *can* or *will be able to* for **future ability** when you are talking about <u>plans or arrangements</u>.	• I **can buy** the tickets *tomorrow*. OR • I**'ll be able to buy** the tickets *tomorrow*.
	BE CAREFUL! Use *will be able to* (but NOT *can*) to talk about <u>things you learn</u>.	• When I finish this course, I**'ll be able to speak** French well. NOT: When I finish this course, I ~~can~~ speak French well.
5	Use *could* or *was/were able to* for **past ability**.	• **Could** he **dance** when he was a child? OR • **Was** he **able to dance** when he was a child?
	BE CAREFUL! Do NOT use *could* in affirmative statements for a <u>single event</u> in the past. Use *was/were able to*.	• After a lot of hard work and dedication, they **were able to win** first prize in the *2002 dance competition*. NOT: . . . they ~~could~~ win first prize . . .
	However, it is possible to use *couldn't* for single past events.	• They **couldn't win** first prize in the *2003 dance competition*.

REFERENCE NOTES

Can and *could* are also used for **permission** (see Unit 14) and for **requests** (see Unit 15).
For a list of **modals and their functions**, see Appendix 19 on page A-8.

EXERCISE 1: Discover the Grammar

Mary Verdi-Fletcher

1955	born in Ohio
1975	graduated from high school got job as keypunch operator
1978	learned to drive
1979	entered Dance Fever Competition
1980	began Dancing Wheels enrolled in Lakeland Community College, Ohio took course in public speaking
1980–1988	worked for Independent Living Center
1984	married Robert Fletcher
1989–1990	tour director for Cleveland Ballet
1990–present	founding director and dancer, Dancing Wheels teaches dance to people with and without disabilities
Some Awards	Invacare Award of Excellence in the Arts (1994) Governor's Award for Outreach (1998) Emmy Award for hosting TV series "Shortcuts to Happiness" (2007)
Other Interests	watching football and soccer games

Look at the information about Mary Verdi-Fletcher. Then check (✓) **True** *or* **False** *for each statement. Check* **?** *if there isn't enough information.*

	True	False	?
1. Verdi-Fletcher was able to get a job after high school.	✓	☐	☐
2. She can't drive a car.	☐	☐	☐
3. She couldn't participate in dance competitions.	☐	☐	☐
4. She can speak foreign languages.	☐	☐	☐
5. She was able to start a dance company.	☐	☐	☐
6. She couldn't finish college.	☐	☐	☐
7. She can probably speak well in front of large groups of people.	☐	☐	☐
8. She's able to help people with disabilities learn to dance.	☐	☐	☐
9. She can play the piano.	☐	☐	☐
10. She's so busy she can't have other interests.	☐	☐	☐

EXERCISE 2: Statements with *Can* and *Could*

(Grammar Notes 1–5)

Complete the paragraphs. Use **can, can't, could,** *or* **couldn't.**

1. For a long time, Jim and Marie _____couldn't_____ agree on a family sport. Jim loves tennis,
   a.

   and Marie takes lessons, but she still _____ play. Marie _____
   b.   **c.**

   swim, but Jim hates the water. They recently took up dancing and discovered a new talent.

   Now, they _____ do the swing *and* spend time together.
   d.

2. Stefan has made a lot of progress in English. Last semester he _____ order a
   a.

   meal in a restaurant or talk on the telephone. His friends helped him do everything. Now he

   _____ speak English in a lot of situations.
   b.

3. Bill almost _____ make his class presentation last semester because he was
   a.

   so nervous. He _____ usually communicate well in small groups, but he still
   b.

   doesn't feel comfortable in big ones. He plans to take a course in public speaking. I'm sure

   that with his dedication he _____ improve quickly.
   c.

4. Last year I _____ dance at all, but when I met Stan, I signed up for a class
   a.

   right away. He _____ really dance, and I wanted to dance with him. Now I
   b.

   _____ do the basic steps. I _____ do the waltz yet, but we're
   c.   **d.**

   planning to waltz at our wedding next month.

EXERCISE 3: Statements and Questions with *Be able to*

(Grammar Notes 2–5)

Complete each conversation. Use the correct form of **be able to** *and the verb in parentheses.*
Choose between affirmative and negative.

1. **AUSTIN:** I heard your sister wanted to take lessons. ____Was____ she ___able to start___?
   a. (start)

   JULIA: Yes, she was. She started last month. She can do the fox-trot now, but even with

   lessons and a lot of practice, she still _____ the waltz.
   b. (do)

2. **EVAN:** _____ you _____ Mrs. Suraikin at the studio yesterday?
   a. (find)

   KAYLA: Yes. She says I _____ in the tango contest next month!
   b. (compete)

   EVAN: Great! We all believe you have the talent to win too.

   KAYLA: Thanks. Mrs. Suraikin really _____ my perceptions of my
   c. (change)

   abilities. Now I think I can too.

3. **EMMA:** _____ you _____ Russian as a child, Olga?
                        a. (speak)

   OLGA: Yes, I was. We spoke it at home, so I _____ it fluently when I
                                                          b. (speak)

   was very young.

   EMMA: Do your children speak Russian too?

   OLGA: Unfortunately, no. We spoke French at home, so they _____ never

   _____ really fluent.
   c. (become)

4. **JENNA:** I _____ the waltz last weekend because I hurt my ankle.
                        a. (practice)

   COLE: That's too bad. _____ you _____ next week?
                                                  b. (practice)

EXERCISE 4: *Can, Could,* or *Be able to*   *(Grammar Notes 3–5)*

Two friends are at a dance performance. Complete their conversations. Use **can, could,** *or*
be able to *and the correct verb from the box. You will use some of the verbs more than once.*
Use **can** *or* **could** *when possible. Choose between affirmative and negative.*

dance	do	get	lend	pay	pronounce	see

1. **NINA:** _____*Can*_____ you _____*see*_____ the stage OK?
                                                                a.

   LEÓN: Yes, I _____ it fine. What about you?
                        b.

   NINA: No. I _____ it very well at all. The man in front of me is too tall.
                        c.

   LEÓN: Change seats with me. You _____ it better then.
                                                    d.

2. **LEÓN:** Wow! This performance is great. This group _____ sure

   _____ beautifully!
   a.

   NINA: I know. I'm glad I _____ tickets. Last year I _____ any.
                                        b.   **c.**

   They were sold out every time I tried.

   LEÓN: What's their name?

   NINA: I'll spell it for you. It's P-i-l-o-b-o-l-u-s. I'm not sure I _____ it correctly!
                                                                                    d.

3. **LEÓN:** It's intermission. Would you like to get something to eat?

   NINA: Oh, I'm afraid I _____ anything. I left my wallet at home by mistake.
                                    a.

   LEÓN: No problem. I _____ you some money.
                                b.

   NINA: Thanks. I _____ you back tomorrow.
                            c.

(continued on next page)

4. **NINA:** This performance makes *me* want to dance. _____ you

_____ the tango?
   a.

   LEÓN: Not yet! But I'm taking dance lessons, so I _____ it soon!
   b.

EXERCISE 5: Editing

Read the review of a dance performance. There are ten mistakes in the use of **can, could,** *and* **be able to.** *The first mistake is already corrected. Find and correct nine more.*

How ~~They Can~~ Do That?
Can They

By Jennifer Andrews

Pilobolus Dance Theatre, photo by John Kane

Last night was the first time I saw the group Pilobolus perform. And what a performance it was! I no can tell you that I fully understood the performance. I *can* to say, however, that the experience was completely wonderful.

Pilobolus is a very unusual group. The performers have no background in dance. When they began, they thought, "Maybe we can't dancing, so why try?" So they just made interesting shapes with their bodies. Well, this group certainly cans dance, and they are able to do much more. The six dancers in the group are athletic, artistic, and very talented. They are able do amazing things with their bodies. In many dances, they move together as a single unit.

My theater companion and I had great seats. We could saw the entire stage (not always true in some theaters). The sound system, though, had a few problems, and we didn't able to hear the music clearly all the time.

Some people in the audience asked: "Is it dance or is it gymnastics?" You can decide for yourself. Many people weren't able to got tickets for the first two performances of this series, but you can still buy tickets for next week. This is the type of dance performance everyone can enjoys.

Highly recommended.

EXERCISE 6: Listening

A | *Karl is interviewing for the job of office manager at Carmen's Dance Studio. What does the interviewer say? Read the statements. Then listen to the conversation. Listen again and circle the correct information.*

1. The office is very (busy) / quiet.

2. Many of the students are <u>foreign / talented</u>.

3. She asks Karl about his <u>computer / math</u> skills.

4. They're thinking of designing a <u>monthly newsletter / new studio</u>.

5. Many of the students take private <u>language / dance</u> lessons.

6. She may need Karl to <u>drive / dance</u> sometimes.

B | *Listen again to the conversation and check (✓) all the things that Karl can do <u>now</u>.*

- ☑ **1.** answer the phones
- ☐ **2.** speak another language
- ☐ **3.** do spreadsheets
- ☐ **4.** type 50 words per minute
- ☐ **5.** design a monthly newsletter
- ☐ **6.** schedule appointments
- ☐ **7.** drive
- ☐ **8.** dance

EXERCISE 7: Pronunciation

A | *Read and listen to the Pronunciation Note.*

> **Pronunciation Note**
>
> In statements:
>
> - *can* is **NOT stressed**, and it's pronounced /kən/
> - *can't* is **stressed**, and it's pronounced /kænt/
>
> EXAMPLES: I **can** dance, but I **can't** sing.
>
> She **can** speak French, but she **can't** speak Spanish.

B | *Listen to the statements. Circle the words you hear.*

1. I <u>can / can't</u> dance.

2. They <u>can / can't</u> speak Chinese.

3. He <u>can / can't</u> fly a plane.

4. We <u>can / can't</u> understand you.

5. She <u>can / can't</u> swim, but she <u>can / can't</u> dive.

6. He <u>can / can't</u> drive.

C | *Listen again and repeat the statements.*

EXERCISE 8: Information Gap: Can they do the tango?

*Students at Carmen's Dance Studio are preparing for a dance recital in June. It is now the end of April. Can students do all the dances featured in the recital at this time? Work in pairs (A and B). **Student A,** follow the instructions on this page. **Student B,** turn to page 188 and follow the instructions there.*

1. Ask your partner for the information you need to complete the schedule below.

   EXAMPLE: **A:** Can the students do the Argentine tango?
   B: No, they can't. But they'll be able to do it by the end of May.

2. Your schedule has the information your partner needs to complete his or her schedule. Answer your partner's questions.

   EXAMPLE: **B:** Can they do the cha-cha?
   A: Yes, they can. They could do it in March.

CARMEN'S DANCE STUDIO
Schedule of Dance Classes

Dances	March	April	May
Argentine tango			✔
Cha-cha	✔		
Fox-trot			
Hip-hop		✔	
Hustle			✔
Mambo			
Merengue	✔		
Salsa			✔
Swing			
Tango		✔	
Waltz			

When you are finished, compare schedules. Are they the same?

EXERCISE 9: Ask and Answer

A | *Work in small groups. Imagine you are planning a class presentation. Look at the list of skills and find someone who can do each one. Add to the list.*

- do research online
- create a website
- make charts and graphs
- do a spreadsheet
- photocopy handouts
- take photographs

- videotape the presentation
- interview people
- give a PowerPoint presentation
- _____
- _____
- _____

EXAMPLE: **A:** Can you do research online?
             B: Sure. But I can't create a website yet.
             C: I can do that. I just learned how.

B | *Report back to the class.*

EXAMPLE: **A:** Theo and Alicia can do research online, but . . .

EXERCISE 10: Writing

A | *Write one or two paragraphs about a person who is or was successful in spite of some kind of disability or problem. Choose someone you know or a famous person.*

EXAMPLE: My aunt had a difficult childhood. She grew up in a poor family. When she was 16, she quit school because she had to stay home and help her mother take care of her younger brothers and sisters. She made all the meals, and by the time she was 18, she could cook and bake very well. She even won a local baking contest. People began ordering cakes from her, and before long she was able to save enough money to start her own small business . . .

B | *Check your work. Use the Editing Checklist.*

Editing Checklist

Did you use . . . ?
- [ ] *can* or *can't* for present ability
- [ ] *be able to* for present ability when this ability comes after hard work
- [ ] *can* or *will be able to* for future ability when you are talking about plans or arrangements
- [ ] *could* or *was/were able to* for past ability
- [ ] the base form of the verb after *can*, *could* or *be able to*

1. The schedule below has the information your partner needs to complete his or her schedule. Answer your partner's questions.

   EXAMPLE: **A:** Can the students do the Argentine tango?
   B: No, they can't. But they'll be able to do it by the end of May.

2. Ask your partner for the information you need to complete your schedule.

   EXAMPLE: **B:** Can they do the cha-cha?
   A: Yes, they can. They could do it in March.

CARMEN'S DANCE STUDIO
Schedule of Dance Classes

Dances	March	April	May
Argentine tango			✓
Cha-cha	✓		
Fox-trot		✓	
Hip-hop			
Hustle			
Mambo		✓	
Merengue			
Salsa			
Swing	✓		
Tango			
Waltz	✓		

When you are finished, compare schedules. Are they the same?

A | Circle the letter of the correct answer to complete each sentence.

1. How many languages can you _____?
   a. speak   **b.** speaks   **c.** speaking

2. After a lot of practice, Steve _____ win his first tennis game.
   a. could   **b.** can   **c.** was able to

3. Keep trying and you _____ do the tango in a just few weeks.
   a. 're able to   **b.** 'll be able to   **c.** can

4. Sorry, I _____ pick up the concert tickets tomorrow.
   a. couldn't   **b.** not able to   **c.** can't

5. They worked hard—that's why they _____ win first prize last night.
   a. able to   **b.** were able to   **c.** can

B | Complete the paragraph with **can, could,** or **be able to** and the verbs in parentheses.
Use **can** or **could** when possible. Choose between affirmative and negative.

As a boy, Carlos Acosta _____ out of trouble, but he sure _____
                              1. (stay)   2. (kick)
a soccer ball. Break dancing (a type of street dancing) was his other hobby. His father

_____ Carlos off the streets, so he put him in ballet school. Carlos had problems
        3. (keep)
at first, but by age 16, he _____ first place in an international dance competition.
                                          4. (win)
Today, Acosta _____ still _____ beautifully. He _____
                                                        5. (dance)   6. (jump)
higher than any other dancer, and he _____ in the air longer too. But, now in
                                                        7. (stay)
his 30s, he _____ much longer. In a few years, he'll return to Cuba. There he
              8. (perform)
_____ his own dance company, and he and his wife _____ a family.
        9. (start)   10. (raise)

C | Find and correct five mistakes.

A: I can't to see the stage. The man in front of me is very tall.

B: Let's change seats. You be able to see from this seat.

A: Thanks. I don't want to miss anything. I no can believe what a great dancer Acosta is.

B: I know. He was so good as a kid that he could win a break dancing contest before he was nine.

A: I didn't know he was a street dancer! Well, I'm glad you were abled to get tickets.

Permission: *Can, Could, May, Do you mind if*
ROOMMATES

STEP 1 GRAMMAR IN CONTEXT

Before You Read

Look at the cartoons. Discuss the questions.

1. Where are these people?
2. What is their relationship?
3. What do two of the people want?
4. How do the others feel about it?

Read

Read the article about getting along with a roommate.

ALWAYS ASK FIRST

Oh, you're awake! **Can I wear** your new jacket today?

Could my friend **stay** here for a few weeks?

Heather immediately liked Tara, her neat, non-smoking college roommate. Their first week together was great. But the second week, the cookies from Heather's mom disappeared. Tara didn't ask Heather, "**Could I have** one?" She just assumed it was all right. Tara's friends always helped themselves to[1] food without asking permission. The third week, Tara looked annoyed whenever Heather's friends stopped by to visit. Heather never asked Tara "Hey, **do you mind if** they **hang out** here for a while?" At home, Heather's friends were always welcome. By October, Heather and Tara weren't speaking to each other. Luckily, their dorm counselor was able to help them fix their relationship with three simple rules.

1. Always ask permission before you touch your roommate's stuff. Say: "My computer isn't working. **Could I use** yours for a few hours?"
2. Establish times when it's OK to have visitors. If it's not "visiting hours," ask your roommate's permission: "**Can** Luis and Ming-Hwa **work** here tonight? We're doing a presentation in class tomorrow."
3. Try to solve problems. Say: "Your music is too loud for me, but you **can borrow** my headphones."

Follow these guidelines, and who knows? You may gain a happier roommate *and* a good friend.

---

[1] **help yourself to something:** to take something you want without permission

After You Read

A | Vocabulary: *Circle the letter of the word or phrase that best completes each sentence.*

1. Ahmed is **annoyed** at his roommate. He is _____ him.
   a. a little angry at
   b. very pleased with
   c. surprised by

2. I have no **guidelines** for this report. Could you give me some _____?
   a. paper
   b. instructions
   c. time

3. Marcia is very **neat**. Her room is always _____.
   a. full of friends
   b. bright
   c. organized

4. I just **assumed** it was OK to eat the cookies because you _____.
   a. told me it was OK
   b. usually don't mind
   c. hid them in your closet

5. We **established** those rules. That means we both _____ to follow them.
   a. agreed
   b. tried
   c. refused

6. For his **presentation**, Raoul _____ about getting along with roommates.
   a. showed a video to his class
   b. talked to his dorm counselor
   c. emailed his best friend

B | Comprehension: *Read each question. Check (✓) all the correct answers.*

Who...?	Heather	Tara	Counselor
1. took the cookies without permission	☐	☐	☐
2. had a lot of visitors without asking first	☐	☐	☐
3. was annoyed	☐	☐	☐
4. helped establish some guidelines	☐	☐	☐

PERMISSION: *CAN, COULD, MAY, DO YOU MIND IF*

Yes /No Questions: *Can / Could / May*

Can / Could / May*	Subject	Base Form of Verb	
Can Could May	I he she we they	stay	here?

Short Answers

Affirmative	Negative
Certainly. Of course. Sure. No problem.	Sorry, but . . .

Can, could, and *may* are modals. Modals have only one form. They do not have *-s* in the third-person singular.

Wh- Questions: *Can / Could / May*

Wh-Word	Can / Could / May	Subject	Base Form of Verb
When	can could may	I he she we they	call?

Statements: *Can / May*

Subject	Can / May (not)	Base Form of Verb	
You He She	can (not) may (not)	stay	here.

Contractions*

cannot OR can not	=	can't

*There is no contraction for *may not*.

Questions: *Do you mind if*

Do you mind if	Subject	Verb	
Do you mind if	I we they	stay	here?
	he she it	stays	

Short Answers

Affirmative	Negative
Not at all. **No**, I **don't**. Go right ahead.	Sorry, but . . .

GRAMMAR NOTES

1   Use the modals **can**, **could**, and **may** to ask **permission**.

     a. Notice that when you use **could** for permission, it is <u>not the past</u>.

     b. **May** is much <u>more formal and polite</u> than *can* and *could*. We sometimes use it when we are speaking to a person in authority (for example, a teacher, police officer, doctor, librarian, counselor, etc.).

     c. We often say **please** when we ask permission. Notice the word order.

- **Can** I **borrow** your book?   LESS FORMAL

- **Could** he **come** tomorrow?

- **May** we **leave**, Professor Lee?   MORE FORMAL
  (student speaking to teacher)

- **Could** I **ask** a question, **please**? OR
- **Could** I **please ask** a question?

---

2   Use the expression **Do you mind if** to ask **permission** when an action may <u>annoy or inconvenience</u> someone.

     BE CAREFUL! Do NOT use **please** with *Do you mind if*.

A: **Do you mind if I clean up** later?
B: Yes, actually, I do. I hate to see a mess in the kitchen.

NOT: Do you mind ~~please~~ if I ask a question?

---

3   There are several **ways to answer** when someone asks permission.

     a. We usually use <u>informal expressions</u> instead of modals in answers.

     b. When we use a <u>modal</u> in an answer, we almost always use **can**. We do NOT use *could*, and we rarely use *may* in short answers.

     BE CAREFUL! When the response to a question with **Do you mind if** is **Not at all**, or **No, I don't**, we're really saying: *It's OK*. We're giving permission.

     c. When we **refuse permission**, we usually <u>apologize</u> and give an <u>explanation</u>.

A: **Could** I close the window?
B: *Sure*. OR *Of course*. OR *Go ahead*.

A: **Could** I borrow this pencil?
B: *Yes*, of course you **can**.
     NOT: Yes, of course you ~~could~~.

A: **May** I see your notes?
B: *Sure* you **can**. RARE: *Yes*, you **may**.

A: **Do you mind if** Ian comes over tonight?
B: *Not at all*. OR *No, I don't*.
     (It's OK for Ian to come over tonight.)

A: **Can** I please use your computer?
B: *I'm sorry*, but I need it today.

REFERENCE NOTES

For general information on **modals**, see Unit 13, Grammar Note 2, on page 179.
Can and **could** are also used for **ability** (see Unit 13) and for **requests** (see Unit 15).
For a list of **modals and their functions**, see Appendix 19 on page A-8.

EXERCISE 1: Discover the Grammar

Read the quiz. Underline all the modals and expressions for permission. Then if you'd like to, you can take the quiz. The answers are below.

Are You a Good Roommate?

Take this short quiz and find out.

1. You want to use your roommate's computer.
   You say:
   ○ **a.** I may use your computer tonight.
   ○ **b.** <u>Can I use</u> your computer tonight?
   ○ **c.** I'm using your computer tonight.

2. You don't have any food in the house.
   You say:
   ○ **a.** Can you make dinner for me?
   ○ **b.** I don't mind eating some of your food.
   ○ **c.** Do you mind if I have some of your food?

3. You may not have time to wash the dishes tonight.
   You say:
   ○ **a.** Could you wash the dishes?
   ○ **b.** I can't wash the dishes.
   ○ **c.** Can I wash the dishes tomorrow?

4. Your roommate asks you: "Could my best friend stay overnight?"
   You answer:
   ○ **a.** Can she stay in a hotel instead?
   ○ **b.** Sure she can!
   ○ **c.** I'm sure she could, but I don't want her to!

5. You can find nothing to wear to the party next Friday.
   You say:
   ○ **a.** Could I borrow your new sweater?
   ○ **b.** I may borrow your new sweater.
   ○ **c.** You could lend me your new sweater.

6. You want to hang your favorite poster in your dorm room.
   You say:
   ○ **a.** Could I hang my poster here?
   ○ **b.** Maybe you could hang my poster here.
   ○ **c.** I assume I can hang my poster here.

ANSWERS: 1. b, **2.** c, **3.** c, **4.** b, **5.** a, **6.** a

EXERCISE 2: Questions and Answers

(Grammar Notes 1–3)

Look at the signs. Complete each conversation. Use the words in parentheses and the correct pronouns. Write appropriate short answers. There can be more than one correct short answer.

1. **PIERRE:** ___Do you mind if___ I ___eat___ my lunch
   a. (do you mind if / eat)
   here while I get on the Internet? I'll be neat.

   ASSISTANT: ___Sorry___. Please look at the sign.
   b.

2. **SÉBASTIEN:** Those guys next door are making a lot of noise!

   _____ they _____ that?
   a. (can / do)
   NATHANIEL: _____. According to the guidelines, it's
   b.
   OK to play music now. It's 8:00 A.M.

   SÉBASTIEN: Well, _____ I _____ your
   c. (can / borrow)
   earplugs? I have to prepare for my English presentation.

3. **CARMEN:** _____ we _____ our bikes
   a. (may / ride)
   on this path?

   GUARD: _____.
   b.

4. **DONOVAN:** _____ I _____ my dog next
   a. (could / bring)
   semester? My roommate doesn't mind.

   COUNSELOR: _____. But some of the other dorms
   b.
   allow pets.

5. **GABRIELLE:** _____ I _____ my cell
   a. (may / use)
   phone in here?

   LIBRARIAN: _____. People get really annoyed by cell
   b.
   phone conversations.

Computer Lab

Quiet
Hours
11:00 p.m. - 7:00 a.m.
Sunday - Saturday

Kent Hall

EXERCISE 3: Questions and Answers

(Grammar Notes 1–3)

Heather and her roommate Tara are planning a party in Kent Hall. Use the words in parentheses to ask for permission. Answer the questions.

1. Tara's friend Troy is in town. She wants him to come to the party.

    TARA: *Do you mind if Troy comes to the party?* _____
                                (do you mind if)

    HEATHER: *Not at all.* _____ I'd love to meet him.

2. Heather wants to borrow her roommate's black sweater.

    HEATHER: I have nothing to wear. _____
                                       (can)

    TARA: _____ I'm planning to wear it myself!

3. Tara's sister is coming from out of town. Tara wants her to stay in their room.

    TARA: _____
                                    (do you mind if)

    HEATHER: _____ She can sleep on the couch.

4. Heather and Tara would like to have the party in the dormitory lounge. Heather asks her dormitory counselor for permission.

    HEATHER: _____
                                    (may)

    COUNSELOR: _____ It's available next Friday. We just have to

    establish some guidelines.

5. Heather and Tara would like to hang decorations from the ceiling of the lounge.

    HEATHER: _____
                                    (could)

    COUNSELOR: _____ Fire regulations won't allow it.

6. Heather and Tara want the party to go until midnight.

    HEATHER: _____
                                    (could)

    COUNSELOR: _____ Quiet hours start at 11:00 on Friday.

7. Tara wants to play some of her friend Erica's CDs at the party.

    TARA: _____
                                    (could)

    ERICA: _____ Which ones should I bring?

8. It's Friday night. A student wants to study in the lounge.

    STUDENT: _____
                                    (can)

    HEATHER: _____ We're having a party. Want to join us?

EXERCISE 4: Editing

Read Emil's English test. There are seven mistakes in the use of **can, could, may,** *and* **do you mind if.** *The first mistake is already corrected. Find and correct six more.*

Class: _English 102_   **Name:** _Emil Kuhn_

Directions: These conversations take place on a train. Find and correct the mistakes.

1. **A:** May we board the train now?

   B: Sorry, you ~~couldn't~~ *can't* board until 12:30.

2. **A:** Can he comes on the train with me?

   B: Sorry. Only passengers can board.

3. **A:** Do you mind if I'm sitting here?

   B: No, I don't. My friend is sitting here.

4. **A:** Could I looked at your newspaper?

   B: Yes, of course you could.

5. **A:** Do you mind if my son play his computer game?

   B: No, not at all. It won't disturb me.

   A: Thanks.

STEP 4 COMMUNICATION PRACTICE

EXERCISE 5: Listening

A | *Read the list. Then listen to the short conversations. Who's speaking? Listen again and write the letter of the people next to the number of each conversation.*

Conversation	People
_d_ 1.	**a.** roommate and roommate
____ 2.	**b.** child and parent
____ 3.	**c.** travel agent and customer
____ 4.	**d.** driver and police officer
____ 5.	**e.** boyfriend and girlfriend's mother
____ 6.	**f.** employee and employer
____ 7.	**g.** student and teacher

B | *Listen again to the conversations and decide if permission was given or refused. Check (✓) the correct column.*

Conversation	Permission Given	Permission Refused
1.	✓	☐
2.	☐	☐
3.	☐	☐
4.	☐	☐
5.	☐	☐
6.	☐	☐
7.	☐	☐

EXERCISE 6: Pronunciation

A | *Read and listen to the Pronunciation Note.*

Pronunciation Note

In **informal conversation**, we often **link** the modals **can**, **could**, and **may** with the pronouns *I* and **he** in questions:

can I	→	"cani"	can he	→	"can'e"	(drop the *h* in *he*)
could I	→	"couldi"	could he	→	"could'e"	(drop the *h* in *he*)
may I	→	"mayi"				

EXAMPLES: **Can I** open the window? → "**Cani** open the window?"
Could he have a cookie? → "**Could'e** have a cookie?"

We do **NOT link** these modals with *you*, *she*, *we*, or *they*.

B | *Listen to the questions. Circle the word you hear.*

1. Can <u>he / she</u> come with us?

2. <u>Could / Can</u> I ask a question?

3. Can <u>he / she</u> sit over there?

4. May <u>she / we</u> call you tonight?

5. Could <u>he / she</u> get a ride with you?

C | *Listen again and repeat the questions.*

EXERCISE 7: Problem Solving

Work in small groups. Read the situations and decide what to say. Think of as many things to say as possible.

1. You have a small apartment. Two of your friends are coming to visit your town for a week, and they want to stay with you. What can you say to your roommate?

   EXAMPLES: Do you mind if Anton and Eva stay here for a week?
   Could Anton practice his guitar in the evening?
   Can Eva keep her bike in the hall?

2. You're visiting some good friends. The weather is very cold, but they don't seem to mind. Their windows are open and the heat is off. You're freezing.

3. You're at a concert with some friends. You like the performer very much. You have your camcorder and your camera with you. Sometimes this performer talks to fans and signs programs after the concert.

4. You have formed a study group with some classmates. You want to use a classroom on Thursday evenings to study. You would like to use one of your school's video cams to practice a presentation. Some of your classmates come directly from work. They would like to eat their dinner in the classroom. What can you say to your teacher?

EXERCISE 8: Role Play: *Could I . . . ?*

Work with a partner. Read the situations. Take turns being Student A and Student B.

Student A	**Student B**
1. You were absent from class yesterday. Student B, your classmate, always takes good notes.	1. Student A is in your class. You're always willing to help your classmates.

   EXAMPLE: **A:** Can I copy your notes from class yesterday?
   B: Sure. Here they are.
   A: Could I call you tonight if I have questions?
   B: Of course.

Student A	**Student B**
2. You're at work. You have a terrible headache. Student B is your boss.	2. Student A is your employee. You have a lot of work for Student A to do today.
3. You're a teenager. You and your friend want to travel to another city to see a concert. You want to borrow your mother's (Student B's) car. Your friend has a license and wants to drive.	3. Student A is your son / daughter. You like this friend, and you have no objection to lending him or her the car. However, you want the friend to be careful.
4. Student B has invited you to a small party. At the last minute, your two cousins show up. They have nothing to do the night of the party.	4. Your party is a small party for a few of your close friends. It's also at a restaurant, and you have already arranged for a certain number of people to attend.

EXERCISE 9: Writing

A | *Write two short notes asking permission. Choose situations from Exercise 8 or use situations of your own. Then exchange notes with two classmates. Write responses to your classmates' notes.*

EXAMPLES:

Ana,
I missed class yesterday.
Can I copy your notes?
Melissa

Sorry, Melissa, but
I missed class too!
Ana

B | *Check your work. Use the Editing Checklist.*

Editing Checklist

Did you . . . ?

☐ use the base form of the verb after **can**, **could**, and **may**

☐ use **can** and **may** (not *could*) in your answers

☐ apologize and give an explanation if you refused permission

A | *Circle the correct words to complete the questions.*

1. Can my brother <u>come / comes</u> to class with me?

2. <u>Could / Do</u> you mind if I call you at home?

3. Could I <u>borrow / borrowed</u> a pen?

4. Do you mind <u>if / when</u> I ask a question?

5. May I <u>shut please / please shut</u> the door?

B | *Read the situations in parentheses. Then complete the questions to ask permission.*

1. Could _____?
   (You want to borrow a pen.)

2. Can _____?
   (Your sister wants to leave.)

3. Do you mind _____?
   (You want to open a window.)

4. Could _____?
   (You and a friend want to come early.)

5. May _____?
   (You want to ask a question.)

C | *Find and correct ten mistakes.*

1. **A:** Do you mind if I changed the date of our next meeting?

   B: Yes, I do. When would you like to meet?

2. **A:** Could I calling you tonight?

   B: Sorry, but you couldn't. I won't be home.

3. **A:** Mom, I may have some more ice cream?

   B: No you mayn't. You've already had a lot. You'll get sick.

4. **A:** Do you mind if my son turn on the TV?

   B: Not at all. I can't study with the TV on.

5. **A:** Can my sister borrows your bike?

   B: Could I letting you know tomorrow?

   A: Sure. No problem.

Requests: *Can, Could, Will, Would, Would you mind*

MESSAGES

Before You Read

Look at the title. Discuss the questions.

1. What do you think it means? Check the list of abbreviations on the next page.
2. Why do people use abbreviations in text messages?
3. Do you use text abbreviations in another language?
4. Do you prefer text messages or email? Why?

Read

Read the email and text messages.

Messages 4 u!

From: RheaJones@island.net
To: MarciaJones@dataline.com
Subject: Requests

Marcia, dear—
Can you **drive** me to the Burtons after work today? They've invited me for dinner. Oh, and **will** you **pick up** something special at the bakery before you come? I told them I'd bring dessert.

Thanks, honey.—Mom

P.S. Here's a little cartoon to cheer you up. :)

"*Would you mind talking to me for a while? I forgot my cell phone.*"

Mom,
I'm sorry, but I can't tonight. I'm working late. Do you want me to ask your favorite son-in-law if he can drive you?
M.
P.S. Thanks for the cartoon. Very funny!

Jsanchez Hi, Marcia. I'll be out of town until Thursday. **Would** you please **copy** and **distribute** the monthly sales report? Thank you. I really appreciate your help! —John

Mjones Hi John. I'd be glad to. I'll text you after I distribute them. Have a good trip. —Marcia

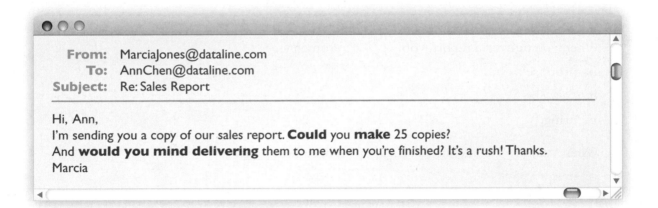

From: MarciaJones@dataline.com
To: AnnChen@dataline.com
Subject: Re: Sales Report

Hi, Ann,
I'm sending you a copy of our sales report. **Could** you **make** 25 copies?
And **would you mind delivering** them to me when you're finished? It's a rush! Thanks.
Marcia

Ejones Mom – I need a ride home from soccer practice 2day. Plz CMB.

Mjones Hi Ethan! I cn pick u up but I'll be late.

Ejones That's OK. CUL8R and TY.

Mjones Jody—**Will** u **cook** dinner 2nite? I'll be home @ 7.

Jjones OK, Mom. I'll get some lasagna out of the freezer.

Mjones TY Jody. ILU.

Jjones ILU2.

Some Abbreviations for Text Messages*			

Abbreviation	Meaning	Abbreviation	Meaning
@	at	CUL8R	See you later
2	to, too	LU	Love you
4	for	Plz	Please
CMB	call me back	TY	Thank you
cn	can	u	you

* We use these abbreviations in informal messages to friends and family.

After You Read

A | Vocabulary: *Circle the letter of the word or phrase that best completes each sentence.*

1. When you **text** someone, you _____ to the person's cell phone.
   a. send photos
   b. write a message
   c. record a message

2. When you **deliver** a report, you _____ it to someone.
   a. promise
   b. describe
   c. bring

3. When you **cheer** someone **up**, that person becomes _____.
   a. upset
   b. happy
   c. smart

4. When you **distribute** something, you _____.
   a. give something to each person in a group
   b. organize it by date
   c. keep a copy on your computer

5. When you **appreciate** what someone does for you, you feel _____.
   a. worried
   b. sorry
   c. thankful

B | Comprehension: *Check (✓)* **True** *or* **False**. *Correct the false statements.*

	True	False
1. Marcia's mother sent Marcia a text message.	☐	☐
2. John needs copies of the sales report.	☐	☐
3. Ann is going to distribute the copies.	☐	☐
4. Marcia is going to make the copies.	☐	☐
5. Ethan needs a ride home from soccer practice.	☐	☐
6. Jody is going to cook dinner tonight.	☐	☐

REQUESTS: *CAN, COULD, WILL, WOULD, WOULD YOU MIND*

Questions: *Can / Could / Will / Would*				Short Answers		
Can / Could / Will / Would*	*You*	**Base Form of Verb**		**Affirmative**	**Negative**	
Can **Could** **Will** **Would**	you	**distribute**	this report for me?	Sure. Certainly. No problem. Of course. I'd be glad to.	I'm sorry, but	I **can't**.
		drive	me to the doctor?			
		pick up	some groceries?		I'm afraid	

*Can, could, will, and *would* are modals. Modals do not have *-s* in the third-person singular.

Questions: *Would you mind*				Short Answers		
Would you mind	**Gerund**			**Affirmative**	**Negative**	
Would you mind	**distributing**	this report for me?		Not at all. I'd be glad to. No problem. Of course not.	I'm sorry, but	I **can't**.
	driving	me to the doctor?				
	picking up	some groceries?			I'm afraid	

GRAMMAR NOTES

1

Use the modals *can*, *could*, *will*, and *would* to make a **request** (ask someone to do something).

- **Can** you **turn on** the TV?
- **Will** you **bring** dessert?

a. *Could* and *would* are <u>more polite</u> than *can* and *will*. We use *could* and *would* to <u>soften requests</u>.

- **Could** you **text** me?
- **Would** you **close** the door?

b. You can also use *please* to make the request <u>more polite</u>. Notice the word order.

- **Would** you **close** the door, *please*? OR
- **Would** you *please* **close** the door?

2

In **affirmative answers** to requests, we usually use <u>expressions</u> such as *sure, certainly, of course,* and *no problem.*

A: **Would** you **shut** the window, please?
B: *Sure.* OR *I'd be glad to.* OR *Of course.*

In **negative answers**, we usually <u>apologize</u> and give an <u>explanation</u>.

A: **Could** you **deliver** this to Ron, please?
B: *I'm sorry, I can't.* I'm expecting a call.

BE CAREFUL! Do NOT use *would* or *could* in response to polite requests.

NOT: Sure I ~~would~~.
NOT: I'm sorry, I ~~couldn't~~.

(continued on next page)

3 We also use **Would you mind** + **gerund** (verb + -ing) to make <u>polite requests</u>. It is even more polite than *could* or *would*.

A: Would you mind waiting? Mr. Caras is in a meeting.

BE CAREFUL! When we <u>answer</u> this type of request with **Not at all** or **Of course not**, it means that we will do what the person requests.

B: Not at all. OR **Of course not.**
(OK. I'll do it.)

In **negative answers**, we usually <u>apologize</u> and give an <u>explanation</u>.

B: I'm sorry, I can't. I have another appointment in half an hour.

REFERENCE NOTES

For general information on **modals**, see Unit 13, Grammar Note 2, on page 179.
Can and **could** are also used for **ability** (see Unit 13) and for **permission** (see Unit 14).
Will is also used for the **future** (see Units 6 and 7).
For a list of **modals and their functions**, see Appendix 19 on page A-8.

STEP 3 FOCUSED PRACTICE

EXERCISE 1: Discover the Grammar

Mike's roommate, Jeff, is having problems today. Underline Jeff's requests. Then circle the letter of the appropriate response to each request.

1. Mike, <u>would you please drive me to Cal's Computer Shop?</u> I have to bring my computer in.
   a. Yes, I would. **(b.)** I'd be glad to.

2. Would you mind lending me five dollars? I'm getting paid tomorrow.
   a. Not at all. **b.** Yes.

3. Mike, can you lend me your laptop for a minute? I have to email my teacher.
   a. Sorry. I'm working on something. **b.** No, I can't.

4. Could you lock the door on your way out? My hands are full.
   a. Yes, I could. **b.** Sure.

5. Jody, can you tell Ethan to come to the phone? It's important.
   a. No problem. **b.** Not at all.

6. Will you pick up some milk on the way home this afternoon?
   a. No, I won't. **b.** I'm sorry, I can't. I'll be at work until 8:00.

7. Would you explain this text message from Jody? She uses weird abbreviations.
   a. I'd be glad to. **b.** No, I wouldn't.

EXERCISE 2: Requests

(Grammar Notes 1, 3)

A | *Look at the pictures. What is each person thinking? Write the letter of the correct thought from the box.*

a. Repair the copier.	d. ~~File these reports.~~	g. Buy some cereal.
b. Call back later.	e. Shut the door.	h. Wait for a few minutes.
c. Get that book.	f. Close the window.	i. Wash your cups and dishes.

1. ___d___

2. _____

3. _____

4. _____

5. _____

6. _____

7. _____

8. _____

9. _____

B | *What are the people in the pictures going to say? Complete their requests. Use the words in parentheses and the information from the pictures.*

1. _____Could you file these reports, please?_____ I've finished reading them.
   (could)

2. _____ I can't think with all that noise in the hall.
   (would)

3. _____ on the way home? We don't have any left.
   (will)

4. _____ It's freezing in here.
   (can)

5. _____ Mr. Rivera is still in a meeting.
   (would you mind)

6. _____ It's getting messy in here.
   (would you mind)

7. _____ I have to leave for a meeting now.
   (could)

8. _____ I can't reach it.
   (can)

9. _____ I need to make copies right away.
   (could)

EXERCISE 3: Requests and Answers

(Grammar Notes 1–3)

Write polite requests. Use **can, could, will, would,** *or* **would you mind** *and the correct form of the words in parentheses. Write appropriate answers.*

1. **MAN:** _____Would you mind lending me your cell phone_____? The battery in mine is dead.
   a. (lend me your cell phone)

   WOMAN: _____No problem_____. But I'm in a hurry.
   b.

   _____?
   c. (please / keep your conversation short)

   MAN: _____. I just need to text my friend.
   d.

2. **STUDENT:** Excuse me, Professor Ruiz. _____?
   a. (explain reflexive pronouns)

   I don't understand them.

   PROFESSOR: _____ right now. I'm expecting a
   b.

   call. _____?
   c. (come back in 20 minutes)

3. **WOMAN:** _____? It's blocking my driveway.
   a. (move your car)

   MAN: _____. I'll do it right away. I'm
   b.

   really sorry. I didn't notice.

4. **MANAGER:** _____? Our sales people need it for
   a. (please / distribute this report)

   their meeting this afternoon.

   ASSISTANT: _____. I can't leave my desk right
   b.

   now. But I can ask Marcia to do it.

EXERCISE 4: Editing

*Read Marcia Jones's response to an email message from her boss. (Her answers are in **red**.)*
There are eight mistakes in making and responding to requests. The first mistake is already
corrected. Find and correct seven more.

Date: 04-11-11   12:14:39 EST
From: MarciaJones@dataline.com
To: JohnSanchez@dataline.com
CC: AnnChen@dataline.com
Subject: sales meeting—Reply

>>><JohnSanchez@dataline.com>   04/11/1110:37 am>>>

The meetings are going well, but they have been extended a day. Could you ~~call please~~ *please call*

Doug Rogers to try to reschedule our sales meeting?

Not at all. I'll do it right away.

We'll need three extra copies of the monthly sales report. Would you ask Ann to take

care of that?

Yes, I would. (Ann—could you do this?)

I won't have time to return Emma Lopes's call this week. Would you mind to call her

and telling her I'll call her back next week?

No problem. Could you email me her phone number?

I hate to ask, but will you mind working on Saturday? We'll need the extra time to go

over the new information I've gotten.

Sorry, but I couldn't. My in-laws are coming for a visit. But Rob Lin says he can come

into the office to help out.

One last thing. I was going to pick up those new business cards, but I won't be back in

time. Would you mind asking the printer to deliver them to the office? I'd really

appreciate that.

Yes, I would. I'll call and ask him to do it right away.

And this will cheer you up—it looks like our office will receive the award for

Communication Excellence this year!

Great! Can I told everyone, or is it a secret?

EXERCISE 5: Listening

A | *Marcia Jones has planned a busy weekend. Read the list. Then listen to the conversations. Listen again and check (✓) the things that belong on her schedule.*

✓ **1.** take Jody to the dentist

☐ **2.** take the kids to the library

☐ **3.** babysit for Kelly's daughter

☐ **4.** go to Kelly's party

☐ **5.** go to the movies

☐ **6.** walk Mom's dog

☐ **7.** pick up the car at the garage

☐ **8.** go to the gym with John

B | *Listen again to the conversations and match each person with the correct information.*

Conversation 1. __d__ Jody   **a.** is going to a party on Saturday night

_____ Ethan   **b.** is going away on Sunday

Conversation 2. _____ Kelly   **c.** is going to the movies on Saturday night

_____ Marcia   **d.** has a dentist appointment on Saturday morning

_____ Ann   **e.** needs a ride to the gym on Saturday afternoon

Conversation 3. _____ Marcia's mother   **f.** is working on a report for school

Conversation 4. _____ John   **g.** sometimes babysits for Marcia

EXERCISE 6: Pronunciation

A | *Read and listen to the Pronunciation Note.*

Pronunciation Note

In **informal conversation**, we often pronounce *could you*, *would you*, *will you*, and *can you* "couldja," "wouldja," "willya," and "canya."

EXAMPLES: **Could you** call me after work? → "**Couldja** call me after work?"
Would you mind driving me home? → "**Wouldja** mind driving me home?"

B | *Listen to the short conversations. Notice the pronunciation of* **could you, would you, will you,** *and* **can you.**

1. **A: Would you** mind texting me when you get home?
   B: Not at all. I know you worry.

2. **A: Can you** lend me a pencil? I lost mine.
   B: Sorry, I can't. I only have one.

3. **A: Could you** explain this cartoon? I don't get it.
   B: No problem! It's a joke about cell phones.

4. **A: Will you** turn the TV down, please? I'm studying.
   B: Sure.

5. **A: Would you** email me a photo of the game?
   B: Sorry, I can't. I didn't have time to take one.

6. **A: Could you** help me with this math problem? I don't understand it.
   B: I'd be glad to.

C | *Listen again to the conversations and repeat the requests. Then practice the conversations with a partner. Take turns making the requests and answering them.*

EXERCISE 7: Making Plans

A | *Fill out your schedule for the weekend.*

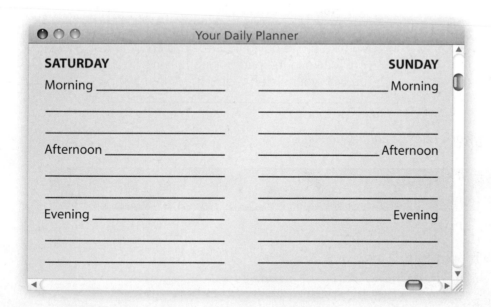

B | *Now work in small groups. Ask group members to help you with some of the things on your schedule.*

> EXAMPLE: **A:** Ali, can you drive me to the mall Saturday morning?
> **B:** Sorry, I can't. I'm working Saturday morning. OR Sure, I'd be glad to.
> **C:** Ria, would you mind . . .

EXERCISE 8: Writing

A | *Read the situations. For each one, write a text message making one or more requests.*

1. Your roommate is going away for the weekend. Your sister from out of town will be visiting you. Write a text message to your roommate.

   EXAMPLE:

   > TO: Viktor M 213-555-4321
   > ────────────────────────────
   > Hi Viktor. My sister is visiting this weekend. W%d u mind lending her your bike? I'd like 2 take her 4 a ride in the park. Thanks. —Kunio

2. You work at a restaurant on Mondays, Wednesdays, and Fridays. You have to go to the dentist, but the dentist can only see you on Wednesday. Write a text message to a co-worker.

3. You're in school. You have to leave class early in order to help your parents. Write a text message to a classmate.

4. You're going to have a party at your home. You've invited 20 people. Write a text message to your neighbor.

B | *Exchange text messages with a partner. Write responses to your partner's requests.*

   EXAMPLE:

   > TO: Kunio 213-555-0507
   > ────────────────────────────
   > Hi Kunio. I'm really sorry, but I can't. My bike broke down this week. U cn rent a bike in the park, though. Have fun with your sister! CUL8R. —Viktor

C | *Check your work. Use the Editing Checklist.*

Editing Checklist
Did you . . . ?
☐ use modals correctly
☐ use a gerund after **Would you mind** . . .
☐ use **please** correctly
☐ apologize and give an explanation when you said **No** to a request

Check your answers on page UR-4.

Do you need to review anything?

A | *Circle the correct words to complete the conversations.*

- **A:** Would you mind <u>to turn / turning</u> off the TV? I'm trying to read.
  1.
  B: <u>Yes, I would. / I'm sorry, I can't</u>. I need to watch the news for a homework assignment.
  2.
- **A:** Will you <u>please text / text please</u> me when you get home?
  3.
  B: <u>Not at all / No problem</u>. I'll probably be home by nine.
  4.
- **A:** Could you <u>picked /pick</u> up some dessert on the way home?
  5.
  B: <u>I'd be glad to / Yes, I could</u>. How about ice cream?
  6.

B | *Read the statements in parentheses. Then complete the questions to make requests.*

1. Would you mind _____?
   (Please lend me five dollars.)

2. Could _____?
   (I'd like you to drive me to school.)

3. Will _____?
   (Please explain this sentence to me.)

4. Can _____?
   (I'd like you to carry this suitcase for me.)

5. Would _____?
   (Please distribute the report.)

6. Would you mind _____?
   (I'd like you to walk the dog tonight.)

C | *Find and correct eight mistakes.*

- **JASON:** Hi Tessa. It's Jason. Could you taking some photos of the game today?

  TESSA: Sorry, Jason, but I couldn't. My camera is broken. Maybe Jeri can help.

- **JASON:** Hi Jeri. Would you came to the game today? I need someone to take photos.

  JERI: Jason, can you mind calling me back in a few minutes? I'm busy right now.

  JASON: Sorry, Jeri, I can't, but I'll email you. Would you give me please your email address?

  JERI: Not at all. It's Rainbows@local.net.

- **JERI:** Hi Jason, it's Jeri. I'm sending you those photos. You could call me when you get them?

  JASON: Thanks, Jeri. The photos are great. Now will teach me how to put them on Facebook?

Advice: *Should, Ought to, Had better*
INTERNET RULES

STEP 1 GRAMMAR IN CONTEXT

Before You Read

Do you communicate with people on the Internet? Discuss the questions.

1. Is it important to be polite on the Internet? Why or why not?
2. Do you behave differently online than face-to-face with people?
3. What are some rules you follow?

Read

🎧 *Read the article about being polite on the Internet. If you don't understand a cyber[1] word, look up its meaning on the next page.*

Netiquette 1💤1
by Emilia Poster

Email, bulletin boards, and chat rooms open up a new world of communication—and sometimes misunderstanding. To avoid problems, you **should know** these simple rules of netiquette:

😉 When **should** you **post** to a bulletin board or chat room? Newbies shouldn't jump in right away—they **ought to lurk** a little first. Look through old messages for answers to common questions. Many websites also have FAQs for basic information. After that, post when you have something new to say. You **should keep** your post short and simple.

😉 **Should** you **use** capital letters to make a strong statement? NO! A MESSAGE ALL IN CAPITAL LETTERS SEEMS LIKE SHOUTING. You **should follow** the normal rules for capital (big) and lowercase (small) letters.

😊 Did someone make you angry? Wait a minute! You**'d better not reply** right away. Count to 10 first. Don't flame another board or chat room member. You **should** never **forget** that people on the Internet are real people with real feelings.

😊 Emoticons can help avoid misunderstandings. You **should learn** how to use them to show your feelings.

😊 Internet safety is part of netiquette. When you post to a bulletin board or a chat room, you **should** always **protect** your identity by using a screen name. Never give your real name or other personal information.

Practice these five rules of netiquette, and most of your emoticons will be smileys! 🙂

---

[1] **cyber:** about computers or the Internet

Cyber Words

bulletin board an Internet site where members can post ideas about a special interest

chat room a site for online conversations in "real" time

emoticon a picture of a feeling, for example:

FAQ Frequently Asked Question

flame to send insulting messages to someone

lurk to read messages on a bulletin board but not post any messages

netiquette Internet etiquette (rules for polite behavior)

newbie (or newb) someone new to an Internet site

post to send messages to a bulletin board or chat room

"Got your e-mail, thanks."

After You Read

A | Vocabulary: *Complete the sentences with the words from the box.*

avoid	behavior	communication	identity	normal	protect

1. Never give your real _____ in a chat room. Always use a screen name.

2. It's _____ for newbies to lurk on a site before they post. Many people do that.

3. Don't go to websites where members often flame other members. _____ those groups. Find groups that practice good netiquette.

4. Do you want to improve your online _____? Emoticons will help others understand what you mean.

5. People's _____ in chat rooms is sometimes different from the way they act in real life.

6. _____ yourself on the Internet. Never tell anyone your passwords. People could steal your identity.

B | Comprehension: *Read the sentences. Check (✓)* **OK** *or* **Not OK.**

	OK	Not OK
1. Read some messages before you post.	☐	☐
2. Reply immediately when you're angry.	☐	☐
3. Use all capital letters in your posts.	☐	☐
4. Use emoticons to show feelings.	☐	☐
5. Use your real name in chat rooms.	☐	☐
6. Learn the rules of netiquette.	☐	☐
7. Flame people when you don't like their messages.	☐	☐
8. Write long, complicated messages.	☐	☐
9. Think about people's feelings when you post a message.	☐	☐

STEP 2 GRAMMAR PRESENTATION

ADVICE: *SHOULD, OUGHT TO, HAD BETTER*

Statements		
Subject	***Should / Ought to / Had better***	**Base Form of Verb**
I You He She We You They	**should (not)** **ought to** **had better (not)**	**reply**.

Contractions		
should not	=	**shouldn't**
had better	=	**'d better**

*Should and ought to are modals. Had better is similar to a modal.
These forms do not have -s in the third-person singular.

Yes / No Questions			Short Answers					
Should	**Subject**	**Base Form of Verb**	**Affirmative**			**Negative**		
Should	I he she we they	**reply**?	**Yes,**	you he she you they	**should.**	**No,**	you he she you they	**shouldn't.**

Wh- Questions				
Wh- Word	**Should**	**Subject**	**Base Form of Verb**	
How When Where	**should**	I he she we they	**send**	it?

GRAMMAR NOTES

1

Use the modals **should** and **ought to** to say that something is **advisable** (a good idea).

- Derek **should answer** that email.
- You **ought to read** the FAQ.

USAGE NOTES:

a. **Should** is much **more common** than *ought to*.

- You **should read** the FAQ.

b. We do NOT usually use the <u>negative</u> of *ought to* in American English. We use **shouldn't** instead.

- We **shouldn't post** long messages.
  NOT COMMON: We ought not to post long messages.

c. We often <u>soften advice</u> with **maybe**, **perhaps**, or **I think**.

- Ryan, **maybe** you **shouldn't spend** so much time on the Internet.

2

Use **had better** (an expression similar to a modal) for **strong advice**—when you believe that something bad will happen if the person does not follow your advice.

- Kids, you**'d better get** offline now or you won't have time for your homework.

USAGE NOTE: The full form *had better* is very formal. We usually use the **contraction**.

- You**'d better choose** a screen name.
  NOT COMMON: You had better choose a screen name.

The <u>negative</u> of *had better* is **had better not**. Notice the word order.

- You**'d better not use** your real name.
  NOT: You ~~had not better~~ use your real name.

BE CAREFUL! *Had better* always refers to the **present** or the **future**, never to the past (even though it uses the word *had*).

- You**'d better not call** them **now**. They're probably sleeping.
- You**'d better post** that **tomorrow** or it'll be late.

3

Use **should** for **questions**. We do not usually use *ought to* or *had better* for questions.

- When **should** I **sign on**?

You can use **should** in **short answers**, but we often use other <u>expressions</u>.

A: **Should I join** this chat room?
B: Yes, you **should**. It's fun.

OR

Why not? Good idea!

(continued on next page)

4 | In **very informal** notes, emails, text messages, and Internet posts, we often use "**oughta**" instead of *ought to* and we use ***better*** instead of *had better*.

BE CAREFUL! Do NOT use these forms in more **formal** writing. Use ***ought to*** and ***had better*** or ***'d better***.

• Newbie, don't post so soon. You **oughta** read the netiquette rules first. You **better not** just jump in.
(informal Internet post)

Q: When should I start to post?
Not: **A:** You ~~oughta~~ read the netiquette rules first. You ~~better not~~ just jump in.
(formal FAQ for the site)

REFERENCE NOTES

For general information on **modals**, see Unit 13, Grammar Note 2, on page 179.
For a list of **modals and their functions**, see Appendix 19 on page A-8.

STEP 3 FOCUSED PRACTICE

EXERCISE 1: Discover the Grammar

Read the posts to an online bulletin board for high school students. Underline the words that give or ask for advice.

Subject: HELP!
From: Hothead

MY BRAIN IS EXPLODING!!! SAVE ME!! <u>What should I do</u>? I'm taking all honors courses this year, and I'm on the debate team, in the school congress, and on the soccer team. OH! And, I'd better not forget piano lessons! I'm so busy I shouldn't even be online now. 😟

From: Tweety

First of all, you should stop shouting. You'll feel better. Then you really ought to ask yourself, "Why am I doing all this?" Is it for you, or are you trying to please somebody else?

From: Loki

Tweety's right, Hothead. Do you really want to do all that stuff? No? You'd better not do it then. You'll burn out before you graduate. 😜

From: gud4me

You're such a loser. You should get a life. I mean a NORMAL life. Do you have any friends? Do you ever just sit around and do nothing?

From: Tweety

Hey, gud4me, no flaming allowed! That's bad cyber behavior. We really shouldn't fight—it never helps communication. Try to help or keep quiet. 🙂

EXERCISE 2: Statements with *Should, Ought to,* and *Had better*   *(Grammar Notes 1–2)*

Read the posts to a chat room about learning English. Complete the posts. Use the correct form (affirmative or negative) of the words in parentheses. Use contractions when possible.

curly: I think I _____*should watch*_____ more movies to improve my English. Any ideas?
            1. (should / watch)

usedit: I loved *The Uninvited*. But you _____ it if you don't like
                                              2. (had better / rent)

scary films.

agurl: That's right. And you _____ the remote in your hand. That
                                    3. (had better / keep)

way you can fast-forward through the scary parts.

592XY: I think you _____ *Groundhog Day*. The same thing
                            4. (ought to / see)

happens again and again. It's an old movie, but it's great listening practice—and it's funny!

pati: You _____ the English subtitles. They really help.
                  5. (should / turn on)

usedit: But you _____ the subtitles right away. First you
                         6. (should / use)

_____ a few times. That's what rewind buttons are for!
    7. (should / listen)

592XY: Good advice. And you really _____ a plot summary before
                                           8. (ought to / read)

you watch. You can find one online. It's so much easier when you know the story.

agurl: Curly, you're a math major, right? Then you really _____
                                                                  9. (ought to / watch)

The Da Vinci Code. It's about solving a mystery with math clues.

curly: Thanks, guys. Those are great ideas. But you _____ me any
                                                            10. (had better / give)

more advice, or I'll never work on my other courses!

EXERCISE 3: Statements with *Should*, *Ought to*, and *Had better*   (Grammar Notes 1–2)

Rewrite the Internet safety tips. Use **should**, **ought to**, *or* **had better**. *Choose between affirmative and negative.*

> **The Internet is a wonderful place to visit and hang out.**
> **Here are some tips to make your trip there a safe one!**

1. **I often use my real name online. Is that a problem?**

   Yes! *You should always use a screen name.*
   _____
   (Always use a screen name.)
   Protect your identity!

2. **Someone in my chat group just asked for my address.**

   _____
   (Don't give out any personal information.)
   People can use it to steal your identity and your money.

3. **My brother wants my password to check out a group before joining.**

   _____
   (Don't give it to anyone.)
   Not even your brother! He might share it, and then people can steal your information.

4. **I sent a file to someone, and she told me it had a virus.**

   _____
   (Get virus protection and use it.)
   A virus can hurt your computer and destroy important files (and other people's too).

5. **I update my virus protection every month. Is that really necessary?**

   Yes! _____
   (Keep your virus protection up-to-date.)
   Remember: *Old* virus protection is *no* virus protection!

6. **I got an email about a home-based business. I could make $15,000 a month.**

   _____
   (Don't believe any "get rich quick" offers.)
   They sound good, but people almost always lose money.

7. **I got an interesting email. I don't know who sent it, but it's got a file attached.**

   _____
   (Don't open any email attachments from strangers.)
   They could contain dangerous viruses.

8. **The Internet sounds too dangerous for me!**

   Not really. _____,
   (Be careful!)
   but enjoy yourself—it's an exciting world out there!

EXERCISE 4: Questions and Short Answers with *Should* (Grammar Note 3)

Complete the posts to an online bulletin board. Use the words from the box to complete the questions. Give short answers.

buy one online	forward the email	~~try to repair it~~
check the spelling	say to make them stop	use my birthday
flame him	start posting	use emoticons

1. **Q:** My computer is seven years old and has problems. _____*Should I try to repair it*_____?

   A: _____*No, you shouldn't*_____. That's very old for a computer! Buy a new one!

2. **Q:** I just joined an online discussion group. When _____?

   Right away?

   A: You should really just read for a while. It's always a good idea to "lurk" before you post.

3. **Q:** I just received a warning about a computer virus. The email says to tell everyone I know

   about it. _____?

   A: _____. These warnings are almost always false.

4. **Q:** I hate to go shopping, but I really need a jacket. _____?

   A: _____. It's safe. Just buy from a company you know.

5. **Q:** I type fast and make spelling mistakes. Is that bad? _____?

   A: _____. Use a spell checker! Mistakes are bad netiquette!

6. **Q:** My friends email me a lot of jokes. I don't want to hurt their feelings, but I *really* don't

   want to keep getting these jokes. What _____?

   A: You should be honest and say you are too busy to read them. These jokes can waste an

   awful lot of time!

7. **Q:** I always forget my password. _____ so I don't forget?

   A: _____. It's too easy to guess. Protect your identity.

8. **Q:** A newb on our board is asking dumb questions. _____?

   A: _____! Your behavior should be as polite online as offline.

9. **Q:** _____ in emails? Those smileys are awfully cute.

   A: Sure, go ahead. They're fun. But don't use them in business emails. ☺

EXERCISE 5: Editing

*Read the posts to a bulletin board for international students in the United States. There are twelve mistakes in the use of **should, ought to,** and **had better**. The first mistake is already corrected. Find and correct eleven more.*

Justme: My friend asked me to dinner, and she told me I should ~~to~~ bring some food! What kind of an invitation is that? What I should bring to this strange dinner party?

Sasha: LOL![1] The invitation is totally normal. Your friend is having a potluck—a dinner party where everybody brings something. It's really a lot of fun. You ought bring a dish from your country. People will enjoy that.

Toby: HELP! My first day of class, and I lost my wallet! What ought I do first? My student ID, credit card, and cash are all gone.

R2D2: First of all, you'd not better panic because you need to be calm so you can speak clearly. You should to call your credit card company right away. Did you lose your wallet at school? Then you ought to going to the Lost and Found Department at your school.

Smiley: What should an international student does to make friends? At my college people always smile and say, "Hi, how are you?" but they don't wait for an answer!

4gud: New students should joining some clubs and international student organizations. They also ought to find a student in each class to study with and ask about homework assignments.

Newguy: Hi. I'm new to this board. I'm from Vietnam, and I'm going to school in Canada next year. How should I will get ready?

Smiley: Welcome Newguy! I'm at school in Montreal, and you won't believe how cold it gets here. You're better bring a lot of warm clothes.

Sasha: You ought check the school's website. They might have a Vietnam Students Association. If they do, you should email the association with your questions. Good luck!

---

[1] **LOL:** abbreviation for *Laughing out Loud*

EXERCISE 6: Listening

A | *A radio show host is giving advice to callers about buying a new computer. Read the questions. Then listen to the show. Listen again and check (✓) all the correct answers.*

Who...?	Amy	Jason	Marta	Tim
1. is the host of the show	☐	☐	☐	☑
2. is calling for the first time	☐	☐	☐	☐
3. asks about repairing an old computer	☐	☐	☐	☐
4. gives information about the normal life of a computer	☐	☐	☐	☐
5. is going to buy a new computer	☐	☐	☐	☐
6. says "always protect your identity"	☐	☐	☐	☐

B | *Read the advice in the list. Listen again to the show and check (✓) the sentences that agree with the host's advice.*

☐ **1.** Repair a seven-year-old computer.

☑ **2.** Read online computer reviews.

☐ **3.** Throw away your old computer.

☐ **4.** Always buy the cheapest computer.

☐ **5.** Order a computer from a big online company.

☐ **6.** Shop at a local computer store.

☐ **7.** Consider a service contract.

☐ **8.** Get the most memory you can afford.

EXERCISE 7: Pronunciation

A | *Read and listen to the Pronunciation Note.*

> **Pronunciation Note**
>
> In **informal conversation**:
>
> • We often pronounce **ought to** "oughta".
>
> • For **had better**, we usually pronounce **had** "d", and sometimes we leave out **had** and just say "better."
>
> **EXAMPLES:** You **ought to** get a new computer. → "You **oughta** get a new computer."
> You **had better** get a flash drive too. → "You**'d better** get a flash drive too." OR
> "You **better** get a flash drive too."

B | *Listen to the conversation. Notice the pronunciation of* **ought to** *and* **had better.**

A: Do you think I **ought to** buy a new computer?

B: I think you**'d better**. Yours is pretty old.

A: What kind should I get?

B: Maybe you **ought to** get a laptop.

A: Good idea. I think I'll look for a used one.

B: You**'d better** not. A lot of used laptops have problems.

A: OK. I guess I **ought to** read some reviews.

B: Yeah, that's what you really **ought to** do.

C | *Listen again to the conversation and repeat each question or statement. Then practice the conversation with a partner.*

EXERCISE 8: Cross-Cultural Comparison

Work with a partner. Imagine that your partner has been offered a job as a computer expert in a country that you know very well. Give some advice about customs there. Then switch roles. Use these topics:

- calling your boss by his or her first name
- shaking hands when you first meet someone
- calling a co-worker by a nickname
- asking for a second helping when you are a guest

- crossing the street before the light turns green

(Add your own topics.)

- _____
- _____

EXAMPLES: You'd better not call your boss by her first name.
You should shake hands when you first meet someone.

EXERCISE 9: Problem Solving

Work in small groups. Each group member chooses a problem to ask the group about. Group members discuss the problem and give advice.

1. I was studying for exams, and I forgot my girlfriend's birthday. She's really angry at me. What should I do?

   EXAMPLE: A: You'd better take her to a nice restaurant.
   B: I think you should apologize and tell her you were really busy.
   C: You'd better not just send her an email. Pick up the phone and call!

2. My best friend from high school is getting married, but I don't have money to travel to her wedding. Should I borrow money for a plane ticket?

3. My boss emails me jokes that aren't really funny. Should I email back and say they're funny?

4. My roommate eats my groceries, and he doesn't clean his room. He's a good friend, and I don't want him to leave. What should I say to him?

5. I work during the day and go to school at night. I don't have much time to go out. How do I make new friends? Should I join online interest groups?

EXERCISE 10: Picture Discussion

Work in pairs. Look at a classroom at the EFL Computer Training Institute. Give advice for ways to improve the institute. Then compare your ideas with the ideas of another pair.

EXAMPLE: **A:** They should empty the trash.
B: Yes, and they ought to . . .

EXERCISE 11: Writing

A | Look at the picture in Exercise 10. Imagine you are a student at that institute. Write an email to Mr. Thompson, the owner of the school, to complain about the institute. Don't flame him; follow the rules of netiquette. Give him advice on improvements the institute should make.

EXAMPLE: Dear Mr. Thompson:
I am a student at the EFL Computer Training Institute. My classes are very good, but the Institute really should make some improvements. First, I think you ought to . . .

B | Check your work. Use the Editing Checklist.

Editing Checklist

Did you use . . . ?
☐ **should** and **ought to** for advice
☐ **had better** for strong advice
☐ the correct written forms of **ought to** and **had better**

A | *Circle the letter of the correct answer to complete each sentence.*

1. Doug should _____ that Internet group. I think he'd like it.

   a. join   **b.** joins   **c.** to join

2. He ought _____ some postings before he posts his own.

   a. read   **b.** reads   **c.** to read

3. He should _____ a long message.

   a. n't post   **b.** no post   **c.** post no

4. He'd _____ give too much personal information. It could be dangerous.

   a. better   **b.** better not   **c.** not better

5. He'd better _____ careful.

   a. be   **b.** not be   **c.** not being

B | *Complete the conversations with the words in parentheses and with short answers.*

- **A:** _____ I _____ Suzanne tomorrow?
                          1. (should / call)

  B: You _____ it tonight. She's been expecting to hear from you.
              2. (had better / do)

- **A:** How _____ I _____ Professor Lions? Email?
                          3. (should / contact)

  B: No. You _____ her. She prefers the phone.
              4. (ought to / call)

- **A:** _____ I _____ her for help?
                          5. (should / ask)

  B: _____, you _____. That's part of her job.
                          6.

- **A:** _____ I _____ it right now?
                          7. (should / do)

  B: _____, you _____. It's much too late.
                          8.

  A: You're right. I _____ until tomorrow morning.
              9. (had better / wait)

C | *Find and correct six mistakes.*

1. Vanessa should gets a new computer. She should no keep her old one.

2. She'd better not buying the first one she sees.

3. She ought read reviews before she decides on one.

4. Ought she get one online or should she goes to a store?

From Grammar to Writing
USING APPROPRIATE MODALS

When you write a note, you do more than give information. You perform social functions such as **asking for permission** and **making requests**. Modals help you perform these functions politely.

EXAMPLE: I want you to call me in the morning. →
Could you **please** call me in the morning?

1 | *Read the first draft of Ed's email to his co-worker, Chen. Work with a partner and decide which sentences should have modals. Underline the sentences.*

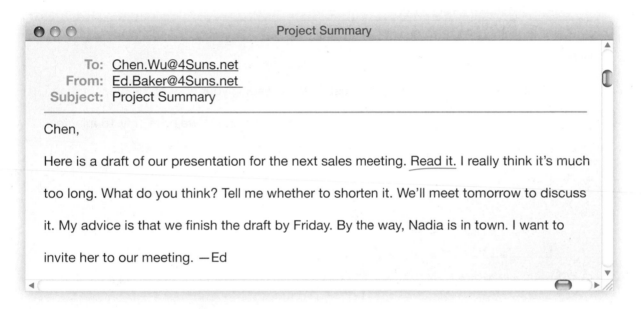

To: Chen.Wu@4Suns.net
From: Ed.Baker@4Suns.net
Subject: Project Summary

Chen,

Here is a draft of our presentation for the next sales meeting. Read it. I really think it's much

too long. What do you think? Tell me whether to shorten it. We'll meet tomorrow to discuss

it. My advice is that we finish the draft by Friday. By the way, Nadia is in town. I want to

invite her to our meeting. —Ed

2 | *Complete Ed's second draft of the email. Use modals to express the functions in parentheses.*

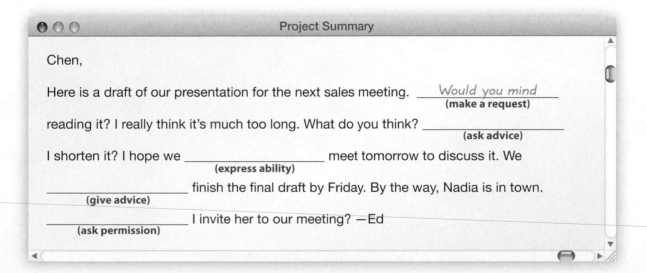

Chen,

Here is a draft of our presentation for the next sales meeting. ___Would you mind___
(make a request)

reading it? I really think it's much too long. What do you think? _____
(ask advice)

I shorten it? I hope we _____ meet tomorrow to discuss it. We
(express ability)

_____ finish the final draft by Friday. By the way, Nadia is in town.
(give advice)

_____ I invite her to our meeting? —Ed
(ask permission)

3 | *Complete Chen's reply to Ed. Use modals to express these ideas:*

- Shorten the presentation. *(advice)*

- I'm not going to meet with you today because of another meeting. *(ability)*

- I'd like to meet tomorrow instead. *(request)*

- Please reserve the conference room for the meeting. *(request)*

- Of course Nadia will come to the meeting. *(permission)*

- I hope we'll all have lunch after the meeting. *(ability)*

⬤ ◯ ◯   Re: Project Summary

To: Ed.Baker@4Suns.net
From: Chen.Wu@4Suns.net
Subject: Re: Project Summary

Hi Ed,

Sorry, I was very busy this morning, so I just finished reading your draft of the presentation.

_____*I think you should shorten it.*_____ Remember we have only 15 minutes.

_____

_____

_____

_____

_____

See you tomorrow morning.

Chen

1. Work with a partner. Choose one of the situations below. Role-play the situation. Use modals to express the ideas.

   Situation 1: A salesperson and his or her boss

   You work in a sales office. Recently a customer complained to your boss because he had to wait for service. You want to meet with your boss to explain what happened. You'd like to bring a co-worker who saw the incident. You think the company needs another receptionist for busy times.

   Situation 2: A student and his or her English teacher

   You would like your English teacher to write a letter of recommendation for you. You want him or her to mention that you have good computer skills and are an A student in the class. You're not sure how many hours to work a week, so you ask your teacher. You want to miss class so that you can go to your job interview.

2. Work with another pair. Watch their role play. Make a list of functions they expressed (for example, advice, ability, request) and the modals they used to express those functions. Discuss your list with them. Did they express what they wanted to?

3. Perform your role play and discuss it with the other pair.

5 | *With your partner, write and answer emails as the characters in your role plays. Use modals and information from the feedback you received on your role play.*

EXAMPLES: Dear Barbara,
Thank you for letting me know about the angry customer. Could you . . . ?

Pete,
Thanks for your email. I'll be able to . . .

APPENDICES

1 Irregular Verbs

Base Form	Simple Past	Past Participle	Base Form	Simple Past	Past Participle
arise	arose	arisen	hang	hung	hung
awake	awoke	awoken	have	had	had
be	was/were	been	hear	heard	heard
beat	beat	beaten/beat	hide	hid	hidden
become	became	become	hit	hit	hit
begin	began	begun	hold	held	held
bend	bent	bent	hurt	hurt	hurt
bet	bet	bet	keep	kept	kept
bite	bit	bitten	kneel	knelt/kneeled	knelt/kneeled
bleed	bled	bled	knit	knit/knitted	knit/knitted
blow	blew	blown	know	knew	known
break	broke	broken	lay	laid	laid
bring	brought	brought	lead	led	led
build	built	built	leap	leaped/leapt	leaped/leapt
burn	burned/burnt	burned/burnt	leave	left	left
burst	burst	burst	lend	lent	lent
buy	bought	bought	let	let	let
catch	caught	caught	lie *(lie down)*	lay	lain
choose	chose	chosen	light	lit/lighted	lit/lighted
cling	clung	clung	lose	lost	lost
come	came	come	make	made	made
cost	cost	cost	mean	meant	meant
creep	crept	crept	meet	met	met
cut	cut	cut	pay	paid	paid
deal	dealt	dealt	prove	proved	proved/proven
dig	dug	dug	put	put	put
dive	dived/dove	dived	quit	quit	quit
do	did	done	read /rid/	read /rɛd/	read /rɛd/
draw	drew	drawn	ride	rode	ridden
dream	dreamed/dreamt	dreamed/dreamt	ring	rang	rung
drink	drank	drunk	rise	rose	risen
drive	drove	driven	run	ran	run
eat	ate	eaten	say	said	said
fall	fell	fallen	see	saw	seen
feed	fed	fed	seek	sought	sought
feel	felt	felt	sell	sold	sold
fight	fought	fought	send	sent	sent
find	found	found	set	set	set
fit	fit/fitted	fit	sew	sewed	sewn/sewed
flee	fled	fled	shake	shook	shaken
fling	flung	flung	shave	shaved	shaved/shaven
fly	flew	flown	shine *(intransitive)*	shone/shined	shone/shined
forbid	forbade/forbid	forbidden	shoot	shot	shot
forget	forgot	forgotten	show	showed	shown
forgive	forgave	forgiven	shrink	shrank/shrunk	shrunk/shrunken
freeze	froze	frozen	shut	shut	shut
get	got	gotten/got	sing	sang	sung
give	gave	given	sink	sank/sunk	sunk
go	went	gone	sit	sat	sat
grind	ground	ground	sleep	slept	slept
grow	grew	grown	slide	slid	slid

(continued on next page)

Base Form	Simple Past	Past Participle		Base Form	Simple Past	Past Participle
speak	spoke	spoken		swing	swung	swung
speed	sped/speeded	sped/speeded		take	took	taken
spend	spent	spent		teach	taught	taught
spill	spilled/spilt	spilled/spilt		tear	tore	torn
spin	spun	spun		tell	told	told
spit	spit/spat	spat		think	thought	thought
split	split	split		throw	threw	thrown
spread	spread	spread		understand	understood	understood
spring	sprang	sprung		upset	upset	upset
stand	stood	stood		wake	woke	woken
steal	stole	stolen		wear	wore	worn
stick	stuck	stuck		weave	wove/weaved	woven/weaved
sting	stung	stung		weep	wept	wept
stink	stank/stunk	stunk		win	won	won
strike	struck	struck/stricken		wind	wound	wound
swear	swore	sworn		withdraw	withdrew	withdrawn
sweep	swept	swept		wring	wrung	wrung
swim	swam	swum		write	wrote	written

2 Non-Action Verbs

Appearance	Emotions	Mental States		Possession and Relationship	Senses and Perceptions	Wants and Preferences
appear	admire	agree	know	belong	feel	desire
be	adore	assume	mean	come from *(origin)*	hear	hope
look *(seem)*	appreciate	believe	mind	contain	notice	need
represent	care	consider	presume	have	observe	prefer
resemble	detest	disagree	realize	own	perceive	want
seem	dislike	disbelieve	recognize	possess	see	wish
signify	doubt	estimate	remember		smell	
	envy	expect	see *(understand)*		sound	
Value	fear	feel *(believe)*	suppose		taste	
cost	hate	find *(believe)*	suspect			
equal	like	guess	think *(believe)*			
weigh	love	hesitate	understand			
	miss	hope	wonder			
	regret	imagine				
	respect					
	trust					

3 Verbs and Expressions Used Reflexively

allow yourself	believe in yourself	forgive yourself	push yourself
amuse yourself	blame yourself	help yourself	remind yourself
ask yourself	buy yourself	hurt yourself	see yourself
avail yourself of	cut yourself	imagine yourself	take care of yourself
be hard on yourself	deprive yourself of	introduce yourself	talk to yourself
be pleased with yourself	dry yourself	kill yourself	teach yourself
be proud of yourself	enjoy yourself	look at yourself	tell yourself
be yourself	feel proud of yourself	prepare yourself	treat yourself
behave yourself	feel sorry for yourself	pride yourself on	wash yourself

4 Transitive Phrasal Verbs

(s.o. = someone   s.t. = something)

PHRASAL VERB	MEANING
ask s.o. **over**	*invite to one's home*
blow s.t. **out**	*stop burning by blowing air on it*
blow s.t. **up**	*make explode*
bring s.o. or s.t. **back**	*return*
bring s.o. **up**	*raise (a child)*
bring s.t. **up**	*bring attention to*
burn s.t. **down**	*burn completely*
call s.o. **back**	*return a phone call*
call s.t. **off**	*cancel*
call s.o. **up**	*contact by phone*
calm s.o. **down**	*make less excited*
carry s.t. **out**	*complete (a plan)*
clean s.o. or s.t. **up**	*clean completely*
clear s.t. **up**	*explain*
close s.t. **down**	*close by force*
count on s.t. or s.o.	*depend on*
cover s.o. or s.t. **up**	*cover completely*
cross s.t. **out**	*draw a line through*
do s.t. **over**	*do again*
drink s.t. **up**	*drink completely*
drop in on s.o.	*visit by surprise*
drop s.o. or s.t. **off**	*take someplace in a car and leave there*
empty s.t. **out**	*empty completely*
figure s.o. **out**	*understand (the behavior)*
figure s.t. **out**	*solve, understand after thinking about it*
fill s.t. **in**	*complete with information*
fill s.t. **out**	*complete (a form)*
find s.t. **out**	*learn information*
get off s.t.	*leave (a bus, a couch)*
get over s.t.	*recover from*
give s.t. **back**	*return*
give s.t. **up**	*quit, abandon*
hand s.t. **in**	*give work (to a boss/teacher), submit*
hand s.t. **out**	*distribute*
hand s.t. **over**	*give*
help s.o. **out**	*assist*
keep s.o. or s.t. **away**	*cause to stay at a distance*
keep s.t. **on**	*not remove (a piece of clothing/ jewelry)*
keep s.o. or s.t. **out**	*not allow to enter*
lay s.o. **off**	*end employment*
leave s.t. **on**	*1. not turn off (a light/radio)*
	2. not remove (a piece of clothing/ jewelry)
leave s.t. **out**	*not include, omit*
let s.o. **down**	*disappoint*
let s.o. or s.t. **in**	*allow to enter*
let s.o. **off**	*allow to leave (from a bus/car)*
light s.t. **up**	*illuminate*
look s.o. or s.t. **over**	*examine*
look s.t. **up**	*try to find (in a book/on the Internet)*

PHRASAL VERB	MEANING
make s.t. **up**	*create*
pass s.t. **on**	*give to others*
pass s.t. **out**	*distribute*
pass s.o. or s.t. **over**	*decide not to use*
pass s.o. or s.t. **up**	*decide not to use, reject*
pay s.o. or s.t. **back**	*repay*
pick s.o. or s.t. **out**	*choose*
pick s.o. or s.t. **up**	*1. lift*
	2. go get someone or something
pick s.t. **up**	*1. get (an idea/a new book)*
	2. answer the phone
point s.o. or s.t. **out**	*indicate*
put s.t. **away**	*put in an appropriate place*
put s.t. **back**	*return to its original place*
put s.o. or s.t. **down**	*stop holding*
put s.t. **off**	*delay*
put s.t. **on**	*cover the body (with clothes/lotion)*
put s.t. **together**	*assemble*
put s.t. **up**	*erect*
set s.t. **up**	*1. prepare for use*
	2. establish (a business)
shut s.t. **off**	*stop (a machine/light)*
straighten s.o. **out**	*change bad behavior*
straighten s.t. **up**	*make neat*
switch s.t. **on**	*start (a machine/light)*
take s.o. or s.t. **back**	*return*
take s.t. **off/out**	*remove*
take over s.t.	*get control of*
talk s.o. **into**	*persuade*
talk s.t. **over**	*discuss*
tear s.t. **down**	*destroy*
tear s.t. **off**	*remove by tearing*
tear s.t. **up**	*tear into small pieces*
think s.t. **over**	*consider*
think s.t. **up**	*invent*
throw s.t. **away/out**	*put in the trash, discard*
try s.t. **on**	*put clothing on to see if it fits*
try s.t. **out**	*use to see if it works*
turn s.t. **around**	*make it work well*
turn s.o. or s.t. **down**	*reject*
turn s.t. **down**	*lower the volume (a TV/radio)*
turn s.t. **in**	*give work (to a boss/teacher), submit*
turn s.o. or s.t. **into**	*change from one form to another*
turn s.o. **off**	*[slang] destroy interest in*
turn s.t. **off**	*stop (a machine/light), extinguish*
turn s.t. **on**	*start (a machine/light)*
turn s.t. **up**	*make louder (a TV/radio)*
use s.t. **up**	*use completely, consume*
wake s.o. **up**	*awaken*
work s.t. **out**	*solve, find a solution to a problem*
write s.t. **down**	*write on a piece of paper*
write s.t. **up**	*write in a finished form*

5 Intransitive Phrasal Verbs

Phrasal Verb	Meaning	Phrasal Verb	Meaning	Phrasal Verb	Meaning
blow up	explode	follow through	complete	look out	be careful
break down	stop working (a machine)	fool around	act playful	make up	end a disagreement, reconcile
		get ahead	make progress, succeed		
burn down	burn completely			pass away	die
call back	return a phone call	get along	have a good relationship	play around	have fun
calm down	become less excited			run out	not have enough
catch on	1. begin to understand	get away	go on vacation	set out	begin an activity or a project
	2. become popular	get back	return		
clear up	become clear	get by	survive	show up	appear
close down	stop operating	get through	finish	sign up	register
come about	happen	get together	meet	sit down	take a seat
come along	come with, accompany	get up	get out of bed	slip up	make a mistake
come by	visit	give up	quit	stand up	rise
come back	return	go ahead	begin or continue to do something	start over	start again
come in	enter			stay up	remain awake
come off	become unattached	go away	leave	straighten up	make neat
come on	do as I say	go on	continue	take off	depart (a plane)
come out	appear	grow up	become an adult	tune in	1. watch or listen to (a show)
come up	arise	hang up	end a phone call		2. pay attention
dress up	wear special clothes	keep away	stay at a distance		
drop in	visit by surprise	keep on	continue	turn up	appear
drop out	quit	keep out	not enter	wake up	stop sleeping
eat out	eat in a restaurant	keep up	go as fast	watch out	be careful
empty out	empty completely	lie down	recline	work out	1. be resolved
find out	learn information	light up	illuminate		2. exercise
fit in	be accepted in a group				

6 Irregular Plural Nouns

Singular	Plural	Singular	Plural	Singular	Plural
half	halves	man	men	deer	deer
knife	knives	woman	women	fish	fish
leaf	leaves	child	children	sheep	sheep
life	lives	foot	feet	person	people
loaf	loaves	tooth	teeth		
shelf	shelves	goose	geese		
wife	wives	mouse	mice		

7 Non-Count Nouns

REMEMBER: Non-count nouns are singular.

Activities	Courses of Study	Food		Ideas and Feelings	Liquids and Gases	Materials	Very Small Things
baseball	archeology	bread	fruit	anger	air	ash	dust
biking	art	broccoli	ice cream	beauty	blood	clay	pepper
exploring	economics	butter	lettuce	fear	gasoline	cotton	rice
farming	English	cake	meat	freedom	ink	glass	salt
football	geography	cheese	pasta	friendship	milk	gold	sand
golf	history	chicken	pizza	happiness	oil	leather	sugar
hiking	mathematics	chocolate	salad	hate	oxygen	paper	
running	music	coffee	soup	hope	paint	silk	Weather
sailing	photography	corn	spaghetti	loneliness	smoke	silver	fog
soccer	psychology	fat	spinach	love	soda	stone	ice
swimming	science	fish	tea	truth	water	wood	rain
tennis		flour	yogurt			wool	snow
							wind

NAMES OF CATEGORIES		OTHER
clothing	(BUT: coats, hats, shoes . . .)	(Some non-count nouns don't fit into any list. You must memorize these non-count nouns.)
equipment	(BUT: computers, phones, TVs . . .)	
food	(BUT: bananas, eggs, vegetables . . .)	
furniture	(BUT: beds, chairs, lamps, tables . . .)	advice
homework	(BUT: assignments, pages, problems . . .)	garbage/trash
jewelry	(BUT: bracelets, earrings, necklaces . . .)	help
mail	(BUT: letters, packages, postcards . . .)	information
money	(BUT: dinars, dollars, euros, pounds . . .)	luggage
time	(BUT: minutes, months, years . . .)	news
work	(BUT: jobs, projects, tasks . . .)	traffic

8 Proper Nouns

REMEMBER: Write proper nouns with a capital letter. Notice that some proper nouns use the definite article *the*.

PEOPLE
- first names — Anne, Eduardo, Mehmet, Olga, Shao-fen
- family names — Chen, García, Haddad, Smith
- family groups — the Chens, the Garcias, the Haddads, the Smiths
- titles — Doctor, Grandma, President, Professor
- title + names — Mr. García, Professor Smith, Uncle Steve

PLACES
- continents — Africa, Asia, Australia, Europe, South America
- countries — Argentina, China, France, Nigeria, Turkey, the United States
- provinces/states — Brittany, Ontario, Szechwan, Texas
- cities — Beijing, Istanbul, Rio de Janeiro, Toronto
- streets — the Champs-Elysées, Fifth Avenue
- structures — Harrods, the Louvre, the Petronas Towers
- schools — Midwood High School, Oxford University
- parks — Central Park, the Tivoli Gardens
- mountains — the Andes, the Himalayas, the Pyrenees
- oceans — the Atlantic, the Indian Ocean, the Pacific
- rivers — the Amazon, the Ganges, the Seine
- lakes — Baikal, Erie, Tanganyika, Titicaca
- canals — the Suez Canal, the Panama Canal
- deserts — the Gobi, the Kalahari, the Sahara

DOCUMENTS
the Bible, the Koran, the Constitution

LANGUAGES
Arabic, Chinese, Portuguese, Russian, Spanish

NATIONALITIES
Brazilian, Japanese, Mexican, Saudi, Turkish

RELIGIONS
Buddhism, Christianity, Hinduism, Islam, Judaism

COURSES
Introduction to Computer Sciences, Math 201

PRODUCT BRANDS
Adidas, Dell, Kleenex, Mercedes, Samsung

TIME
- months — January, March, December
- days — Monday, Wednesday, Saturday
- holidays — Bastille Day, Buddha Day, Christmas, Hanukah, New Year's Day, Ramadan

9 Adjectives That Form the Comparative and Superlative in Two Ways

ADJECTIVE	COMPARATIVE	SUPERLATIVE
cruel	crueler/more cruel	cruelest/most cruel
deadly	deadlier/more deadly	deadliest/most deadly
friendly	friendlier/more friendly	friendliest/most friendly
handsome	handsomer/more handsome	handsomest/most handsome
happy	happier/more happy	happiest/most happy
likely	likelier/more likely	likeliest/most likely
lively	livelier/more lively	liveliest/most lively
lonely	lonelier/more lonely	loneliest/most lonely
lovely	lovelier/more lovely	loveliest/most lovely
narrow	narrower/more narrow	narrowest/most narrow
pleasant	pleasanter/more pleasant	pleasantest/most pleasant
polite	politer/more polite	politest/most polite
quiet	quieter/more quiet	quietest/most quiet
shallow	shallower/more shallow	shallowest/most shallow
sincere	sincerer/more sincere	sincerest/most sincere
stupid	stupider/more stupid	stupidest/most stupid
true	truer/more true	truest/most true

10 Irregular Comparisons of Adjectives, Adverbs, and Quantifiers

ADJECTIVE	ADVERB	COMPARATIVE	SUPERLATIVE
bad	badly	worse	the worst
far	far	farther/further	the farthest/furthest
good	well	better	the best
little	little	less	the least
many/a lot of	—	more	the most
much*/a lot of	much*/a lot	more	the most

*Much is usually only used in questions and negative statements.

11 Participial Adjectives

-ed	-ing	-ed	-ing	-ed	-ing
alarmed	alarming	disturbed	disturbing	moved	moving
amazed	amazing	embarrassed	embarrassing	paralyzed	paralyzing
amused	amusing	entertained	entertaining	pleased	pleasing
annoyed	annoying	excited	exciting	relaxed	relaxing
astonished	astonishing	exhausted	exhausting	satisfied	satisfying
bored	boring	fascinated	fascinating	shocked	shocking
charmed	charming	frightened	frightening	surprised	surprising
confused	confusing	horrified	horrifying	terrified	terrifying
depressed	depressing	inspired	inspiring	tired	tiring
disappointed	disappointing	interested	interesting	touched	touching
disgusted	disgusting	irritated	irritating	troubled	troubling

12 Order of Adjectives Before a Noun

REMEMBER: We do not usually use more than three adjectives before a noun.

1. **Order of Adjectives from Different Categories**

Adjectives from different categories usually go in the following order. Do not use a comma between these adjectives.

OPINION	SIZE*	AGE	SHAPE	COLOR	ORIGIN	MATERIAL	NOUNS USED AS ADJECTIVES	
beautiful	enormous	antique	flat	blue	Asian	cotton	college	
comfortable	huge	modern	oval	gray	European	gold	flower	
cozy	little	new	rectangular	green	Greek	plastic	kitchen	+ NOUN
easy	tall	old	round	purple	Pacific	stone	mountain	
expensive	tiny	young	square	red	Southern	wooden	vacation	

*EXCEPTION: Big and small usually go first in a series of adjectives: a **small** comfortable apartment

EXAMPLES: I bought an **antique Greek flower** vase. NOT: a ~~Greek antique~~ flower vase
She took some **easy college** courses. NOT: some ~~college easy~~ courses
We sat at an **enormous round wooden** table. NOT: a ~~wooden enormous round~~ table

2. **Order of Adjectives from the Same Category**

Adjectives from the same category do not follow a specific order. Use a comma between these adjectives.

EXAMPLES: We rented a **beautiful, comfortable, cozy** apartment. OR
We rented a **cozy, comfortable, beautiful** apartment. OR
We rented a **comfortable, cozy, beautiful** apartment.

13 Verbs Followed by Gerunds (Base Form of Verb + -ing)

acknowledge	can't help	discuss	feel like	limit	prevent	resent
admit	celebrate	dislike	finish	mention	prohibit	resist
advise	consider	endure	forgive	mind (object to)	put off	risk
allow	delay	enjoy	go	miss	quit	suggest
appreciate	deny	escape	imagine	permit	recall	support
avoid	detest	excuse	justify	postpone	recommend	tolerate
ban	discontinue	explain	keep (continue)	practice	report	understand

14 Verbs Followed by Infinitives (To + Base Form of Verb)

agree	can('t) afford	deserve	hurry	neglect	promise	threaten
aim	can't wait	expect	intend	offer	refuse	volunteer
appear	claim	fail	learn	pay	request	wait
arrange	choose	help	manage	plan	rush	want
ask	consent	hesitate	mean (intend)	prepare	seem	wish
attempt	decide	hope	need	pretend	struggle	would like

15 Verbs Followed by Gerunds or Infinitives

begin	continue	like	remember*	stop*
can't stand	forget*	love	regret*	try
	hate	prefer	start	

*These verbs can be followed by either a gerund or an infinitive, but there is a big difference in meaning (see Unit 32).

16 Verbs Followed by Object + Infinitive

advise	convince	get	need*	persuade	require	want*
allow	encourage	help*	order	prefer*	teach	warn
ask*	expect*	hire	pay*	promise*	tell	wish
cause	forbid	invite	permit	remind	urge	would like*
choose*	force			request		

*These verbs can also be followed by an infinitive without an object (example: ask to leave or ask someone to leave).

17 Adjective + Preposition Combinations

accustomed to	bad at	curious about	good at	responsible for	sorry for/about
afraid of	bored with/by	different from	happy about	sad about	surprised at/
amazed at/by	capable of	disappointed with	interested in	safe from	about/by
angry at	careful of	excited about	nervous about	satisfied with	terrible at
ashamed of	certain about	famous for	opposed to	shocked at/by	tired of
aware of	concerned about	fond of	pleased about	sick of	used to
awful at	content with	glad about	ready for	slow at/in	worried about

18 Verb + Preposition Combinations

admit to	believe in	deal with	look forward to	rely on	thank someone for
advise against	choose between	dream about/of	object to	resort to	think about
apologize for	complain about	feel like	pay for	succeed in	wonder about
approve of	count on	insist on	plan on	talk about	worry about

19 Modals and Their Functions

FUNCTION	MODAL OR EXPRESSION	TIME	EXAMPLES
Ability	**can** **can't**	Present	• Sam **can swim**. • He **can't skate**.
	could **couldn't**	Past	• We **could swim** last year. • We **couldn't skate**.
	be able to* **not be able to***	All verb forms	• Lea **is able to run** fast. • She **wasn't able to run** fast last year.
Permission	**can** **can't** **could** **may** **may not**	Present or future	• **Can** I **sit** here? • **Can** I **call** tomorrow? • Yes, you **can**. • No, you **can't**. Sorry. • **Could** he **leave** now? • **May** I **borrow** your pen? • Yes, you **may**. • No, you **may not**. Sorry.
Requests	**can** **can't** **could** **will** **would**	Present or future	• **Can** you **close** the door, please? • Sure, I **can**. • Sorry, I **can't**. • **Could** you please **answer** the phone? • **Will** you **wash** the dishes, please? • **Would** you please **mail** this letter?
Advice	**should** **shouldn't** **ought to** **had better**** **had better not****	Present or future	• You **should study** more. • You **shouldn't miss** class. • We **ought to leave**. • We'd **better go**. • We'd **better not stay**.
Necessity	**have to*** **not have to***	All verb forms	• He **has to go** now. • I **had to go** yesterday. • I **will have to go** soon. • He **doesn't have to go** yet.
	have got to* **must**	Present or future	• He's **got to leave!** • You **must use** a pen for the test.
Prohibition	**must not** **can't**	Present or future	• You **must not drive** without a license. • You **can't drive** without a license.

*The meaning of this expression is similar to the meaning of a modal. Unlike a modal, it has -s for third-person singular.
**The meaning of this expression is similar to the meaning of a modal. Like a modal, it has no -s for third-person singular.

FUNCTION	MODAL OR EXPRESSION	TIME	EXAMPLES
Possibility	must must not have to*	Present	• This **must be** her house. Her name is on the door. • She **must not be** home. I don't see her car. • She **had to know** him. They went to school together.
	have got to* may may not might might not could	Present or future	• He**'s got to be** guilty. We saw him do it. • She **may be** home now. • It **may not rain** tomorrow. • Lee **might be sick** today. • He **might not come** to class. • They **could be** at the library. • It **could rain** tomorrow.
Impossibility	can't	Present or future	• That **can't be** Ana. She left for France yesterday. • It **can't snow** tomorrow. It's going to be too warm.
	couldn't	Present	• He **couldn't be** guilty. He was away . . .

*The meaning of this expression is similar to the meaning of a modal. Unlike a modal, it has -s for third-person singular.

20 Spelling Rules for the Simple Present: Third-Person Singular (*He, She, It*)

1. Add -*s* for most verbs.

work	work**s**
buy	buy**s**
ride	ride**s**
return	return**s**

2. Add -*es* for verbs that end in -*ch*, -*s*, -*sh*, -*x*, or -*z*.

watch	watch**es**
pass	pass**es**
rush	rush**es**
relax	relax**es**
buzz	buzz**es**

3. Change the *y* to *i* and add -*es* when the base form ends in **consonant** + *y*.

study	stud**ies**
hurry	hurr**ies**
dry	dr**ies**

Do not change the *y* when the base form ends in **vowel** + *y*. Add -*s*.

play	play**s**
enjoy	enjoy**s**

4. A few verbs have **irregular forms**.

be	**is**
do	**does**
go	**goes**
have	**has**

21   Spelling Rules for Base Form of Verb + -*ing* (Progressive and Gerund)

1. Add -*ing* to the base form of the verb.

read	read**ing**
stand	stand**ing**

2. If the verb ends in a **silent -e**, drop the final -*e* and add -*ing*.

leave	leav**ing**
take	tak**ing**

3. In **one-syllable** verbs, if the last three letters are a consonant-vowel-consonant combination (CVC), double the last consonant and add -*ing*.

   C V C
   ↓ ↓ ↓
   s i t   sit**ting**

   C V C
   ↓ ↓ ↓
   p l a n   plan**ning**

   Do not double the last consonant in verbs that end in -*w*, -*x*, or -*y*.

sew	sew**ing**
fix	fix**ing**
play	play**ing**

4. In verbs of **two or more syllables** that end in a consonant-vowel-consonant combination, double the last consonant only if the last syllable is stressed.

admít	admit**ting**	*(The last syllable is stressed.)*
whísper	whisper**ing**	*(The last syllable is not stressed, so don't double the -**r**.)*

5. If the verb ends in -*ie*, change the *ie* to *y* before adding -*ing*.

die	d**ying**
lie	l**ying**

> **Stress**
> ′ shows main stress.

22   Spelling Rules for Base Form of Verb + -*ed* (Simple Past and Past Participle of Regular Verbs)

1. If the verb ends in a **consonant**, add -*ed*.

return	return**ed**
help	help**ed**

2. If the verb ends in -*e*, add -*d*.

live	live**d**
create	create**d**
die	die**d**

3. In **one-syllable** verbs, if the last three letters are a consonant-vowel-consonant combination (CVC), double the last consonant and add -*ed*.

   C V C
   ↓ ↓ ↓
   h o p   hop**ped**

   C V C
   ↓ ↓ ↓
   g r a b   grab**bed**

   Do not double the last consonant in verbs that end in -*w*, -*x*, or -*y*.

bow	bow**ed**
mix	mix**ed**
play	play**ed**

4. In verbs of **two or more syllables** that end in a consonant-vowel-consonant combination, double the last consonant only if the last syllable is stressed.

prefér	prefer**red**	*(The last syllable is stressed.)*
vísit	visit**ed**	*(The last syllable is not stressed, so don't double the -**t**.)*

5. If the verb ends in **consonant + y**, change the *y* to *i* and add -*ed*.

worry	worr**ied**
carry	carr**ied**

6. If the verb ends in **vowel + y**, add -*ed*. (Do not change the *y* to *i*.)

play	play**ed**
annoy	annoy**ed**

   Exceptions:

lay	la**id**
pay	pa**id**
say	sa**id**

23 Spelling Rules for the Comparative (-er) and Superlative (-est) of Adjectives

1. With **one-syllable** adjectives, add *-er* to form the comparative. Add *-est* to form the superlative.

cheap	cheap**er**	cheap**est**
bright	bright**er**	bright**est**

2. If the adjective ends in *-e*, add *-r* or *-st*.

nice	nice**r**	nice**st**

3. If the adjective ends in **consonant** + *y*, change *y* to *i* before you add *-er* or *-est*.

pretty	prett**ier**	prett**iest**

   EXCEPTION:

shy	shy**er**	shy**est**

4. If a one-syllable adjective ends in a consonant-vowel-consonant combination (CVC), double the last consonant before adding *-er* or *-est*.

   C V C
   ↓ ↓ ↓

b i g	big**ger**	big**gest**

   Do not double the consonant in adjectives ending in *-w* or *-y*.

slow	slow**er**	slow**est**
gray	gray**er**	gray**est**

24 Spelling Rules for Adverbs Ending in *-ly*

1. Add *-ly* to the corresponding adjective.

nice	nice**ly**
quiet	quiet**ly**
beautiful	beautiful**ly**

2. If the adjective ends in **consonant** + *y*, change the *y* to *i* before adding *-ly*.

easy	eas**ily**

3. If the adjective ends in *-le*, drop the *e* and add *-y*.

possible	possib**ly**

   Do not drop the *e* for other adjectives ending in *-e*.

extreme	extreme**ly**

   EXCEPTION:

true	tru**ly**

4. If the adjective ends in *-ic*, add *-ally*.

basic	basic**ally**
fantastic	fantastic**ally**

25 Spelling Rules for Regular Plural Nouns

1. Add *-s* to most nouns.

book	books
table	tables
cup	cups

2. Add *-es* to nouns that end in *-ch*, *-s*, *-sh*, or *-x*.

watch	watch**es**
bus	bus**es**
dish	dish**es**
box	box**es**

3. Add *-s* to nouns that end in **vowel** + *y*.

day	day**s**
key	key**s**

4. Change the *y* to *i* and add *-es* to nouns that end in **consonant** + *y*.

baby	bab**ies**
city	cit**ies**
strawberry	strawberr**ies**

5. Add *-s* to nouns that end in **vowel** + *o*.

radio	radio**s**
video	video**s**
zoo	zoo**s**

6. Add *-es* to nouns that end in **consonant** + *o*.

potato	potato**es**
tomato	tomato**es**

   EXCEPTIONS: kilo—kilos, photo—photos, piano—pianos

1. SIMPLE PRESENT, PRESENT PROGRESSIVE, AND IMPERATIVE

Contractions with *Be*

I am	=	I'm
you are	=	you're
he is	=	he's
she is	=	she's
it is	=	it's
we are	=	we're
you are	=	you're
they are	=	they're

SIMPLE PRESENT	**PRESENT PROGRESSIVE**
I'm a student.	I'm studying here.
He's my teacher.	He's teaching verbs.
We're from Canada.	We're living here.

I am not	=	I'm not		
you are not	=	you're not	OR	you aren't
he is not	=	he's not	OR	he isn't
she is not	=	she's not	OR	she isn't
it is not	=	it's not	OR	it isn't
we are not	=	we're not	OR	we aren't
you are not	=	you're not	OR	you aren't
they are not	=	they're not	OR	they aren't

SIMPLE PRESENT	**PRESENT PROGRESSIVE**
She's not sick.	She's not reading.
He isn't late.	He isn't coming.
We aren't twins.	We aren't leaving.
They're not here.	They're not playing.

Contractions with *Do*

do not	=	don't
does not	=	doesn't

SIMPLE PRESENT	**IMPERATIVE**
They don't live here.	Don't run!
It doesn't snow much.	

2. SIMPLE PAST AND PAST PROGRESSIVE

Contractions with *Be*

was not	=	wasn't
were not	=	weren't

Contractions with *Do*

did not	=	didn't

SIMPLE PAST	**PAST PROGRESSIVE**
He wasn't a poet.	He wasn't singing.
They weren't twins.	They weren't sleeping.
We didn't see her.	

3. FUTURE

Contractions with *Will*

I will	=	I'll
you will	=	you'll
he will	=	he'll
she will	=	she'll
it will	=	it'll
we will	=	we'll
you will	=	you'll
they will	=	they'll
will not	=	won't

FUTURE WITH *WILL*
I'll take the train.
It'll be faster that way.
We'll go together.
He won't come with us.
They won't miss the train.

Contractions with *Be going to*

I am going to	=	I'm going to
you are going to	=	you're going to
he is going to	=	he's going to
she is going to	=	she's going to
it is going to	=	it's going to
we are going to	=	we're going to
you are going to	=	you're going to
they are going to	=	they're going to

FUTURE WITH *BE GOING TO*
I'm going to buy tickets tomorrow.
She's going to call you.
It's going to rain soon.
We're going to drive to Boston.
They're going to crash!

4. PRESENT PERFECT AND PRESENT PERFECT PROGRESSIVE

Contractions with *Have*

I have	=	I**'ve**
you have	=	you**'ve**
he has	=	he**'s**
she has	=	she**'s**
it has	=	it**'s**
we have	=	we**'ve**
you have	=	you**'ve**
they have	=	they**'ve**
have not	=	**haven't**
has not	=	**hasn't**

You**'ve** already **read** that page.
We**'ve been writing** for an hour.
She**'s been** to Africa three times.
It**'s been raining** since yesterday.
We **haven't seen** any elephants yet.
They **haven't been living** here long.

5. MODALS AND SIMILAR EXPRESSIONS

cannot or can not	=	**can't**
could not	=	**couldn't**
should not	=	**shouldn't**
had better	=	**'d better**
would prefer	=	**'d prefer**
would rather	=	**'d rather**

She **can't** dance.
We **shouldn't go**.
They**'d better decide**.
I**'d prefer** coffee.
I**'d rather take** the bus.

27 Capitalization and Punctuation Rules

	USE FOR . . .	**EXAMPLES**
capital letter	• the pronoun *I* • proper nouns • the first word of a sentence	• Tomorrow **I** will be here at 2:00. • His name is **Karl**. He lives in **Germany**. • **When** does the train leave? **At** 2:00.
apostrophe (')	• possessive nouns • contractions	• Is that **Marta's** coat? • **That's** not hers. **It's** mine.
comma (,)	• after items in a list • before sentence connectors *and*, *but*, *or*, and *so* • after the first part of a sentence that begins with *because* • after the first part of a sentence that begins with a preposition • after the first part of a sentence that begins with a time clause or an *if* clause	• He bought **apples**, **pears**, **oranges**, and **bananas**. • They watched TV, **and** she played video games. • *Because* it's raining, we're not walking to the office. • *Across from* the post office, there's a good restaurant. • *After* he arrived, we ate dinner. • *If* it rains, we won't go.
exclamation mark (!)	• at the end of a sentence to show surprise or a strong feeling	• You're here! That's great! • Stop! A car is coming!
period (.)	• at the end of a statement	• Today is Wednesday.
question mark (?)	• at the end of a question	• What day is today?

28 Pronunciation Table

These are the pronunciation symbols used in this text. Listen to the pronunciation of the key words.

VOWELS

Symbol	Key Word	Symbol	Key Word
i	beat, feed	ə	banana, among
ɪ	bit, did	ɚ	shirt, murder
eɪ	date, paid	aɪ	bite, cry, buy, eye
ɛ	bet, bed	aʊ	about, how
æ	bat, bad	ɔɪ	voice, boy
ɑ	box, odd, father	ɪr	beer
ɔ	bought, dog	ɛr	bare
oʊ	boat, road	ɑr	bar
ʊ	book, good	ɔr	door
u	boot, food, student	ʊr	tour
ʌ	but, mud, mother		

CONSONANTS

Symbol	Key Word	Symbol	Key Word
p	pack, happy	ʃ	ship, machine, station, special, discussion
b	back, rubber		
t	tie	ʒ	measure, vision
d	die	h	hot, who
k	came, key, quick	m	men
g	game, guest	n	sun, know, pneumonia
tʃ	church, nature, watch	ŋ	sung, ringing
dʒ	judge, general, major	w	wet, white
f	fan, photograph	l	light, long
v	van	r	right, wrong
θ	thing, breath	y	yes, use, music
ð	then, breathe	t̪	butter, bottle
s	sip, city, psychology		
z	zip, please, goes		

29 Pronunciation Rules for the Simple Present: Third-Person Singular (He, She, It)

1. The third-person singular in the simple present always ends in the letter -s. There are, however, three different pronunciations for the final sound of the third-person singular.

/s/	/z/	/ɪz/
talks	loves	dances

2. The final sound is pronounced /s/ after the voiceless sounds /p/, /t/, /k/, and /f/.

top	tops
get	gets
take	takes
laugh	laughs

3. The final sound is pronounced /z/ after the voiced sounds /b/, /d/, /g/, /v/, /m/, /n/, /ŋ/, /l/, /r/, and /ð/.

describe	describes
spend	spends
hug	hugs
live	lives
seem	seems
remain	remains
sing	sings
tell	tells
lower	lowers
bathe	bathes

4. The final sound is pronounced /z/ after all **vowel sounds**.

agree	agrees
try	tries
stay	stays
know	knows

5. The final sound is pronounced /ɪz/ after the sounds /s/, /z/, /ʃ/, /ʒ/, /tʃ/, and /dʒ/. /ɪz/ adds a syllable to the verb.

miss	misses
freeze	freezes
rush	rushes
massage	massages
watch	watches
judge	judges

6. *Do* and *say* have a change in vowel sound.

do	/du/	does	/dʌz/
say	/seɪ/	says	/sɛz/

30 Pronunciation Rules for the Simple Past and Past Participle of Regular Verbs

1. The regular simple past and past participle always end in the letter *-d*. There are three different pronunciations for the final sound of the regular simple past and past participle.

/t/	/d/	/ɪd/
raced	lived	attended

2. The final sound is pronounced /t/ after the voiceless sounds /p/, /k/, /f/, /s/, /ʃ/, and /tʃ/.

hop	hopped
work	worked
laugh	laughed
address	addressed
publish	published
watch	watched

3. The final sound is pronounced /d/ after the voiced sounds /b/, /g/, /v/, /z/, /ʒ/, /dʒ/, /m/, /n/, /ŋ/, /l/, /r/, and /ð/.

rub	rubbed
hug	hugged
live	lived
surprise	surprised
massage	massaged
change	changed
rhyme	rhymed
return	returned
bang	banged
enroll	enrolled
appear	appeared
bathe	bathed

4. The final sound is pronounced /d/ after all **vowel sounds**.

agree	agreed
die	died
play	played
enjoy	enjoyed
snow	snowed

5. The final sound is pronounced /ɪd/ after /t/ and /d/. /ɪd/ adds a syllable to the verb.

start	started
decide	decided

GLOSSARY OF GRAMMAR TERMS

action verb A verb that describes an action.
- *Alicia **ran** home.*

adjective A word that describes a noun or pronoun.
- *That's a **great** idea.*
- *It's **wonderful**.*

adverb A word that describes a verb, an adjective, or another adverb.
- *She drives **carefully**.*
- *She's a **very** good driver.*
- *She drives **really** well.*

adverb of frequency An adverb that describes how often something happens.
- *We **always** watch that program.*

adverb of manner An adverb that describes how someone does something or how something happens. It usually ends in *-ly*.
- *He sings **beautifully**.*

adverb of time An adverb that describes when something happens.
- *We'll see you **soon**.*

affirmative A statement or answer meaning *Yes*.
- *He **works**.* (affirmative statement)
- *Yes, he **does**.* (affirmative short answer)

article A word that goes before a noun. The indefinite articles are *a* and *an*.
- *I ate **a** sandwich and **an** apple.*

The definite article is *the*.
- *I didn't like **the** sandwich. **The** apple was good.*

auxiliary verb (also called **helping verb**) A verb used with a main verb. *Be, do,* and *have* are often auxiliary verbs. Modals (*can, should, may . . .*) are also auxiliary verbs.
- *I **am** exercising right now.*
- ***Does** he exercise every day?*
- *She **should** exercise every day.*
- *They**'ve** learned how to swim.*
- *They **can** swim very well.*
- *We **may** go to the pool tomorrow.*

base form The simple form of a verb without any endings (*-s, -ed, -ing*) or other changes.
- ***be, have, go, drive***

capital letter The large form of a letter. The capital letters are: *A, B, C, D, . . .*
- ***A**licia lives in the **U**nited **S**tates.*

clause A group of words that has a subject and a verb. A sentence can have one or more clauses.
- ***We are leaving now.*** (one clause)
- ***When he calls, we'll leave.*** (two clauses)

common noun A word for a person, place, or thing (but not the name of the person, place, or thing).
- *Teresa lives in a **house** near the **beach**.*

comparative The form of an adjective or adverb that shows the difference between two people, places, or things.
- *Alain is **shorter** than Brendan.* (adjective)
- *Brendan runs **faster** than Alain.* (adverb)

comparison A statement that shows the difference between two people, places, or things. A comparison can use comparative adjectives and comparative adverbs. It can also use *as . . . as*.
- *Alain is **shorter than** Brendan.*
- *Alain isn't **as tall as** Brendan.*
- *He runs **faster than** Brendan.*

consonant A letter of the alphabet. The consonants are:
- *b, c, d, f, g, h, j, k, l, m, n, p, q, r, s, t, v, w, x, y, z*

continuous See **progressive**.

contraction A short form of a word or words. An apostrophe (') replaces the missing letter or letters.
- ***she's*** = *she is*
- ***hasn't*** = *has not*
- ***can't*** = *cannot*
- ***won't*** = *will not*

count noun A noun that you can count. It has a singular and a plural form.
- *one **book**, two **books***

G-1

definite article   *the*
This article goes before a noun that refers to a specific person, place, or thing.

- *Please bring me **the book** on the table. I'm almost finished reading it.*

dependent clause   (also called **subordinate clause**) A clause that needs a main clause for its meaning.

- ***When I get home**, I'll call you.*

direct object   A noun or pronoun that receives the action of a verb.

- *Marta kicked **the ball**. I saw **her**.*

formal   Language used in business situations or with adults you do not know.

- *Good afternoon, Mr. Rivera. Please have a seat.*

gerund   A noun formed with verb + -*ing*.
It can be the subject or object of a sentence.

- ***Swimming** is great exercise.*
- *I enjoy **swimming**.*

helping verb   See **auxiliary verb**.

imperative   A sentence that gives a command or instructions.

- ***Hurry!***
- ***Don't touch that!***

indefinite article   *a* or *an*
These articles go before a noun that does not refer to a specific person, place, or thing.

- *Can you bring me **a book**? I'm looking for something to read.*

indefinite past   Past time, but not a specific time. It is often used with the present perfect.

- *I've already **seen** that movie.*

indefinite pronoun   A pronoun such as *someone, something, anyone, anything, anywhere, no one, nothing, nowhere, everyone,* and *everything.* An indefinite pronoun does not refer to a specific person, place, or thing.

- ***Someone** called you last night.*
- *Did **anything** happen?*

indirect object   A noun or pronoun (often a person) that receives something as the result of the action of the verb.

- *I told **John** the story.*
- *He gave **me** some good advice.*

infinitive   *to* + base form of the verb

- *I want **to leave** now.*

infinitive of purpose   *(in order) to* + base form
This form gives the reason for an action.

- *I go to school **(in order) to learn** English.*

informal   Language used with family, friends, and children.

- *Hi, Pete. Sit down.*

information question   See **wh- question**.

inseparable phrasal verb   A phrasal verb whose parts must stay together.

- *We **ran into** Tomás at the supermarket.*

intransitive verb   A verb that does not have an object.

- *We **fell**.*

irregular   A word that does not change its form in the usual way.

- ***good → well***
- ***bad → worse***

irregular verb   A verb that does not form its past with -*ed*.

- ***leave → left***

main clause   A clause that can stand alone as a sentence.

- *When I get home, **I'll call you**.*

main verb   A verb that describes an action or state. It is often used with an auxiliary verb.

- *She **calls** every day.*
- *Jared is **calling**.*
- *He'll **call** again later.*
- *Does he **call** every day?*

modal   A type of auxiliary verb. It goes before a main verb or stands alone as a short answer. It expresses ideas such as ability, advice, obligation, permission, and possibility. *Can, could, will, would, may, might, should, ought to,* and *must* are modals.

- ***Can** you swim?*
- *Yes, I **can**.*
- *You really **should** learn to swim.*

negative   A statement or answer meaning *No.*

- *He **doesn't** work. (negative statement)*
- ***No**, he **doesn't**. (negative short answer)*

non-action verb (also called **stative verb**) A verb that does not describe an action. It describes such things as thoughts, feelings, and senses.
- I **remember** that word.
- Chris **loves** ice cream.
- It **tastes** great.

non-count noun A noun that you usually do not count (air, water, rice, love, . . .). It has only a singular form.
- The **rice** is delicious.

noun A word for a person, place, or thing.
- My **sister**, **Anne**, works in an **office**.
- She uses a **computer**.

object A noun or pronoun that receives the action of a verb. Sometimes a verb has two objects.
- She wrote **a letter to Tom**.
- She wrote **him a letter**.

object pronoun A pronoun (me, you, him, her, it, us, them) that receives the action of a verb.
- I gave **her** a book.
- I gave **it** to **her**.

paragraph A group of sentences, usually about one topic.

participial adjective An adjective that ends in -ing or -ed. It comes from a verb.
- That's an **interesting** book.
- She's **interested** in the book.

particle A word that looks like a preposition and combines with a main verb to form a phrasal verb. It often changes the meaning of the main verb.
- He looked the word **up**.
  (He looked for the meaning in the dictionary.)
- I ran **into** my teacher.
  (I met my teacher accidentally.)

past participle A verb form (verb + -ed). It can also be irregular. It is used to form the present perfect. It can also be an adjective.
- We've **lived** here since April.
- She's **interested** in math.

phrasal verb (also called **two-word verb**) A verb that has two parts (verb + particle). The meaning is often different from the meaning of its separate parts.
- He **grew up** in Texas. (became an adult)
- His parents **brought** him **up** to be honest. (raised)

phrase A group of words that forms a unit but does not have a main verb. Many phrases give information about time or place.
- **Last year**, we were living **in Canada**.

plural A form that means two or more.
- There **are** three **people** in the restaurant.
- **They are** eating dinner.
- **We** saw **them**.

possessive Nouns, pronouns, or adjectives that show a relationship or show that someone owns something.
- Zach is **Megan's** brother. (possessive noun)
- Is that car **his**? (possessive pronoun)
- That's **his** car. (possessive adjective)

predicate The part of a sentence that has the main verb. It tells what the subject is doing or describes the subject.
- My sister **works for a travel agency**.

preposition A word that goes before a noun or a pronoun to show time, place, or direction.
- I went **to** the bank **on** Monday. It's **next to** my office.
- I told him **about** it.

Prepositions also go before nouns, pronouns, and gerunds in expressions with verbs and adjectives.
- We rely **on** him.
- She's accustomed **to** getting up early.

progressive (also called **continuous**) The verb form be + verb + -ing. It focuses on the continuation (not the completion) of an action.
- She**'s reading** the paper.
- We **were watching** TV when you called.

pronoun A word used in place of a noun.
- That's my brother. You met **him** at my party.

proper noun A noun that is the name of a person, place, or thing. It begins with a capital letter.
- **Maria** goes to **Central High School**.
- It's on **High Street**.

punctuation Marks used in writing (period, comma, . . .). They make the meaning clear. For example, a period (**.**) shows the end of a sentence. It also shows that the sentence is a statement, not a question.

quantifier A word or phrase that shows an amount (but not an exact amount). It often comes before a noun.

- Josh bought **a lot of** books last year, but he only read **a few**.
- He doesn't have **much** time.

question See **yes/no question** and **wh- question**.

question word See **wh- word**.

reciprocal pronoun A pronoun (*each other or one another*) that shows that the subject and object of a sentence refer to the same people and that these people have a two-way relationship.

- Megan and Jason have known **each other** since high school.
- All the students worked with **one another** on the project.

reflexive pronoun A pronoun (*myself, yourself, himself, herself, itself, ourselves, yourselves, themselves*) that shows that the subject and the object of the sentence refer to the same people or things.

- He looked at **himself** in the mirror.
- They enjoyed **themselves** at the party.

regular A word that changes its form in the usual way.

- **play** —> play**ed**
- **fast** —> fast**er**
- **quick** —> quick**ly**

sentence A group of words that has a subject and a main verb. It begins with a capital letter and ends with a period (**.**), question mark (**?**), or exclamation point (**!**).

- **Computers are** very useful.

EXCEPTION: In imperative sentences, the subject is *you*. We do not usually say or write the subject in imperative sentences.

- **Call** her now!

separable phrasal verb A phrasal verb whose parts can separate.

- Tom **looked** the word **up** in a dictionary.
- He **looked** it **up**.

short answer An answer to a *yes/no* question.

- **A:** Did you call me last night?
  B: No, I didn't. OR **No.**

singular one

- They have **a sister**.
- **She** works in **a hospital**.

statement A sentence that gives information. In writing, it ends in a period.

- Today is Monday.

stative verb See **non-action verb**.

subject The person, place, or thing that the sentence is about.

- **Ms. Chen** teaches English.
- **Her class** is interesting.

subject pronoun A pronoun that shows the person or thing (*I, you, he, she, it, we, they*) that the sentence is about.

- **I** read a lot.
- **She** reads a lot too.

subordinate clause See **dependent clause**.

superlative The form of an adjective or adverb that is used to compare a person, place, or thing to a group of people, places, or things.

- Cindi is **the best** dancer in the group. (adjective)
- She dances **the most gracefully**. (adverb)

tense The form of a verb that shows the time of the action.

- **simple present:** Fabio **talks** to his friend every day.
- **simple past:** Fabio **talked** to his teacher yesterday.

third-person singular The pronouns *he*, *she*, and *it* or a singular noun. In the simple present, the third-person-singular verb ends in *-s*.

- **Tomás works** in an office. (Tomás = he)

time clause A clause that begins with a time word such as *when, before, after, while,* or *as soon as*.

- I'll call you **when I get home**.

time expression A phrase that describes when something happened or will happen.

- We saw Tomás **last week**.
- He'll graduate **next year**.

transitive verb A verb that has an object.

- She **paints** beautiful pictures.

two-word verb See **phrasal verb**.

verb   A word that describes what the subject of the sentence does, thinks, feels, senses, or owns.

- They **run** two miles every day.
- I **agree** with you.
- She **loved** that movie.
- We **smell** smoke.
- He **has** a new camera.

vowel   A letter of the alphabet. The vowels are:

- **a, e, i, o, u**.

wh- question   (also called **information question**) A question that begins with a *wh-* word. You answer a *wh-* question with information.

- **A: Where** are you going?
  B: To the store.

wh- word   (also called **question word**) A word such as *who, what, when, where, which, why, how,* and *how much.* It often begins a *wh-* question.

- **Who** is that?
- **What** did you see?
- **When** does the movie usually start?
- **How** long is it?

yes/no question   A question that begins with a form of *be* or an auxiliary verb. You can answer a *yes/no* question with *yes* or *no*.

- **A: Are** you a student?
  B: Yes, I am. OR **No**, I'm not.
- **A: Do** you come here often?
  B: Yes, I do. OR **No**, I don't.

UNIT REVIEW ANSWER KEY

Note: In this answer key, where a short or contracted form is given, the full or long form is also correct (unless the purpose of the exercise is to practice the short or contracted forms).

UNIT 1

A 1. are you taking   4. 's talking
2. don't   5. Do
3. often speak

B 1. are . . . doing   6. looks
2. 'm . . . playing   7. doesn't taste
3. Do . . . want   8. are . . . shouting
4. don't eat   9. Are
5. 'm feeling OR feel   10. talk

C I live in Qatar, but right now I ~~stay~~ *'m staying* in Wisconsin.

I'm studying English here. I ~~have~~ *'m having* a good time this summer, but in some ways it's a pretty strange

experience. Summer in Wisconsin ~~feel~~ *feels* like winter in Qatar! Every weekend, I go to the beach with some

classmates, but I ~~go never~~ *never go* into the water—it's too

cold! I'm ~~enjoy~~ *enjoying* my time here though, and my culture shock is going away fast.

UNIT 2

A 1. b   3. a   5. a
2. c   4. c   6. c

B 1. Did . . . go   5. went
2. called   6. did . . . see
3. didn't answer   7. saw
4. Yes . . . did   8. didn't like

C The poet Elizabeth Alexander was born in New

York City, but she didn't ~~grew~~ *grow* up there. Her father

~~taked~~ *took* a job with the government, and her family

moved to Washington, D.C. As a child, she ~~have~~ *had* a loving family. Her parents were active in the civil

rights movement, and Elizabeth ~~gots~~ *got* interested in African-American history. In her first book, she wrote about important African leaders. She met Barack Obama at the University of Chicago. They

both ~~teached~~ *taught* there in the 1990s. On January 20, 2009,

she ~~reads~~ *read* a poem at President Obama's inauguration.

UNIT 3

A 1. Did . . . hear   6. was raining
2. saw   7. was finishing
3. turned   8. was leaving OR left
4. Were . . . driving   9. stopped
    OR Did . . . drive   10. looked
5. was working

B 1. . . . Danielle was watching TV, I was studying.
2. I closed my book . . . the show *Dr. Davis* came on.
3. Dr. Davis was talking to his patient when the electricity went off.
4. . . . the electricity went off, we lit some candles.
5. We were talking (OR We talked) about a lot of things . . . we were waiting for the lights to come on.

C When I turned on the TV for the first episode of

Dr. Davis, I ~~unpacked~~ *was unpacking* boxes in my freshman dorm room. I stopped and watched for an hour. After that,

I ~~wasn't missing~~ *didn't miss* a single show while I was attending school. While I was solving math problems, Dr.

Davis was solving medical mysteries. And *just* ~~while~~ *when* my dumb boyfriend broke up with me, the beautiful Dr. Grace left Davis for the third time. I even watched the show from the hospital when I

~~was breaking~~ *broke* my leg. The show just ended. I was sad

when I ~~see~~ *saw* the last episode, but I think it's time for some real life!

UNIT 4

A 1. did   3. Did   5. used to
2. used to   4. play   6. used to

B 1. used to look   5. used to play
2. used to have   6. used to practice OR
3. used to let OR   would practice
    would let   7. Did . . . use to go
4. wouldn't get   8. used to love

C Celine Dion was born in Quebec, Canada. When

she ~~used to be~~ *was* five, her family opened a club, and

Celine used to ~~sang~~ *sing* there. People from the

community ~~would to come~~ *would come* to hear her perform.

At the age of 12, Celine wrote her first songs. Her
family ~~used to record~~ one and sent it to a manager. *(recorded)*

At first Celine used to ~~singing~~ only in French. After *(sing)*
she learned English, she became known in more

countries. As a child, Celine Dion ~~would be~~ poor, but *(was)*
she had a dream—to be a singer. Today she is one
of the most successful singers in the history of pop
music.

UNIT 5

A 1. h   3. f   5. g   7. c
   2. d   4. a   6. e   8. b

B 1. work   4. did she leave   6. is her boss
   2. did she   5. start   7. does
   3. told

C **A:** What did you ~~did~~ with my math book? I can't *(do)*
   find it.

   B: Nothing. Where ~~you saw~~ it last? *(did you see)*

   A: In the living room. I was watching *Lost* on TV.
   ~~What~~ Zack's phone number? *(What's)*

   B: I'm not sure. ~~Why you~~ want to know? *(Why do you)*

   A: He took the class last year. I'll call him. Maybe
   he still has his book.

   B: Good idea. What time does he ~~gets~~ out of *(get)*
   work?

UNIT 6

A 1. 're going   3. is going to   5. is giving
   2. 'll   4. 's going to

B 1. are . . . going to do OR are . . . doing
   2. 're going to feel OR you'll feel
   3. is going to arrive OR will arrive
   4. is going to get
   5. 'll see
   6. 's going to cry
   7. does . . . start OR will . . . start OR is . . . starting
   8. Is . . . going to call OR Will . . . call OR Is . . .
   calling
   9. won't forget OR isn't going to forget
   10. 'll speak

C 1. When will Ed ~~gets~~ home tomorrow? *(get)*
   2. The movie starts at 7:30, so I think I ~~go~~. *('ll go OR 'm going to go)*
   3. Do you want to go with me, or are you ~~study~~ *(studying OR going to study)*
   tonight?
   4. What ~~you are~~ going to do next weekend? *(are you)*
   5. I'm going ⌃ be home all day. *(to)*

UNIT 7

A 1. graduate   4. Will   6. until
   2. finish   5. learning   7. Are you
   3. When

B 1. works OR 's working
   2. won't register OR isn't going to register
   3. 'll spend OR 's going to spend
   4. studies OR is studying
   5. won't look OR isn't going to look
   6. graduates
   7. 'll take OR 's going to take

C **A:** Are you going to call Phil when ~~we'll~~ finish *(we)*
   dinner?

   B: No, I'm too tired. I'm just going to watch TV
   ~~after~~ I go to sleep. *(before)*

   A: Before I wash the dishes, I'm going ⌃ answer *(to)*
   some emails.

   B: I'll help you ×as soon as ~~I'll drink~~ my coffee. *(I drink)*

   A: No rush. I have a lot of emails. I won't be ready
   to clean up until ~~you'll~~ finish. *(you)*

UNIT 8

A 1. for   4. for   6. For
   2. since   5. Since   7. Since
   3. for

B 1. 've been   4. 've competed
   2. haven't had   5. 's won
   3. has loved   6. haven't seen

C 1. Marta and Tomás ~~lived~~ here since they got *(have lived)*
   married in 1998.
   2. Tomás has been a professional tennis player
   since he ~~has come~~ to this country. *(came)*
   3. He has won several competitions ~~for~~ then. *(since)*
   4. Since I have known Tomás, he ~~had~~ three *(has had)*
   different coaches.
   5. I haven't ~~see~~ Marta for several weeks. *(seen)*
   6. She ~~have~~ been in Brazil since April 1. *(has)*
   7. I've wanted to visit Brazil ~~since~~ years, but I *(for)*
   haven't had any vacation time since I got this
   new job.

UNIT 9

A 1. already   3. yet   5. told
    2. still   4. Has   6. yet

B 1. has already graduated OR has graduated already

    2. still haven't had

    3. Have . . . delivered . . . yet

    4. still hasn't set

    5. 's already started OR 's started already

    6. still haven't arrived

    7. has arrived yet

    8. have . . . met . . . yet

C **A:** I can't believe it's the 10th already. And we still
      haven't
      ~~didn't~~ finished planning.

   B: We haven't checked the guest list for a while.
       replied
       Who hasn't ~~replies~~ yet?

   A: Sally hasn't called about the invitation ~~already~~. *yet*
       I wonder if she's coming.

   B: Maybe she just forgot. Have you called ~~yet her~~? *her yet*

   A: I've already ~~call~~ her a couple of times. She *called*
       still hasn't
       ~~hasn't still~~ called back.

UNIT 10

A 1. ever   3. been   5. lately
    2. just   4. Has   6. has

B 1. Have . . . seen   5. 've . . . wanted
    2. 've . . . been   6. has taken
    3. has . . . read   7. 's . . . shown
    4. 's given

C 1. I've ~~lately~~ traveled a lot. *lately*

    just returned
    2. We've ~~returned just~~ ^ from an African safari.

    had
    3. I've never ~~have~~ so much fun before.

    ever been
    4. Have you ~~been ever~~ on a safari?

    been OR *gone*
    5. No, but I've recently ~~went~~ hot-air ballooning.

    have
    6. My wife and I ~~has~~ decided to go next summer.

    seen
    7. I've ~~saw~~ a lot of great photos on a hot-air
      ballooning website.

UNIT 11

A 1. When did you move to Vancouver?

    2. How long have you been an engineer?

    3. Did you work in Vancouver for a long time?

    4. When did you get married?

    5. How many years have you lived in Singapore?

    6. Has your wife lived in Singapore long?

B 1. 've been   6. was
    2. saw   7. has learned
    3. 've crossed   8. ordered
    4. haven't seen   9. didn't learn
    5. took

C Tina and Ken lived apart for a while, but then

Tina found a job in Singapore. She ~~has moved~~ there *moved*
last month. Here are some of their thoughts:

KEN: I'm so glad Tina is finally here. Last year
was
~~has been~~ the hardest time of my life.

TINA: Before I got here, I didn't ~~understood~~ Ken's *understand*
       've been
experiences. But I ~~was~~ in culture shock since I
arrived
~~arrive~~, and I'm learning a new job too! Now I know
what a rough time Ken had at first.

UNIT 12

A 1. has written   4. has read
    2. has chosen   5. 've had
    3. 've been reading   6. 've taken

B 1. have . . . lived (OR been living)

    2. 've been

    3. 've been enjoying

    4. Have . . . read

    5. has . . . written

    6. 've been trying

    7. 've been studying

    8. has . . . been

    9. Has . . . chosen

    hasn't written
C 1. Janet ~~hasn't been writing~~ a word since she sat
      down at her computer.

                     's had
    2. Since I've known Dan, he's ~~been having~~ five
      different jobs.

      been drinking
    3. I've ~~drunk~~ coffee all morning. I think I've
      had
      ~~been having~~ at least 10 cups!

              living
    4. We've been ~~lived~~ here for several years, but
      we're moving next month.

UNIT 13

A 1. a 2. c 3. b 4. c 5. b

B 1. couldn't stay
2. could kick
3. couldn't keep
4. was able to win
5. can . . . dance
6. can jump
7. can stay
8. can't perform
9. can start
10. can raise

C A: I can't ~~to~~ see the stage. The man in front of me is very tall.

B: Let's change seats. You ^'ll^ be able to see from this seat.

A: Thanks. I don't want to miss anything. I ~~no can~~ ^can't^ believe what a great dancer Acosta is.

B: I know. He was so good as a kid that he ~~could~~ ^was able to^ win a breakdancing contest before he was nine.

A: I didn't know he was a street dancer! Well, I'm glad you were ~~abled~~ ^able^ to get tickets.

UNIT 14

A 1. come 3. borrow 5. please shut
2. Do 4. if

B 1. I borrow a pen
2. my sister leave
3. if I open a window
4. my friend and I (OR me and a friend OR we) come early
5. I ask a question

C 1. A: Do you mind if I ~~changed~~ ^change^ the date of our next meeting?
B: ~~Yes, I do.~~ *Not at all.* OR *No, I don't.* OR *No problem.* When would you like to meet?

2. A: Could I ~~calling~~ ^call^ you tonight?
B: Sorry, but you ~~couldn't~~ ^can't^. I won't be home.

3. A: Mom, ~~I may~~ ^may I^ have some more ice cream?
B: No you ~~mayn't~~ ^may not^. You've already had a lot. You'll get sick.

4. A: Do you mind if my son ~~turn~~ ^turns^ on the TV?
B: ~~Not at all.~~ *Sorry, (but)* I can't study with the TV on.

5. A: Can my sister ~~borrows~~ ^borrow^ your bike?
B: Could I ~~letting~~ ^let^ you know tomorrow?
A: Sure. No problem.

UNIT 15

A 1. turning off
2. I'm sorry, I can't
3. please text
4. No problem
5. pick
6. I'd be glad to

B 1. lending me five dollars
2. you drive me to school
3. you (please) explain this sentence to me (please)
4. you carry this suitcase for me
5. you (please) distribute the report (please)
6. walking the dog tonight

C

JASON: Hi Tessa. It's Jason. Could you ~~taking~~ ^take^ some photos of the game today?

TESSA: Sorry, Jason, but I ~~couldn't~~ ^can't^. My camera is broken. Maybe Jeri can help.

JASON: Hi Jeri. Would you ~~came~~ ^come^ to the game today? I need someone to take photos.

JERI: Jason, ~~can~~ ^would^ you mind calling me back in a few minutes? I'm busy right now.

JASON: Sorry, Jeri, I can't, but I'll email you. Would you ~~give me please~~ ^please give me^ your email address?

JERI: ~~Not at all.~~ *Sure* OR *No problem* OR *Of course* OR *Certainly* It's Rainbows@local.net.

JERI: Hi Jason, it's Jeri. I'm sending you those photos. ~~You could~~ ^Could you^ call me when you get them?

JASON: Thanks, Jeri. The photos are great. Now will ^you^ teach me how to put them on Facebook?

UNIT 16

A 1. a 2. c 3. a 4. b 5. a

B 1. Should . . . call
2. 'd better do
3. should . . . contact
4. ought to call
5. Should . . . ask
6. Yes . . . should
7. Should . . . do
8. No . . . shouldn't
9. 'd better wait

C 1. Vanessa should ~~gets~~ ^get^ a new computer. She should ~~no~~ ^not^ keep her old one.

2. She'd better not ~~buying~~ ^buy^ the first one she sees.

3. She ought ^to^ read reviews before she decides on one.

4. ~~Ought~~ ^Should^ she get one online or should she ~~goes~~ ^go^ to a store?

UNIT 17

A 1. a   2. b   3. c   4. c   5. a

B 1. Music is   4. Clothing shows
    2. photographs show   5. Food goes
    3. Money makes

C One night in ~~june~~ *June* 1,400 ~~Years~~ *years* ago, a volcano erupted in today's El Salvador and buried a village of the great Mayan civilization. Archeologists have already found many large ~~building~~ *buildings* from this time, but only a ~~little~~ *few* homes of farmers and workers. The village of El Ceren contains perfect examples of ~~a great deal of~~ *many OR a lot of* everyday objects. The archeologists have found some knives (with ~~foods~~ *food* still on them), ~~much~~ *many OR a lot of* pots made of ~~clays~~ *clay*, a lot *of* garden tools, a little fabric, and a book. On the wall of one room, they found a few ~~word~~ *words* in an unknown language. There is still a lot to learn from this time capsule, called "the Pompeii of Latin America."

UNIT 18

A 1. a   3. Ø   5. Some   7. the
    2. a   4. an   6. Ø   8. the

B 1. the   2. the   3. a   4. a   5. an

C Yesterday I downloaded ~~the~~ *some* movies. We watched *a* comedy and ~~a~~ *an* Argentinian thriller. *The* comedy was very funny. I really enjoyed it. The thriller wasn't that good. There wasn't enough action in it. Tonight I think I'd rather read ~~the~~ book than watch a movie. I recently bought ~~the~~ *a* book of fables and a mystery. I think I'll read ~~a~~ *the* mystery before I go to bed.

UNIT 19

A 1. annoying   4. hard
    2. late   5. surprisingly
    3. perfect

B 1. interesting old house
    2. big cheerful yellow kitchen OR cheerful big yellow kitchen
    3. peaceful residential street
    4. nice young international students
    5. didn't seem friendly at all (OR at all friendly)
    6. cute little Greek restaurant
    7. really beautiful garden
    8. wonderful old round wooden table
    9. decide pretty quickly
   10. rent awfully fast

C The conditions in Parker Dorm are pretty ~~shocked~~ *shocking*. The rooms are ~~terrible~~ *terribly* small, and the furniture is incredibly ugly. The locks on the doors don't work ~~good~~ *well*, so your stuff is never ~~safely~~ *safe*. The dorm counselors are great—they're all really nice, friendly people—but they can't make up for the ~~badly~~ *bad* conditions.

UNIT 20

A 1. as   4. less
    2. better   5. longer
    3. more   6. the more impatient

B 1. more expensive than   4. more convenient
    2. bigger   5. farther
    3. larger than

C Last night, I had dinner at the new Pasta Place on the corner of Main Street and Grove. This new Pasta Place is just as good ~~than~~ *as* the others, and it has just as many sauces to choose from. No one makes a ~~more good~~ *better* traditional tomato sauce *than* them. But there are much ~~interestinger~~ *more interesting* choices. Their mushroom cream sauce, for example, is as ~~better~~ *good* as I've ever had. Try the mushroom and tomato sauce for a healthier ~~than~~ meal. It's just as delicious. The new branch is already popular. The later it is, *the* longer the lines. My recommendation: Go early for a ~~more short~~ *shorter* wait. And go soon. This place will only get more ~~popular~~ and more popular!

UNIT 21

A 1. shortest   4. rainiest
    2. biggest   5. most expensive
    3. driest   6. cheapest

B 1. the coldest   5. the least fun
    2. the most fantastic   6. the best
    3. the most popular   7. the funniest
    4. the most crowded

C Small towns aren't *the* most dynamic places to visit, and that's just why we love to vacation on Tangier Island. This tiny island is probably the ~~less~~ *least* popular vacation spot in the United States. Almost no one comes here. But it's also one of the ~~most~~ safest places to visit. And you'll find some of the ~~goodest~~ *best* seafood and the *most* beautiful beaches here. It's one of the easiest ~~place~~ *places* to get around (there are no cars on the island). If you get bored, just hop on the ferry. You're only a few hours from Washington, D.C., and a few more hours from New York and the ~~excitingest~~ *most exciting* nightlife ever.

A 1. well
2. doesn't run
3. more accurately
4. of
5. as well as
6. the more tired he gets
7. harder
8. better

B 1. well
2. faster
3. the most accurately
4. the hardest
5. the worst

C Last night's game was a very exciting one. The Globes played the best they've played all season. But they still didn't play as ~~good~~ *well* as the Stars. The Stars hit the ball more ~~frequent~~ *frequently* and ran ~~more fast~~ *faster* than the Globes, and their pitcher, Kevin Rodriguez, threw the ball more accurately. Their catcher, Scott Harris, handled ~~better the ball~~ *the ball better* than the Globes' catcher. The Globes are good, but they are ~~less good than~~ *not as good as* the Stars. All in all, the Stars just keep playing ~~good~~ *better* and better. And the better they play, the ~~hardest~~ *harder* it is for their fans to get tickets! These games sell out quicker than hotcakes, so go early if you want to get a chance to see the Stars.

UNIT 23

A 1. not liking
2. smoking
3. feeling
4. joining
5. swimming
6. not eating
7. improving

B 1. Laughing is
2. suggests OR suggested watching
3. Telling . . . helps OR will help
4. advises OR advised against drinking
5. enjoy taking
6. think about smoking

C 1. You look great. Buying these bikes ~~were~~ *was* a good idea.
2. I know. I'm happy about ~~lose~~ *losing* weight too. ~~Didn't~~ *Not* exercising was a bad idea.
3. It always is. Hey, I'm thinking of ~~rent~~ *renting* a movie. What do you suggest ~~to see~~ *seeing*?
4. I've been looking forward to ~~see~~ *seeing* *Grown Ups*. Have you seen it yet?
5. Not yet. Do you recommend it? You're so good at ~~choose~~ *choosing* movies.

UNIT 24

A 1. to get
2. to meet
3. to finish
4. to go
5. to play
6. to call

B 1. invited Mary to visit us
2. agreed to come
3. wants to make new friends
4. told her to come early
5. decided not to invite Tom
6. needs to finish his project

C 1. **A:** I want ^*to* invite you to my party.
   B: Thanks. I'd love ~~coming~~ *to come*.
2. **A:** I plan ~~to not~~ *not to* get there before 8:00.
   B: Remember ~~getting~~ *to get* the soda. Don't forget!
3. **A:** Sara asked ~~I~~ *me* to help her.
   B: I agreed ~~helping~~ *to help* her too.
4. **A:** I promised ^*to* pick up some ice cream.
   B: OK. But let's do it early. I prefer ~~don't~~ *not to* arrive late.

UNIT 25

A 1. get
2. in order not
3. to take
4. too
5. clearly enough

B 1. easy enough to figure out
2. too hard for me to use
3. too fast for me to understand
4. too far for us to walk
5. in order not to be late
6. early enough for us to walk
7. too heavy for us to cross
8. my phone to get directions
9. clearly enough for it to work
10. a taxi to save time

C Is 16 too young ~~for~~ *to* drive? It's really hard to ~~saying~~ *say*. Some kids are mature enough to drive at 16, but some aren't. I think most 16 year-olds are still too immature ^*to* drive with friends in the car, though. It's ~~for them easy~~ *easy for them* to forget to pay attention with a lot of kids in the car. In order ~~preventing~~ *to prevent* accidents, some families have a "no friends" rule for the first year. I think that's a reasonable idea.

A
1. starting
2. to finish
3. trying
4. to join
5. seeing
6. to call
7. Studying

B
1. doing
2. to take
3. working OR to work
4. sitting
5. taking
6. to get
7. studying

C It's difficult to study in a foreign country, so

students need ~~preparing~~ *to prepare* for the experience. Most people look forward to living abroad, but they

worry about ~~don't feel~~ *not feeling* at home. They're afraid of not understanding the culture, and they don't want

~~making~~ *to make* mistakes. It's impossible to avoid ~~to have~~ *having* some problems at the beginning. No one escapes from feeling some culture shock, and it's important

~~realizing~~ *to realize* this fact. But soon most people stop ~~to feel~~ *feeling* uncomfortable and start to feel more at home in the new culture.

A
1. each other
2. himself
3. one another
4. herself
5. myself
6. ourselves
7. yourselves
8. itself

B
1. talk to each other
2. greet each other
3. help yourself
4. enjoying themselves
5. drove herself

C When I first met Nicole, I told myself, "I'm not

going to like working with ~~herself~~ *her*." I was really

wrong. Nicole has helped ~~myself~~ *me* out with so many

things. When she ~~oneself~~ *herself* didn't know something, she

always found out for me. That way, both of ~~ourselves~~ *us* learned something. After I learned the job better, we

helped ~~each other's~~ *each other OR one another* out. Now the job ~~themselves~~ *itself* isn't that challenging, but I'm really enjoying myself.

Everyone here likes ~~each another~~ *one another OR each other*. That makes it a great place to work. I feel lucky to be here.

A
1. out
2. up
3. on
4. out
5. up
6. over

B
1. Joe gets up early.
2. He turns on the TV OR He turns the TV on.
3. He sits down with Ana.
4. They get along well.
5. They look over his schedule OR They look his schedule over.
6. They talk it over.
7. They put it away.
8. They put on their coats OR They put their coats on.

C As soon as Ina wakes up, she finds Abby's leash

and puts it ~~away~~ *on* her. Then the two of them set *out* for

their morning walk ~~out~~. They keep ~~up~~ *on* walking until they get to the park, where there are a lot of other dogs and their owners. Abby is a very friendly animal,

and she gets ~~well along~~ *along well* with other dogs. Ina loves dogs and always had one when she was growing

~~over~~ *up*. There is a saying that "A dog is a man's best friend," but Ina knows it's a woman's best friend too. "I enjoy playing with Abby," she says, "and just being

with her cheers ~~up me~~ *me up*." Abby obviously enjoys being with Ina too. The two have become really good friends and have improved each other's lives a lot.

A
1. don't have to
2. Does
3. can't
4. 've got to
5. had
6. have

B
1. don't have to do
2. have to pick up
3. 've . . . had to stand
4. don't have to wait OR won't have to wait
5. can't smoke
6. has to move OR will have to move
7. can't sit
8. have to have OR 'll have to have
9. had to eat OR 'll have to eat

C
1. He can't ~~boards~~ *board* the plane yet.
2. Passengers ~~must not~~ *don't have to* stay in their seats when the seat belt light is off.
3. Passengers: Please note that you ~~gotta~~ *have to OR must* pay extra for luggage over 50 pounds.
4. You don't ~~have got to~~ *have to* show your passport right now, but please have it ready.
5. Paul ~~will has~~ *will have OR has* to unpack some of his stuff. His suitcase is much too heavy.

UNIT 30

A **1.** a   **2.** b   **3.** c   **4.** a   **5.** c

B **1.** 're supposed to be

   2. isn't supposed to start

   3. are . . . supposed to sit

   4. 're supposed to go

   5. Was (OR Am) . . . supposed to wear

   6. 're (OR were) supposed to wear

   7. isn't (OR wasn't) supposed to rain

   8. was (OR is) supposed to be

C **1.** Dahlia was ~~suppose~~ *supposed* to drive. She was
   ~~supposed not~~ *not supposed* to fly.

   2. She ~~is~~ *was* going to wear her blue dress, but she
   changed her mind.

   3. What are we supposed to ~~doing~~ *do* after the
   ceremony?

   4. My parents ~~will~~ *were* supposed to fly home
   tomorrow, but they're staying another day.

   5. It was ~~no~~ *not* supposed to be this cold, and it
   ~~didn't suppose~~ *wasn't supposed* to rain.

UNIT 31

A **1.** Will   **5.** get
   2. might   **6.** could
   3. going to   **7.** Maybe
   4. may

B **1.** Are . . . going to go
   2. may OR might OR could
   3. Is . . . going to be
   4. may not OR might not
   5. are . . . going to
   6. may OR might OR could stay
   7. may not OR might not open
   8. may OR might OR could open

C Suddenly, weather forecasts all over the world are predicting terrible storms. Climatologist Jack Hall understands weather trends, and he thinks that a new ice age could ~~be~~ begin very quickly. His son Sam is in New York with his high school class. One student is sick and ~~mayn't~~ *may not* live without medicine. ~~May~~ *Will* those kids survive by themselves? They ~~maybe~~ *may* OR *might* not. Jack bundles up and starts walking to New York to save them. There ~~might could~~ *may* OR *might* OR *could* be a happy ending. Or the world could end. You'll have to watch to find out!

UNIT 32

A **1.** must   **4.** can't
   2. has got to   **5.** Could
   3. could   **6.** could

B **1.** couldn't be   **5.** can't be
   2. could be   **6.** Could . . . lead
   3. could . . . want   **7.** might know
   4. Could . . . be

C **1.** Jason has been coughing all morning. He
   might ~~having~~ *have* a cold.

   2. Diana must not ~~likes~~ *like* fish. She left most of it on
   her plate.

   3. ~~May~~ *Could* OR *Can* the package be from your parents?

   4. That's impossible! It ~~might not~~ *couldn't* OR *can't* be true.

   5. Is the bank still open? That's a good question.
   I don't know. It might ᐱ *be*.

   6. She ~~could~~ *couldn't* OR *can't* be a thief! I trust her completely!

   7. It's got ᐱ *to* be a joke. I don't believe it's serious.

CREDITS

INDEX

This index is for the full and split editions. All entries are in the full book. Entries for Volume A of the split edition are in black. Entries for Volume B are in red.